CHASING

DIRTY

MONEY

The Fight Against
Money Laundering

INSTITUTE FOR INTERNATIONAL ECONOMICS

CHASING DIRTY MONEY

THE FIGHT AGAINST MONEY LAUNDERING

Peter Reuter and Edwin M. Truman

Washington, DC
November 2004

Peter Reuter is a professor in the School of Public Affairs and in the Department of Criminology at the University of Maryland. Since July 1999, he has been the editor of the Journal of Policy Analysis and Management. He was a senior economist in the Washington office of the RAND Corporation (1981–93). He founded and directed RAND's Drug Policy Research Center (1989–93). His early research focused on the organization of illegal markets and resulted in the publication of Disorganized Crime: The Economics of the Visible Hand (MIT Press, 1983), which won the Leslie Wilkins award for the most outstanding book of the year in criminology and criminal justice. He has served as a consultant to numerous government agencies (including the US General Accounting Office, the White House Office of National Drug Control Policy, the National Institute of Justice, and the Substance Abuse and Mental Health Services Administration) and to foreign organizations including the United Nations Drug Control Program and the British Department of Health.

Edwin M. Truman, senior fellow, was assistant secretary of the US Treasury for international affairs (1998–2000). He was staff director of the Division of International Finance of the Board of Governors of the Federal Reserve System (1987–98) and director of the division from 1977 to 1987. From 1983 to 1998, he was one of three economists on the staff of the Federal Open Market Committee. He has been a member of numerous international groups working on international economic and financial issues, including the Financial Stability Forum's Working Group on Highly Leveraged Institutions (1999–2000), the G-22 Working Party on Transparency and Accountability (1998), the G-10-sponsored Working Party on Financial Stability in Emerging Market Economies (1996–97), the G-10 Working Group on the Resolution of Sovereign Liquidity Crises (1995–96), and the G-7 Working Group on Exchange Market Intervention (1982–83). He has published on international monetary economics, international debt problems, economic development, and European economic integration.

INSTITUTE FOR INTERNATIONAL ECONOMICS
1750 Massachusetts Avenue, NW
Washington, DC 20036-1903
(202) 328-9000   FAX: (202) 659-3225
www.iie.com

C. Fred Bergsten, Director
Valerie Norville, Director of Publications and Web Development
Edward Tureen, Director of Marketing

Typesetting by Circle Graphics
Printing by Automated Graphic Systems, Inc.

Printed in the United States of America

06 05 04   5 4 3 2 1

Library of Congress Cataloging-in-Publication Data

Reuter, Peter
    Chasing dirty money : progress on anti-money laundering / Peter Reuter, Edwin M. Truman.
        p. cm.
    Includes bibliographical references and index.
    ISBN 0-88132-370-5
    1. Money laundering. 2. Money laundering—Prevention. 3. Money laundering—United States—Prevention. I. Truman, Edwin M. II. Title.

HV6768.T78 2004
363.25'968—dc22   2004054940

To
Caroline Isber and Tracy Philbrick Truman

To
Caroline Isber and Tracy Philbrick Truman

Contents

Preface

The structure and functioning of the international financial system in an increasingly globalized world has received considerable attention from the Institute for International Economics throughout its existence. Morris Goldstein has written extensively on the topic, including *The Case for an International Banking Standard* in 1997, which was shortly adopted by the world's authorities. Wendy Dobson and Gary C. Hufbauer analyzed *World Capital Markets: Challenge to the G-10* in 2001. Kimberly A. Elliott previewed some of the issues addressed in this study in her *Corruption and the Global Economy* in 1997.

This study by Peter Reuter and Ted Truman addresses an additional and extremely important element of the international financial system: money laundering. Money laundering is a quintessential global issue that combines many of our previous themes. But combating it requires a cooperative, global, and special anti–money laundering (AML) regime, and this study provides the first comprehensive effort to assess the effectiveness of the existing regime. The authors first describe the activity of money laundering. They then provide an overview of the global AML regime as it has evolved over the past 15 years. Finally, they assess the regime's effectiveness in addressing three underlying goals: reducing crime, protecting the integrity of the core financial system, and controlling three types of global "public bads"—terrorism, corruption, and failed states. They find evidence the regime has helped increase the integrity of the banking system in the United States and many major financial centers. However, there is an absence of systematic evidence that it has made money laundering more than marginally more difficult for those who need to clean dirty money or finance terrorism.

The authors conclude with recommendations for improvements in the US and global AML regime during its next phase, which will probably be one of consolidation following its rapid expansion to date. They stress the need for increased international cooperation on tax evasion, not covered by the current US AML regime, to solidify support for the international AML regime. They emphasize the role for greater financial as well as technical assistance for poorer countries to tighten the global fight against money laundering and terrorism financing. They recommend that the United States volunteer for an IMF/World Bank assessment of its own financial system, including regulations affecting money laundering and terrorism, because of the central global role of the United States. They also recommend the revival of the National Money Laundering Strategy, which the United States previously submitted to the Congress and published regularly, but with changes from those produced from 1999 to 2003. They conclude with a systematic research agenda to identify the costs of the AML regime and improve its efficiency going forward.

Peter Reuter is a professor in the School of Public Policy and the Department of Criminology at the University of Maryland. He is a widely cited expert on drug policy and coauthor of *Drug War Heresies: Learning from Other Vices, Times, and Places* (Cambridge University Press, 2001). Edwin M. Truman has been a senior fellow at the Institute for International Economics since 2001, following a distinguished career of more than 25 years in the US government, principally the Federal Reserve and the Treasury. This is his second major Institute study, following *Inflation Targeting in the World Economy*, which was published in 2003.

The Institute for International Economics is a private, nonprofit institution for the study and discussion of international economic policy. Its purpose is to analyze important issues in that area and to develop and communicate practical new approaches for dealing with them. The Institute is completely nonpartisan.

The Institute is funded largely by philanthropic foundations. Major institutional grants are now being received from the William M. Keck, Jr. Foundation and the Starr Foundation. A number of other foundations and private corporations contribute to the highly diversified financial resources of the Institute. About 18 percent of the Institute's resources in our latest fiscal year were provided by contributors outside the United States, including about 8 percent from Japan. Major support for this project was provided by Carla A. Hills and Roderick M. Hills.

The Institute's Board of Directors bears overall responsibilities for the Institute and gives general guidance and approval to its research program, including the identification of topics that are likely to become important over the medium run (one to three years), and which should be addressed by the Institute. The director, working closely with the staff and outside Advisory Committee, is responsible for the development of particular projects and makes the final decision to publish an individual study.

The Institute hopes that its studies and other activities will contribute to building a stronger foundation for international economic policy around the world. We invite readers of these publications to let us know how they think we can best accomplish this objective.

C. FRED BERGSTEN
Director
November 2004

Acknowledgments

We worked on this study for three years, which was much longer than we anticipated at the start. Once we got into it, the topic expanded. In the process of our work, we were fortunate in the substantial assistance, encouragement, and advice we received from a wide range of people who have been active participants in the anti–money laundering regime, mostly in the United States and the United Kingdom, but in other countries as well. We spoke with more than 75 bank officials, financial regulators, other government officials, international officials, consultants, prosecutors, and investigators. Many of them had worn several hats, and some participated in our two study group meetings. They were all very generous with their time and advice, but there are too many of them to name separately. None should feel responsible for the views or conclusions expressed in this study, but we acknowledge their substantive contributions.

We do want to thank explicitly five people who read and commented on our final manuscript: Michael Levi, Robert E. Litan, Daniel K. Tarullo, David R. Truman, and William F. Wechsler. Their guidance was much appreciated, but they, too, should not be held responsible for any of our sins of omission or commission. Three major contributors to this study were Frank Gaenssmantel, Fabrizio Iacobellis, and Jeri Smith-Ready. Without their diligent research assistance and dedication, this study would have taken many more months, if not years. We also thank Valerie Norville and her team of Marla Banov, Madona Devasahayam, and Kathryn Sweetman, who skillfully guided the final birthing process.

Our final thanks go to our spouses for whose support and toleration we are continually grateful and to whom we have dedicated the product of our collaboration.

1

Chasing Dirty Money

Money laundering is the conversion of criminal incomes into assets that cannot be traced back to the underlying crime. Over the past three decades, the number and scope of laws and regulations aimed at combating money laundering have expanded dramatically.

The anti–money laundering (AML) effort by the United States began with the passage in 1970 of the Bank Secrecy Act, which was largely domestic in nature and covered only depository institutions. Since then, anti–money laundering has become a highly structured international regime that regulates a wide variety of institutions. Not all of them—casinos are an example—are normally viewed as part of the financial system.

The emergence of international terrorism as a major policy concern in recent years has led to a further ratcheting up to cover yet more institutions and activities. Box 1.1 examines the connections between the AML regime and efforts to combat terrorist financing.

Growth of the global anti–money laundering regime has generated relatively little public controversy. The banking sector initially resisted increased government interference in its relationships with clients, but the sector has since learned how to accommodate AML requirements in ways that impose relatively modest costs and inconveniences on both banks and their customers. Fears about the effects on the international competitiveness of US banks have also faded as other nations have imposed similar regimes. Privacy considerations have rarely been a major issue, despite the fact that the structure represents a considerable investment of public authority and public and private resources in the collection of information.

Notwithstanding the increased authority and investment represented by the anti–money laundering regime, few assessments have been carried out

Box 1.1 Anti–money laundering and combating terrorism financing

The attack on the United States on September 11, 2001, led to stepped-up efforts to move the war against terrorism and its financing to the forefront of national and international anti–money laundering regimes. However, long before the tragic events of 9/11, international initiatives to control money laundering incorporated efforts to combat terrorist financing. For example, a number of countries already had explicitly included the financing of terrorism as a predicate or underlying offense in their anti–money laundering regimes, and the Financial Action Task Force (FATF) and the Egmont Group of Financial Intelligence Units (FIUs) reviewed a number of cases involving terrorist financing. The United States reported to the FATF that it designated 30 foreign organizations as terrorist organizations in 1997, and seized $1.4 million in cash and property in connection with an antiterrorism case in 1998. In 2000, the United States and the FATF highlighted the potential connection between the financing of terrorism and *hawala* and other informal value transfer systems.

The tools developed nationally and internationally as part of the anti–money laundering regime can also be used in dealing with the financing of terrorism. First, regime tools can be used as investigative devices to learn something not only about the origins of funds but also their destinations. Customer due diligence, for example, can help determine not only who customers are but also what they do, where their money comes from, what they are doing with it, and where it is transferred to. Second, the regime can be used as a prosecutorial device, as in a 1998 US confiscation case involving a scheme to finance terrorism in the Middle East, or in the more recent US case involving a Chicago-based charitable organization, Benevolence International Foundation (even though the money laundering charge in that case was dropped as part of a plea bargain). Third, combating the financing of terrorism involves close international cooperation in the exchange of information, blocking funds, and closing down channels used to transfer funds.

(box continues next page)

of either its achievements or consequences. This study's aim is to begin the task of evaluating the effectiveness of the global anti–money laundering regime. It describes the phenomenon of money laundering itself, to the extent that the available fragments of information allow, as well as the status of the current AML regime. This is followed by an analysis of its effectiveness in achieving three goals: reducing crime, protecting the integrity of the core financial system, and controlling three types of global "public bads"—terrorism, corruption, and failed states. The study concludes with recommendations on how the AML system and analysis of its effectiveness could both be improved.

The process of preparing this study revealed that there is a dearth of quantitative data about money laundering and efforts to control it. Nor has there been much analysis of what few data exist. The available information consists of case descriptions, raw accounts of law enforcement events (such as convictions on money-laundering charges or numbers of reports of suspicious activities), and anecdotes from investigators, prosecutors, or, on rare occasions, the criminals themselves. The academic literature falls

Box 1.1   *(continued)*

There are differences as well, of course, between the general anti–money laundering regime and the specific variant applied to terrorist financing. First, terrorist financing generally (although not exclusively) involves financial flows that originate in legitimate activities to support illegitimate activities, rather than the reverse process in which funds from illicit activities are made to appear licit. Although most other money laundering originates with illegitimate activities, even here one traditional technique is the exploitation of legitimate activities, especially those handling large amounts of cash such as casinos or grocery stores. This points to the importance of financial institutions not only knowing their customers but also knowing what those customers are doing, where they get their money, and where it is being sent.

Second, terrorist financing typically involves smaller amounts of money than does traditional money laundering, often far less than $100,000. Combating such relatively small-scale laundering can be far more difficult—sometimes like looking for a needle in the haystack.

Third, the stakes are higher in combating terrorist financing in that the amounts involved may be small, but the potential benefits to society from prevention and confiscation are huge. Thus, the objective is not to contain or reduce but to eliminate the activity because the benefit-cost ratio of doing so is high.

Finally, while the goal in most other money-laundering activities can be linked to some degree or other to the profit motive, in terrorist financing the profit motive (other than cost minimization) is largely replaced by noneconomic motives, particularly political ones. This may further hamper detection.

The basic question is the extent to which the authorities can proactively use the anti–money laundering regime to attack and eliminate terrorist financing and terrorism itself. The simple answer is that the regime can make a major contribution to combating terrorism, but some of the differences sketched out above imply the need for, at the very least, more intense application of existing anti–money laundering instruments as well as the use of supplementary mechanisms.

---

into three broad categories: (1) practical law review articles primarily directed toward identifying the necessary components of an effective AML regime and explaining the complex statutes in force to control money laundering; (2) criminological and historical analyses, many of which are highly judgmental and value-driven; and (3) crude economic analyses of the extent of money laundering.

Money Laundering and Its Control

Money laundering is conventionally divided into three phases: *placement* of funds derived from an illegal activity, *layering* of those funds by passing them through many institutions and jurisdictions to disguise their origin, and *integration* of the funds into an economy where they appear to be legitimate. Although the anti–money laundering regime has many objectives— including the aforementioned goals of reducing crime, preserving financial system integrity and controlling terrorism, corruption, and failed states—

those objectives are for the most part compatible and do not present operational conflicts.

No credible estimates are available as to the volume of money laundering, or its distribution across countries and activities (chapter 2). Certainly the aggregate annual figure is in the hundreds of billions of dollars, but whether that figure is a small number of hundreds or more than a trillion is unknown. The vagueness of such estimates is a result both of disagreements over how to conceptualize money laundering and of weaknesses in the techniques used to quantify it. As a consequence, estimated changes in the volume of money laundered cannot be used as a measure to judge the effectiveness of the global anti–money laundering regime.

Moreover, aggregate figures conceal as much as they reveal. The adverse social consequences of a million dollars laundered to finance a terrorist act, on the one hand, and a million-dollar embezzlement, on the other, are so different that adding together the two figures would not produce a useful statistic for policy purposes. What is needed—but not available—is reliable figures for the major types of offenses that generate the total amount.

Money can be laundered in many different ways that can involve a variety of businesses and professions (chapter 3). Major drug traffickers face a unique money-laundering problem—namely, the need to clean large quantities of currency (much of it in small bills) on a frequent basis. Most other criminal offenses generate funds that can be more easily concealed. Surprisingly little evidence exists that much money laundering involves professionals who provide services to multiple clients. Many cases involve laundering by the offenders themselves (in embezzlement cases, for example) or relationships between an offender and someone who carries out a few transactions solely for that person.

The underlying or "predicate" crimes that make it necessary to launder proceeds can be divided into five categories: drug trafficking, other "blue-collar" crimes, white-collar crimes, bribery and corruption, and terrorism. These crimes differ in terms of their reliance on cash, the quantities of money involved, the severity of their negative social impact, and whom they affect. As a result, policy decisions may have different consequences for each category. At least for some activities and offenders—most notably major drug traffickers—good-quality money-laundering services appear to be hard to find. They are certainly expensive, with regular reports of laundering costs as high as 4 to 8 percent of the gross amounts.

As discussed in chapter 4, the AML regime consists of a prevention pillar (customer due diligence, reporting, regulation and supervision, and sanctions) and an enforcement pillar (a list of predicate crimes, investigation, prosecution and punishment, and confiscation). Globally, the prevention pillar has developed more rapidly, while in many nations the enforcement pillar is weak. International financial institutions—primarily the International Monetary Fund (IMF) and the World Bank—now play a major role in assessing primarily the implementation of the prevention pillar throughout the world.

Chapter 4 describes in considerable detail the AML regime in the United States and its evolution. It summarizes the prevention pillar's coverage of various financial and nonfinancial entities, and then contrasts prevailing coverage with that of the mid-1980s. An examination of the five national money-laundering strategies presented to the US Congress between 1999 and 2003 reinforces a number of key points about the structure and evolution of the US regime, particularly the two-pillar framework and the elements of each pillar. The chapter also reviews efforts over the past 15 years to establish a global AML regime and compares and contrasts the US AML regime with regimes in other countries. The chapter concludes with consideration of the gross financial cost of the US AML regime to the government, private-sector institutions, and the general public. On the basis of several assumptions and a few rough guesses, the conclusion is that the cost is substantial but not overwhelming—on the order of $7 billion in 2003, or about $25 per capita.

Chapters 5 through 7 assess the effectiveness of the global AML regime and its progress with respect to the three goals of reducing crime, protecting the integrity of the core financial system, and controlling terrorism, corruption, and failed states. Applying a single framework to assess an AML regime with respect to each of these goals is not the best way to carry out such an evaluation; instead, those measures deemed most appropriate to judge the effectiveness with respect to each goal are used on a case-by-case basis. Under current circumstances, only indirect measures of effectiveness can be applied.

Chapter 5 argues that enforcement activities under the US AML regime have not been intense. While the number of suspicious activity reports filed has risen rapidly in recent years, as has the value of assets confiscated, total seizures and forfeitures amount to an extremely small sum (approximately $700 million annually in the United States) when compared with the crude estimates of the total amounts laundered. Moreover, there has not been an increase in the number of federal convictions for money laundering. A very speculative estimate of the risk of conviction faced by money launderers is about 5 percent annually. Data from other industrialized nations indicate even lower levels of enforcement.

It is natural for economists to think of the AML regime as an effort to control an illegal market, in this case the market for money-laundering services. However, using that framework to understand better the functioning and effectiveness of the AML regime results in surprising findings. The available evidence suggests that most money laundering is not carried out as a separate activity by professionals, but rather is often part of the underlying offense or involves ad hoc assistance. This implies that price signals may be very weak and that market analysis may not provide useful insights. On the other hand, it may well be that the market framework needs to be more thoroughly analyzed, a worthwhile task for future study. Both theoretical and empirical work is needed to determine whether it is in fact useful to think of money-laundering controls in terms of the demand for, and supply of, illegal services with an implicit or explicit price.

For this study, assessing the effectiveness of the AML regime in reducing crime meant relying on indirect indicators such as suspicious activity reports, prosecutions and convictions, forfeitures and seizures, and prices paid for money-laundering services. The indicators provide some support for the proposition that the AML regime has contributed to the overall effectiveness of law enforcement by providing an additional tool.

With respect to protecting the integrity of the core financial system (chapter 6), the AML regime established in major jurisdictions over the past 15 years has changed how banks and other financial institutions do business. Today's AML regime has induced banks to take their obligation to avoid direct contact with criminal money seriously. Banks generally have implemented reporting systems and developed monitoring techniques that make them much less attractive for the placement phase of money laundering. However, while the global system that has emerged presents tangible obstacles to using banks and mainstream financial institutions for the placement of funds, the effectiveness of the AML regime with respect to the layering phase of money laundering is much more difficult to assess.

The AML regime today appears to be reasonably effective in protecting the integrity of the core financial system in major financial centers. However, it was not possible for this study to apply systematically the preferred assessment instrument, which is close examination and cross-classification of money-laundering cases, to determine the size of the financial institutions involved and the nature of their involvement.

With respect to each of the global "public bads"—terrorism, corruption, and failed states—chapter 7 concludes that each is individually complex enough that an AML regime can only contribute modestly to combat it. On terrorism, for example, the standard of zero tolerance, while defensible, is essentially impossible to achieve. By the indicator of amounts frozen or seized, the global AML regime has had limited success in combating terrorism since the end of 2001. Moreover, international cooperation in this area has been uneven.

Conclusions and Recommendations

The anti–money laundering regime and its associated laws and regulations represent a means to multiple ends. Money laundering is not itself the target; the regime primarily aims to reduce the activities that generate the money to be laundered (e.g., drug dealing, corruption, terrorism). Preserving the integrity of the core financial system is a different type of AML goal, as the aim is not so much to reduce money laundering as to move it to other channels.

A central policy question is whether the anti–money laundering regime needs to expand further, given the regime's rapid growth across countries and financial and nonfinancial businesses and professions in recent years. To date, very modest evidence that a particular channel (for example, real estate brokers or life insurance agents) has been used to launder money has provided a justification for bringing that channel into the net of AML regulation. Little systematic evidence has been advanced that these extensions of the AML regime, with the costs they impose on legitimate businesses and their customers, will do more than marginally inconvenience those who need to launder the proceeds of their crimes.

In the years ahead, it is likely that the pace of expansion of the AML regime will slow and that the focus will shift to improving global implementation of the current regime. As part of this consolidation process, increased cooperation will be important in a number of areas. Cooperation between the public and private sectors is critical, since the current flow of information is primarily from private to public, without significant feedback. Another important area for cooperation involves technical and financial assistance to poorer jurisdictions, in which an effective AML regime is essentially a luxury good.

The international community will also have to continue to grapple with the substantial differences in objectives, regulatory structures, and philosophies that impede effective coordination. Ratification and implementation by the major nations of the new UN Convention Against Corruption will be an important signal of willingness to cooperate on these matters.

For its part, the United States faces numerous challenges going forward, such as satisfying the revised Forty Recommendations issued in 2003 by the Financial Action Task Force, which was established by the G-7 summit in Paris in 1989 to examine measures to combat money laundering. Among the recommendations that have prompted debate in the United States are those to expand coverage of the AML regime to lawyers, accountants, and auditors, and to deal with special purpose vehicles, legal structures that are sometimes used to disguise beneficial owners of assets.

The United States also needs to demonstrate its commitment to a strong global AML regime by voluntarily submitting to a full IMF/World Bank assessment of its financial sector, including regulations affecting money laundering and terrorism financing. For the same reason, the United States should expand the list of crimes committed abroad (including tax evasion) that can lead to money-laundering prosecutions domestically.

Another recommendation is that the US executive branch resume preparing a National Money Laundering Strategy on a regular basis, but in a different manner than the five strategies produced from 1999 to 2003. While the strategy does not need to be redone annually, it should provide systematic reports on progress in implementing the objectives identified in preceding strategies, along with more analytical assessments of how well the system is working.

The US government should also find ways to encourage better use of the database of suspicious activity reports, which at present appears to be an evidentiary supplement rather than a source of new cases. Banking regulators need to create a database of cases involving financial institutions to examine the extent of the money-laundering threat to the core financial system and to assess progress in containing that threat.

Finally, the global AML regime needs to be strengthened through development of a systematic research program using economic tools, starting with more sophisticated assessment of the costs of the AML regime. Other important research-related activities include creating a database of existing cases that provides a detailed description of the prices, methods, and predicate crimes involved. This would represent a first step toward analyzing the existence and mechanics of the market for money-laundering services. The market-model framework for money laundering needs to be better developed; of particular importance is whether the model can incorporate more opportunistic modes of converting the proceeds of crime into forms that cannot be traced.

Scholars are inclined to emphasize the importance of research, but in the case of money laundering and finding ways to combat it, the need for greater research is particularly acute. The fact is that, to date, an elaborate system of laws and regulations that affects the lives of millions of people and imposes several billion dollars in costs annually on the American public has been based to a substantial degree on untested assumptions that do not look particularly plausible. While the failure to evaluate systematically the AML regime has not as yet impeded its expansion either in the United States or elsewhere, at some stage it should and most likely will. The system needs careful examination before any further expansion is actively contemplated.

2

How Much Money Is Laundered?

Conceptually, money laundering is straightforward: the effort to conceal the origins of illegally obtained funds that have been converted for legitimate purposes. As defined by the US General Accounting Office (GAO 1996, 1): "Money laundering is the act of converting money gained from illegal activity, such as drug smuggling, into money that appears legitimate and in which the source cannot be traced to the illegal activity." Terrorism financing requires inverting this definition, as it more typically involves money from legal pursuits that is converted into forms that facilitate acts of violence for political purposes.

Estimating how much money is actually laundered in the United States, any other country, or globally is extremely difficult. A sustained effort between 1996 and 2000 by the Financial Action Task Force (FATF) to produce such estimates failed.[1] In fact, no direct estimates exist of how much money passes through the financial system, whether broadly or narrowly defined, for the purposes of converting illegal gains into a nontraceable form. Financial firms lack both incentive and tools to estimate the extent of laundering in their accounts, so it is unlikely that any such figure will ever be produced, though changes in technology might help financial institutions in this respect.

What *is* known is the amount of laundered money the US government identifies through its investigations. According to the 2002 *National Money Laundering Strategy*—an annual report from 1999 to 2003 by the US Treasury to Congress on anti–money laundering efforts—seizures of money

---

1. One of the authors of this study (Peter Reuter) was involved in the latter stages of this effort, which did not result in any official publication.

laundering–related assets in fiscal 2001 amounted to $386 million, while the corresponding figure for forfeited assets was $241 million. Considering the billions of laundered dollars believed to be out there, a few hundred million dollars annually is a negligible share of the true total.

A number of estimates have been published of the potential demand for money laundering, i.e., the quantity of funds generated through either crime or legal activities that are concealed from authorities in order to evade taxes as well as what Vito Tanzi (1980) in his classic article calls "various governmental restrictions on the activities of economic agents." Estimating this demand can be done through either a macroeconomic or microeconomic approach. The various macroeconomic methods might be expected to produce a rough upper bound of how much money is laundered, simply because it is impossible to make fine distinctions in these studies. The microeconomic method, which involves summing up the income generated by major crime categories, provides a loose lower bound on the demand for money-laundering services.

A review of the two methods comes to a simple conclusion: neither yields estimates of the volume of laundered money that can be considered as anything more than an indicative order of magnitude. Such figures are useful to confirm that the phenomenon of money laundering is of sufficient scale to warrant public policy attention, but their quality is not good enough to provide guidance for policy. Moreover, the macroeconomic estimates are methodologically flawed, while the available microeconomic estimates lack credible empirical foundations.

These negative conclusions regarding the accuracy of these estimates are based on a fairly detailed and technical review. Confronting this reality is critical because ignorance about the volume of money laundering is an important conditioning reality for policymakers as well as for any assessment of the AML regime's effectiveness. Without a measure of how much money is laundered, the most obvious and direct outcome measure for an anti–money laundering regime—reductions in the targeted activity—is not available. More indirect measures must be developed. It seems unlikely to us that direct measurement of the total volume can be improved in the foreseeable future. Even measures of predicate crimes, the principal targets of the control regime, are crude.

Such a negative assessment, however, does not imply an endorsement of policymaking-by-anecdote in this or any other area. To the contrary, a recurring theme in this study is that better use could and should be made of available data on particular aspects of money laundering, and greater thought should be given to collecting and assembling relevant statistics that aid policymakers. Even these efforts, however, are unlikely to produce a global aggregate of the amount of money laundered that can be used to monitor progress in control efforts. As discussed in chapters 5 and 8, more disaggregated measures are needed to assess the seriousness of the money-laundering problem.

Macroeconomic Estimates

The macroeconomic approach to measuring the extent of money laundering is based on a broad definition that assumes that any revenue on which no tax is paid—be it from a legal or illegal activity—will need to be laundered in some way.[2] In this view, the demand for money laundering is related to the monetary component of the so-called underground economy.

The study of what has been called the underground, shadow, or hidden economy first emerged in the late 1970s (Gutmann 1977, Feige 1979). It has since evolved into a considerable body of literature that proposes a host of different techniques for estimating the size of the phenomenon. More recently, one particular estimation method, the currency-demand approach, has been applied frequently enough to allow for comparison of many different countries over one or two decades.

The first step of this method, developed by Tanzi (1980), estimates a currency-demand function for the concerned country. The dependent variable is the ratio of currency holdings to a broad measure of the money supply such as M2, and on the right-hand side of the equation are series for the following:

- tax rates (higher taxes are expected to induce use of currency to evade them),

- share of wages and salaries in personal income (these types of income are more often than others paid in cash),

- interest rates (as the opportunity cost of holding currency), and

- real per capita income (as a proxy for financial infrastructure, the degree of urbanization and mobility; higher income decreases the use of cash).

The second step, which is based on the estimated equation and actual values of M2, can determine for each year the level that currency holdings would have been with taxes at either the lowest level of the sample period or at zero. The difference between this estimated figure and the actual observed cash holdings is then attributed either to the entire underground economy when a zero tax rate is used, or to its increase since the year with taxes at their lowest level. Assuming that income velocity of currency circulation is the same in the underground and legal economies, the third

---

2. Theoretically, it would seem reasonable to assume that no taxes are paid on income from illegal activities, but there are rare exceptions, such as when an offender chooses to launder criminal earnings through a legitimate business and pay some taxes.

Table 2.1 Taxonomy of underground economy activities

Activities	Monetary transactions		Nonmonetary transactions	
Illegal activities	Trade in stolen goods, drug manufacturing and dealing, prostitution, gambling, smuggling, fraud		Barter (drugs, stolen goods, smuggling, etc.); production of drugs for own use; theft for own use	
	Tax evasion	**Tax avoidance**	**Tax evasion**	**Tax avoidance**
Legal activities	Unreported income from self-employment; wages, salaries, and assets from unreported work related to legal goods and services	Employee discounts, fringe benefits	Barter of legal services and goods	All do-it-yourself work and neighbor help

Sources: Mirus and Smith (1997) and Schneider and Enste (2000).

step computes the corresponding estimates of the total volume of the underground economy or its increase.[3]

What is the currency-demand approach measuring, and how well does it match the broad working definition of money laundering used in this study? Clearly, the estimates are measures of a cash-based underground economy dependent on particular levels of taxes and extent of tax evasion, which is in line with the definition. Tanzi (1980) himself defines the underground economy as the "gross national product that, because of unreporting and/or underreporting, is not measured by official statistics." The impact of tax evasion on national accounts is unclear, and depends on both the particular taxes evaded (e.g., personal income taxes may be more easily evaded than property taxes) and on the methods used for estimating each of the components of the national accounts. As a result, Tanzi's definition is probably too general to match the specifics of his own method, but precise enough to provide a reasonable upperbound estimate of total money laundered.

Friedrich Schneider and Dominik Enste (2000) also apply the currency-demand approach. They present a "reasonable consensus definition" of the underground economy based on an earlier schematization by Rolf Mirus and Roger Smith (1997). Their taxonomy (table 2.1) better describes what the currency-demand approach estimates, and also illustrates conceptually a broad measure of money laundered. Schneider and Enste distinguish between monetary and nonmonetary transactions. The latter, by definition, cannot be measured by the currency-demand approach and cannot in the first instance give rise to any money to be laundered. Schneider and Enste also

---

3. A more restricted variation on this method is the currency-ratio approach described in Feige (1997). It uses the ratio of currency to demand deposits and makes the restricting assumption that this ratio is affected only by changes in the underground economy.

distinguish between legal and illegal activities. With the reasonable assumption that no taxes are paid on illegal activities, it is the sum of the legal and illegal categories of monetary transactions in the underground economy that give rise to money laundering in its broadest definition.[4]

Schneider and Enste provide roughly comparable estimates of the underground economy for many countries based on the currency-demand approach. Using their 2000 study as well as a later paper by Schneider (2002), table 2.2 shows figures for 21 member countries of the Organization for Economic Cooperation and Development (OECD) for selected years since 1989. The figures illustrate the extraordinary magnitude of money-laundering estimates using this approach. On the basis of these estimates, the combined underground economies of these 21 countries in 1997 totaled more than $3 trillion annually, and for single nations the underground economy represented an average of 16 to 17 percent of GDP. For all the years listed, the amounts estimated are more than 7 percent of global GDP, and since 1994 the figure exceeds 10 percent for most years.[5] This is substantially above the 2 to 5 percent of global GDP cited in 1998 by Michel Camdessus, then managing director of the International Monetary Fund, as a "consensus range" for the scale of money-laundering transactions. Even this lower guesstimate was described by Camdessus (1998) as "beyond imagination."

Differences across countries may be partly explained by differences in taxpayer cultures and by tax rates themselves. For example, southern European nations (Greece, Italy, Portugal, Spain) and Belgium, all of which are thought of as having a tradition of low tax compliance, have the highest proportion of GDP estimated as coming from the underground economy, with figures above 20 percent for all years since 1994. The heavily taxed Scandinavian countries follow them closely. The United States, Austria, and Switzerland have much lower rates, less than 10 percent.

Not surprisingly, considering the size of US GDP, the United States leads the field in absolute terms, with $650 billion to $800 billion in 1995 dollars, followed by Japan and Germany. Italy and Spain are the only countries with both underground economies accounting for more than 20 percent of GDP and contributions to the worldwide underground economy in absolute numbers of more than $100 billion.

The absolute and percentage estimates are shocking if taken as measures of money laundering. However, they are frail even in their own terms as measures of what evades government taxation and other restrictions, and even more frail as the basis for estimating the volume of money laundered.

---

4. Transaction measures are broader than value-added measures, however, in that the former encompass the gross expenditures at all stages in the production of output, while the latter are net of inputs. Thus, gross transaction measures of the underground economy tend to overstate its size relative to value-added measures of the total economy.

5. Based on world GDP in constant 1995 dollars. See World Bank (2003b).

Table 2.2 Estimates of the underground economies of 21 OECD countries, 1989–2001

Country	1989 Percent of GDP	1989 Billions of dollars	1991 Percent of GDP	1991 Billions of dollars	1994 Percent of GDP	1994 Billions of dollars	1997 Percent of GDP	1997 Billions of dollars	1999 Percent of GDP	1999 Billions of dollars	2001[a] Percent of GDP	2001[a] Billions of dollars
Australia	10.1	32.2	13.0	41.5	13.0	46.8	13.9	56.7	14.3	64.1	14.1	66.0
Austria	*8.3*	16.8	7.1	15.6	9.9	22.9	8.9	21.6	*9.6*	24.8	*10.5*	28.2
Belgium	19.3	48.1	20.8	54.3	21.4	57.6	22.4	64.7	22.2	67.4	22.0	70.2
Canada	12.8	67.9	13.5	70.4	14.6	82.3	14.8	90.9	16.0	106.1	15.8	111.1
Denmark	10.8	17.5	15.0	24.8	17.6	30.9	18.1	34.4	18.0	35.9	17.9	37.1
Finland	13.4	17.9	16.1	20.2	*18.2*	22.7	*18.9*	27.0	18.1	28.4	18.0	30.1
France	9.0	129.2	13.8	205.3	14.3	218.4	14.7	235.2	15.2	258.8	15.0	268.7
Germany	*11.4*	250.7	12.5	291.8	13.1	316.6	15.0	376.8	*15.5*	403.5	*16.0*	431.2
Greece	22.6	25.0	24.9	28.4	26.0	29.9	*29.0*	36.1	28.7	38.1	28.5	41.1
Ireland	11.0	5.4	14.2	7.7	15.3	9.3	16.1	12.7	15.9	15.0	15.7	17.6
Italy	22.8	230.3	24.0	250.6	25.8	275.0	27.3	308.9	27.1	317.3	27.0	331.1
Japan	8.8	412.4	9.5	483.5	*10.6*	552.3	*11.1*	618.7	11.2	622.1	11.1	628.6
Netherlands	11.9	42.7	12.7	48.5	13.6	55.2	13.5	59.9	13.1	62.4	13.0	64.8
New Zealand	9.2	4.8	9.0	4.6	11.3	6.5	11.9	7.5	12.8	8.4	12.6	8.6
Norway	14.8	17.8	16.7	21.1	17.9	25.3	19.4	31.2	19.1	31.8	19.0	32.8
Portugal	15.9	15.0	17.2	17.3	*22.1*	23.1	*23.1*	26.7	22.7	28.1	22.5	29.4
Spain	16.1	84.8	17.3	96.7	22.3	126.8	23.1	143.7	22.7	153.2	22.5	162.4
Sweden	15.8	36.5	17.0	39.2	18.3	42.4	19.8	49.1	19.2	51.3	19.1	53.5
Switzerland	*7.2*	21.4	6.9	21.1	8.7	26.6	8.0	25.1	*8.3*	27.0	*9.3*	31.6
United Kingdom	9.6	99.3	11.2	114.9	12.4	135.9	13.0	155.5	12.7	159.5	12.5	165.4
United States	6.7	429.4	8.2	532.0	9.4	671.7	8.8	699.0	8.7	752.1	8.7	793.1
European Union members	14.1	1,019.2	16.0	1,215.3	17.9	1,366.6	18.8	1,552.4	18.6	1,643.8	18.6	1,730.8
Total		2,004.9		2,389.6		2,778.1		3,081.4		3,255.5		3,402.7
Average	12.7		14.3		16.0		16.7		16.7		16.7	

a. Estimates for 2001 are preliminary.

Note: Data for the underground economy as a percent of GDP are the average of the cited and the following year for all countries for 1991; all countries except Austria, Germany, and Switzerland for 1989, 1999, and 2001; for Finland, Japan, and Portugal for 1994; and for Finland, Greece, Japan, New Zealand, and Portugal for 1997. All exceptions referenced in this note are in *italics* in the table. Absolute numbers are in constant 1995 dollars.

Sources: Underground economy as percent of GDP: Schneider and Enste (2000) and Schneider (2002). Absolute numbers calculated from official GDP data in World Bank (2003b).

By definition, the entire right-hand, nonmonetary side of table 2.1 is not included in these estimates of money laundering, as these items were excluded by the estimation method used by Schneider and Enste (2000) and do not fit conceptually.

Moreover, the currency-demand approach has been extensively and convincingly critiqued (Tanzi 1999). First, its strong focus on taxes to explain the size of the underground economy ignores the criminal trades, which are not a function of tax rates but of other factors (such as the demand for illegal drugs); it measures only the lower left-hand side of table 2.1. For example, removing legal restrictions on casino gaming in the 1990s in many American states may have reduced the size of the illegal gambling sector. Second, the currency-demand approach assumes that the underground economy consists of only cash transactions. Studies in Norway have suggested that cash may account for only about 80 percent of such activities (Isachsen and Strom 1980, 1985). Moreover, some money laundering, such as that associated with financial fraud, is done primarily, if not exclusively, in noncash monetary transactions such as electronic transfers. Third, the currency-demand approach assumes that income velocity is the same in the hidden and the official sectors. As the two are likely to have very different structures, that assumption is almost certainly false.

Fourth, the estimates presented in table 2.2 are based on the strong assumption of no underground economy in the year with lowest taxation. When designing the currency-demand approach, Tanzi explained that predicting a currency-to-M2 ratio based on the lowest level of taxation over the sample period would indicate the increase in the underground economy since the year of that lowest tax level. Theoretically, Tanzi maintained, one would need to put taxes at zero to estimate the entire underground economy. Schneider and Enste are less explicit in laying out the framework for their econometric work, but they do mention that a weak point of the approach is the assumption of no underground economy in the base year. The fact that the already enormous estimates would be further inflated if based on a currency-to-M2 ratio predicted with zero taxes raises serious doubts about the accuracy of the estimates.

Finally, substantial amounts of currency are held outside certain countries. For countries with currencies used internationally (the United States, Germany [prior to 1999], the euro countries, the United Kingdom, Japan, and Switzerland to some degree), this factor might change the results substantially, because currency held abroad should be excluded to obtain a net volume of the domestic underground economy. If currency abroad is not part of the domestic underground economy, it might well be in the foreign underground economy. This implies that this method is not reliable for purposes of measuring the volume of money laundering in the countries issuing international currencies, but in principle may be appropriate for constructing a global aggregate if one could reallocate the currency appropriately.

Unfortunately, there are no promising ways around these problems. For example, it is difficult to find a proxy for illegal activities to include in the equation. Nor is there any promising approach for estimating income velocity in the hidden sector.

The reliance on currency as the basis for measuring money laundering resulting from illegal drugs imparts the right bias by excluding the nonmonetary sector and taking into account the huge amounts of cash in the drug trade. That advantage will be lost with other macroeconomic approaches.

There are contending macroeconomic approaches. One alternative method is based on the discrepancies between different components of national income accounts. For example, nonreporting or underreporting may affect income statistics differently than other national accounts categories such as consumption. Second, one can compare official data on the labor force with data based on household surveys, and take the difference as an indicator of underground economic activity. The third alternative option is the so-called physical input approach. Based on total real physical inputs (most typically electricity), it estimates total GDP, subtracts official GDP from it, and attributes the difference to underground activity. Lastly, the underground economy has been estimated with an econometric method that allows for estimating an unobserved variable "between" certain observable causes and effects.[6]

When used individually, all of the alternative approaches have obvious and very substantial shortcomings. For example, simple comparisons of different national accounts categories may not be meaningful because this procedure conflates measurement error with unrecorded activity. Labor surveys may be biased, physical inputs measure only "underground industrial" activity, and the associated econometric modeling requires a set of strong assumptions.

The results themselves also reduce the credibility of the various economic approaches. Derek Blades and David Roberts (2002) make telling comments in reviewing various estimates. Their main critique is that nonobserved activities are highly concentrated in certain sectors of the economy, such as retail trade, taxis, trucking, and restaurants, while other sectors such as power generation, heavy industry, or air transport are intrinsically less vulnerable. Taking this into account, the high estimates of the size of underground economies would imply that much larger shares of the susceptible sectors are underground, which hardly seems credible.

Considering, then, that the different shortcomings tend to bias the results, and sometimes in different directions, it is best to take the different figures with several grains of salt. At best, the various estimates suggest that there is substantial potential demand for money-laundering services, but there is little basis for concluding whether it amounts to hundreds of billions or trillions of dollars.

---

6. See Dixon (1999) for a brief review of various methods.

Before moving to the discussion of microeconomic estimates of the amount of money laundering, it is important to recognize the substantial work that has been done on estimating underground economic activities in the context of the compilation of national economic accounts. Most countries today use the national accounting standards and definitions set out in the System of National Accounts (1993), and referred to as SNA93. A compatible but somewhat more specific set of rules is in force for countries in the European Union (EU), namely the European System of Accounts (Eurostat 1995), known as ESA95. To determine what needs to be included in complete national accounts, both systems use the notion of a "production boundary." Everything that lies within the boundary is considered to have been produced, with some value added to it, and is to be included in the accounts, while everything beyond the boundary does not count as production or value added and is to be excluded. Presented in a very simplified way, according to SNA93 and ESA95, all goods and services produced with inputs of capital, labor, or any materials lie within the production boundary, with the sole exception of housing services provided by owner-occupiers. Goods that are not produced with such inputs, such as natural resources, are considered outside the boundary.[7] The point is that for both SNA93 and ESA95 the concept of a production boundary is independent of whether an activity is illegal or performed in violation of certain regulations. Thus, many national statistical agencies have made considerable efforts to estimate nonobserved economic activity in order to include it in their GDP estimates. In particular, they have attempted to define in detailed fashion the different sectors of the underground economy, and to develop particular methods to measure each sector. Consequently, the findings are much more reliable than estimates based on general macroeconomic approaches such as those discussed above.

Were they easily available and comparable, the national estimates could be useful for developing an overall measure of money laundering. However, although there has been considerable study and assessment by national and international agencies of all the particular methods of examining underground economies,[8] practices at national levels vary widely. The most inclusive effort to collect and compare national practices and estimation results to date is a study by the UN Economic Commission for Europe (UNECE 2002). The study includes detailed reports by 29 countries about their methods of estimating underground activity. Eight are developed market economies and OECD members that are part of the principal focus

---

7. See Blades and Roberts (2002) for a simple representation of the production boundary. A more detailed account can be found in Jackson (2000, 120–34).

8. The most complete overview is probably the *Handbook for Measurement of the Non-Observed Economy* published by the OECD (2002) in cooperation with the International Monetary Fund, International Labor Organization, and the Statistical Committee of the Commonwealth of Independent States.

of attention in this study: Belgium, Canada, Finland, Germany, Ireland, Italy, the United Kingdom, and the United States.

Unfortunately, most of these countries, while adjusting for a host of different nonobserved activities, usually estimate these types of economic activities in a way that does not allow identification of a total figure for the underground economy (for example, as a percentage of GDP). The first exception is Italy, where the estimate of the underground economy as a proportion of total estimated GDP was 15 percent for 1998, i.e., a little more than half of what currency-demand-based macroeconomic estimates suggested for 1997 and 1999. The second exception is the United States, but in this case the efforts are limited to a survey of the literature discussed below in the section on microestimates. Moreover, US figures primarily cover the period around 1980 and are thus outdated for purposes of this study.

Apart from these two countries, only Belgium and Canada provided estimates for the UNECE study of the correction in national accounts for nonobserved activities. In Belgium, these activities were reported to account for 3 to 4 percent of total estimated GDP in 1997, and in Canada less than 2.7 percent in 1992. The figures for these two countries (less so for Italy) are substantially below the estimates in table 2.2, demonstrating yet again the weakness of the currency-demand approach.

Studies on underground economies related to national accounts also have their weaknesses when used to measure the scale of money laundering, specifically with regard to certain important types of illegal activities. First, some activities like theft or extortion do not fall within the production boundary. Second, even for the countries that do report on illegal activities, the UNECE (2002) study reports that the estimates "can only be regarded as indicative" due to "difficulties in measurement." Third, notwithstanding such exceptions as the United Kingdom and the United States, most OECD members do not list any estimates for illegal activities at all, which again limits comparability.[9]

Two main lessons emerge from our review of attempts to estimate the amount of money laundering in the context of national accounts. On the one hand, insofar as data are available, they only reinforce the previous skepticism about the results from currency-demand estimation methods. On the other, the data show that there are sophisticated methods available that can be refined and may contribute to more meaningful estimates in the future of the size of the underground economy and volume of money laundering.

---

9. One reason for the limited coverage in OECD countries may be the confusion in EU norms. While the ESA95 (enacted in a Council Regulation in 1996) requires inclusion of illegal activities, a Commission Decision of 1994 excludes them from what is required of states to ensure complete national accounts (Art. 1 Commission Decision 94/168/EC, Euratom). Interestingly, Calzaroni (2001) notes that the Italian approach to estimating underground activity explicitly states that illegal activities are not included in line with EU requirements.

Microeconomic Estimates

The microeconomic approach to estimating the demand for money laundering is in a sense a complement to the macroeconomic approaches, which pay limited attention to estimating total earnings from criminal activities, aside from tax evasion. The microeconomic approach focuses on different types of crimes and on estimating the incomes from each. These estimates normally do not include the informal economy or activities that, though legal, are not reported in order to evade taxes. However, in principle it would be possible to graft those estimates onto such measures. The problems associated with the microeconomic approach basically involve the paucity and unreliability of the data. In other words, what little data are available are not worth much.

There have been two systematic efforts to provide estimates of incomes generated by a broad range of criminal activities in the United States. Carl Simon and Ann Witte (1982) cobbled together figures for the late 1970s. Indicative of the uncertainty of their results, which they acknowledge, is the basis for their estimate for income from prostitution. They started with estimates of the number of acts of prostitution and the number that a full-time prostitute would commit in the course of a year. This calculation resulted in an estimate of full-time-equivalent prostitutes of 80,000 to 500,000. Add in considerable uncertainty about the annual earnings of a prostitute, and the result is an estimate of income that spans approximately an order of magnitude.

Under the auspices of the President's Commission on Organized Crime, Wharton Econometrics Forecasting Associates, a US research firm, also developed estimates of incomes from many different criminal activities (Godshaw, Koppel, and Pancoast 1987). In its final report in 1987, the commission stated that organized crime produced an annual net income of approximately $47 billion, costing Americans $18.2 billion and more than 400,000 legitimate jobs. These criminal groups—including traditional mobsters, motorcycle gangs, and other emerging ethnic crime groups—had nearly 300,000 members, with an additional half million people employed in part-time, crime-related jobs. Nine of the commission's 18 members, it should be pointed out, said that the final report's account of the income sources of organized crime was inadequate.

The estimates used for this study for the proceeds from 34 crimes in the United States cover one or more years during the period from 1965 to 2000. The 30 sources used include both public agencies and private organizations. For most crimes, estimates were available for only a few years. There were data for 10 or fewer crimes for 14 of the years, for 11 to 15 crimes for 19 of the years, and for up to 22 crimes for the remaining 4 years. Sixteen crimes had 10 or fewer years of data, while only nine crimes had more than 25 years' worth. The results are presented in table 2.3 and figure 2.1. Simple linear projections were used to impute the missing years to generate estimates for all crimes for all years; some of the projections cover large gaps.

Table 2.3 Estimated earnings from criminal activity in the United States, 1965–2000 (billions of current dollars)

	Tax evasion included		Tax evasion excluded	
Year	Estimated criminal income	Percent of GDP	Estimated criminal income	Percent of GDP
1965	49	6.8	18	2.5
1970	74	7.1	26	2.5
1975	118	7.2	45	2.7
1980	196	7.0	78	2.8
1985	342	8.1	166	4.0
1990	471	8.1	209	3.6
1995	595	8.0	206	2.8
2000	779	7.9	224	2.3

Note: Non–tax evasion crimes included trafficking in illicit drugs, human trafficking, burglary, larceny-theft, motor vehicle theft, robbery, fraud, arson, nonarson fraud, counterfeiting, illegal gambling, loan sharking, and prostitution. Tax evasion crimes included federal income, federal profits, and excise tax evasion.

Sources: Office of National Drug Control Policy (2000, 2001); Simon and Witte (1982); GAO (1980); Federal Bureau of Investigation's annual Uniform Crime Reports; Internal Revenue Service; International Organization on Migration; Abt, Smith, and Christiansen (1985); Kaplan and Matteis (1967); Carlson et al. (1984); and Key (1979).

A glimpse at one of the more complete years is presented in table 2.4. It reveals the general composition of the US criminal economy according to these estimates. In 1990, the most lucrative crime (in aggregate) was drug trafficking (cocaine, heroin, marijuana, and other), which resulted in approximately $97 billion in revenues. Fraud generated $60 billion while gambling generated less than $8 billion. The total for all crimes with available data amounted to roughly $470 billion, approximately 8 percent of US GDP in 1990. To obtain a smoother time series for comparison, data points were interpolated for the 18 crimes with the most consistently available figures (table 2.3). According to these data, criminal income in the United States rose from just under 7 percent of GDP in 1965 to around 8 percent in 1985, with the largest increase occurring in the early 1980s. However, when tax evasion estimates were removed from the totals, the criminal share of US GDP ranged from 2.5 to 4 percent, peaking in the late 1980s before dropping to the levels of the late 1960s.

The fraud estimate, by far the largest single item in most years, is particularly frail. It comes from a report by the Association of Certified Fraud Examiners (2002), which sent survey forms to 10,000 of its members, fewer than 10 percent of whom responded. Respondents provided specific information about cases of which they were aware. But they also were asked to estimate the percentage of revenues that would be lost in 2002 as a result of occupational fraud and abuse. As the median figure was 6 percent, using an estimate for US GDP of $10.4 trillion in 2002 leads to an estimate of $625 billion. No effort was made to adjust for nonresponse or to ask whether respondents were in fact in a position to make such estimates. Nor did the

Figure 2.1   Estimated criminal income as percent of US GDP, 1965–2000

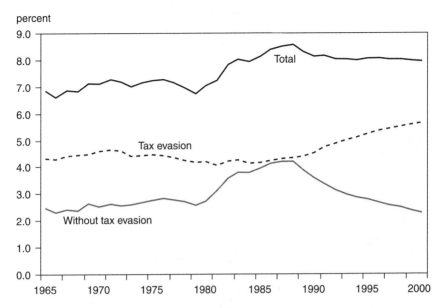

Source: See table 2.3.

study consider whether GDP was the correct base to use for these calculations. If each examiner estimated the share of the flow through his or her corporation, then the right base was much larger, namely the total volume of transactions through corporations.

Revenues from crimes involving stolen goods (burglary, larceny, and robbery) are probably overestimated, since they are based on the reported value of the stolen property. A victim may inflate the worth of an item to receive a higher insurance payment. Even if the claimed amount is accurate, a fence or pawnbroker is unlikely to pay a thief the retail value for pilfered goods; indeed, the standard figure used in research studies is that fences pay 20 to 30 percent of the market value of the good, depending on how easily it can be resold (Muscato 2003).

Even the estimates of revenues from drug sales, by far the most systematically developed, have very broad confidence intervals, though the government only publishes point estimates. One can get a sense of the uncertainty of these revenue estimates by examining revisions in the related estimates of the number of drug addicts that are published as part of the same studies. When calculated in 2000, the estimated number of heroin addicts for 1992 was 630,000; in 2001 this 1992 figure was revised up to 945,000 (Office of National Drug Control Policy 2000, 2001). Nor is this an isolated example. The 2000 estimate for frequent methamphetamine users in 1998 was

Table 2.4 Estimated criminal proceeds in the United States, 1990

Crime	Proceeds in billions of current dollars	Percent of total
Tax evasion	262.2	55.7
Cocaine trafficking	61.3	13.0
Fraud (nonarson)	59.3	12.6
Heroin trafficking	17.6	3.7
Prostitution	14.7	3.1
Loan sharking	14.0	3.0
Marijuana trafficking	13.5	2.9
Motor vehicle theft	8.0	1.7
Illegal gambling	7.6	1.6
Other drug trafficking	4.8	1.0
Larceny/theft	3.8	0.8
Burglary	3.5	0.7
Robbery	0.5	0.2
Human trafficking	0.2	0.04
Counterfeiting	0.1	0.02
Fraud arson	0.04	0.008
Total	471.1	

Sources: Office of National Drug Control Policy (2000, 2001); Simon and Witte (1982); GAO (1980); Federal Bureau of Investigation's annual *Uniform Crime Reports*; Internal Revenue Service; International Organization on Migration; Abt, Smith, and Christiansen (1985); Kaplan and Matteis (1967); and Carlson et al. (1984).

356,000; one year later the figure was revised to 659,000. Estimating the prevalence of rare behavior, particularly one that leads to erratic lifestyles, is difficult, resulting in a corresponding uncertainty. Taking into account the range in estimates in the numbers of drug addicts, the $70 billion estimate of revenues from drug sales in 2000 is probably best thought of as somewhere between $35 billion and $105 billion, with no particular central tendency (Office of National Drug Control Policy 2000, 2001).

Many of the estimates of criminal earnings have no known provenance. The demand for numbers generates a supply (Reuter 1986). If having an approximation of total income from the smuggling of human beings (for example, illegal immigrants) is useful for a congressional hearing or regulatory proceeding, then an organization will be found to produce such a number. In reality, however, there are no shortcuts to reliably generating this figure, and quantity and price estimates are critical. As it stands, there are only broad estimates of the numbers of illegal immigrants, even broader estimates of how many have purchased services from smugglers, and yet broader estimates of how much they paid on average. While it is possible to do surveys in immigrant communities and obtain reasonable response rates even from illegal immigrants (DaVanzo et al. 1994), it is not known whether questions about the immigrant experience will generate meaningful data.

Outside of the United States, estimates of criminal earnings are sparser and often equally implausible. Blades and Roberts (2002) report a small number of such estimates for OECD and transition economies. Their figures, admittedly partial and essentially guesstimates, are usually in the range of 0.5 to 1.0 percent of GDP.

Even taken at face value, these numbers are only weakly related to money laundering. Much of this income is earned by people who use the cash to directly purchase legal goods without making use of any financial institution. Small-time thieves earning $25,000 annually are unlikely to make use of a bank or any other means of storing or transferring value.[10] It is impossible to estimate or even guess what share of these revenues will require laundering.

Moreover, it is important in the context of estimating amounts of money to be laundered to distinguish gross revenues from criminal activities and the profits, after covering costs, from those activities. If criminals use cash to purchase legitimate goods, such as airline tickets for couriers, then that money laundering is quite different from most conventional notions of the activity. In fact, the legitimate nonlabor inputs to criminal activity constitute a very modest share of total costs; almost all expenses are those of purchasing criminal labor, but the distinction may be important for some offenses such as cigarette smuggling. A central question, then, is how much of the income needs to be laundered? Perhaps money is laundered only when it is exchanged into a different currency or when it tries to crawl up into the legitimate world—the "above-ground" economy. By definition, laundering turns dirty money into clean money. If the revenue from a criminal transaction remains in the underground economy, it can stay dirty without stigma.

Conclusions

Neither of the two broad approaches to estimating how much money is laundered—examining incomes in the broadly defined underground economy or incomes from criminal activities—provides numbers that meet minimal standards for policy guidance. The findings can support only the broadest statements about the extent of money-laundering activities. The underground economy, and even the criminal economy, probably amount to hundreds of billions of dollars each in the United States. However, this statement provides no possible guidance for assessing the effectiveness of

---

10. In most jurisdictions, the use of money acquired by illegal means to cover "living expenses" or operating costs is technically considered (self-) money laundering and often can be prosecuted under anti–money laundering statutes. However, this is not an aspect of the general phenomenon of money laundering that by itself would rise to the level of a public policy problem.

money-laundering controls by comparing the volume of money laundered across time or nations. If an estimate rises by 10 percent from one year to the next, it is as likely to be the result of changes in coverage or estimating technique as any change in the actual size of the underground economy or of criminal earnings.

Moreover, as will be discussed in more detail in chapter 3, there are very different social consequences of money laundering associated with different offenses. Such offenses vary in the amount of associated harm per million dollars, in their underlying nature, and in their distribution across different segments of society. Therefore, a national estimate of the total volume of money laundered would not necessarily have much value in guiding policy or assessing policy effectiveness. For example, if an annual estimate declined due to a reduction in large-value corporate fraud, but at the same time low-value terrorism financing increased, policymakers would not likely take any satisfaction from the reduction in the global aggregate. This underlines the basic point that controlling money laundering is a tool directed at many, varied objectives. What is important, at least in terms of measurement issues, is the amount of money laundered in connection with an activity that the anti–money laundering regime is specifically aiming to combat.

3

Money Laundering:
Methods and Markets

Money laundering is usually described as having three sequential elements—placement, layering, and integration—as defined in a report by the Board of Governors of the Federal Reserve System (2002, 7):

> The first stage in the process is placement. The placement stage involves the physical movement of currency or other funds derived from illegal activities to a place or into a form that is less suspicious to law enforcement authorities and more convenient to the criminal. The proceeds are introduced into traditional or nontraditional financial institutions or into the retail economy. The second stage is layering. The layering stage involves the separation of proceeds from their illegal source by using multiple complex financial transactions (e.g., wire transfers, monetary instruments) to obscure the audit trail and hide the proceeds. The third stage in the money laundering process is integration. During the integration stage, illegal proceeds are converted into apparently legitimate business earnings through normal financial or commercial operations.

Not all money-laundering transactions involve all three distinct phases, and some may indeed involve more (van Duyne 2003). Nonetheless, the three-stage classification is a useful decomposition of what can sometimes be a complex process.

In contrast to most other types of crime, money laundering is notable for the diversity of its forms, participants, and settings. It can involve the most respectable of banks unwittingly providing services to customers with apparently impeccable credentials. For example, Richard Scrushy, chairman and CEO of HealthSouth, a major health care corporation, was indicted on 85 counts, including fraud and money laundering. His financial executives pleaded guilty to using false earnings reports to mislead banks into providing a $1.25 billion credit line. Scrushy himself is alleged

Box 3.1   Laundering methods of a drug trafficker

"Rick" launched his own drug trafficking operation using the funds of the cartel he once served. With the help of former associates, he used several methods to launder the proceeds. Cash shipments arrived by boat or plane and were promptly placed by couriers into a range of bank accounts (a process known as "smurfing"), an activity that corresponds to the placement phase of money laundering. An agent then moved the funds to the personal accounts of overseas intermediaries, each of whom arranged to transfer the funds back into the country into accounts at the national central bank, which granted authorization.

At this point, Rick would call the intermediary to cancel the transfer. The funds were then withdrawn in cash from the intermediary's account and wired back in country to other accounts, using the authorization from the national central bank to explain the origin of the funds. Without knowing it, the central bank was giving legitimacy to drug monies.

After this layering phase, Rick purchased real estate with the funds, using lawyers, bank managers, and other professionals, which moves the process to the integration phase. He offered unusually high commission rates (3 to 5 percent) to gain the cooperation of the professionals with whom he was doing business. The real estate purchases were usually made in the names of other individuals or companies.

Eventually, several of the banks noticed that his account activities were rather odd and notified the national financial intelligence unit. An investigation revealed that Rick's scheme had laundered tens of millions of dollars over several years.

Source: Egmont Group (2000).

---

to have used personal checks, cashiers' checks, and wire transfers to purchase nearly $10 million worth of high-value goods and real estate during the layering phase of this laundering operation.

Money laundering can also involve small nonfinancial businesses knowingly providing similar services to violent criminals, as in the case of truckers smuggling large bundles of currency out of the country for drug traffickers.

Money laundering does not require international transactions; there are instances of purely domestic laundering.[1] Nonetheless, a large number of cases do involve the movement of funds across national borders. Though governments have unique police powers at the border, those same borders can impede the flow of information. Thus the description and analysis in this chapter place heavy emphasis on the international dimensions of money laundering.

---

1. Just to cite one example, in the *United States v. Clyde Hood et al., Central District of Illinois,* an indictment returned on August 18, 2000, charged the defendants with fraud for collecting checks from investors, who were promised a 5,000 percent return. Funds were deposited in checking accounts and used to incorporate and support participants' businesses, as well as to purchase real estate, all within the Mattoon, Illinois, area.

Several officials of the Washington, DC Teachers Union (WTU), including president Barbara A. Bullock, were implicated in a recent scandal involving the theft of $4.6 million.

The astonishingly simple scheme had several concurrent elements. One involved Bullock's chauffeur, Leroy Holmes, who in February 2003 pleaded guilty to laundering more than $1.2 million. Many of the more than 200 checks Holmes cashed were made out to creditors such as Verizon or the DC Treasurer, with the original payee's name crossed out and replaced with Holmes' name. He often left Independence Federal Savings Bank with his pockets stuffed with as much as $20,000 worth of bills. The bank never filed either the required currency transaction report or suspicious activity report and may face investigation for colluding in the union's money-laundering plan.

In addition, the WTU made several payments totaling $450,000 for the "consulting services" of a phony company called Expressions Unlimited. One of the company's partners, Michael Martin, claimed to be Bullock's hairdresser but has since pleaded guilty to money-laundering conspiracy charges.

Union credit cards were used to buy expensive clothing, electronic equipment, artwork, and other costly items. As of February 2004, Bullock had been sentenced to nine years in prison following a guilty plea, and four others had been indicted.

Source: Washington Post (various editions, 2003 and 2004).

Boxes 3.1 through 3.4 are examples of money laundering that illustrate the variety of clients, providers, and methods involved. The chapter then goes into more detail about the "market" for money laundering—what is known about the providers and prices they charge. The final section presents a typology of offenses intended to provide a structure for policy analysis in dealing with the heterogeneous set of offenses that engender money laundering.

Laundering Mechanisms

A striking feature of money laundering is the number of different methods used to carry it out. Some of the major mechanisms described below are associated with only one of the three phases of money laundering, while others are usable in any of the phases of placement, layering, and integration.

Four methods of money laundering—cash smuggling, casinos and other gambling venues, insurance policies, and securities—are described below in some detail. A number of others that may be of importance are listed in box 3.5. The descriptions draw heavily on the FATF's annual typologies reports, which list notable cases that illustrate the variety of laundering techniques used.

Box 3.3   "Underground" banking that finances human smuggling

A South Asian man ran a small business with an annual turnover of around $150,000. His banks were understandably surprised to see that between $1.7 million and $3.5 million flowed annually through his private accounts for three years. Their suspicious transaction reports triggered investigations that revealed that the suspect's business was the headquarters of an international "underground bank" with "branches" in several Central Asian and European countries. Along with small amounts intended to support relatives in the transferring parties' home countries, this illegal banking system was used to transfer large sums for smuggling people into Europe. In May 2000, the suspect and one of his branch managers were arrested. He had squirreled away around $140,000 in cash in a safe and had purchased his home for $400,000 in cash shortly before his arrest.

Source: FATF (2002b).

Cash Smuggling

One of the oldest placement techniques, common smuggling of currency, seems to be on the rise. Bulk shipments are driven across the border or hidden in cargo, even though it is illegal to export more than $10,000 in currency from the United States without filing a Report of International Transportation of Currency or Other Monetary Instruments (CMIR). Criminals have even been known to purchase shipping businesses so that they can store cash inside the goods. Individual couriers transport cash in checked or carry-on baggage or on their persons. Smugglers can also simply use the mail or a shipping company such as UPS or FedEx. US customs officials spend most of their resources inspecting people and cargo coming *into* the United States, so it is relatively easy to ship currency to another country.[2] Also, cash stockpiling (allowing cash to accumulate while waiting for a smuggling opportunity) is thought to have increased, particularly in port or border regions. If cash smuggling has grown overall, it may be partially attributed to the success of banks' antilaundering measures.

Casinos and Other Gambling Venues

Casinos.   Chips are bought with cash, then after a period of time during which gambling may or may not take place, the chips are traded in for a check from the casino, perhaps in the name of a third party. When a casino

---

2. The authority to search in the United States does not distinguish between entry and exit. However, historically there has been more interest in preventing the entry than the exit of inappropriate goods and people. Nonetheless, the US Customs Service does occasionally use its authority for exit inspections.

has establishments in different countries, it may serve as an unwitting international launderer if a customer requests that his or her credit be made available in a casino establishment in another country. In addition, tokens themselves may be used to purchase goods and services or drugs.

Horse racing.   Winning tickets are bought at a slight premium, allowing the winner to collect his or her money without tax liability and enabling the launderer to collect a check from the track. Relevant taxes will be deducted from this amount.

Lotteries.   As at horse tracks, winning tickets are purchased from the winners as they arrive at the lottery office to collect their winnings. In a case believed to be a common type of operation, a launderer placed many low-risk bets at various bookmakers within his city, ending up with a long-term 7 percent loss rate—an unusual pattern and poor record for a professional gambler. He had the checks for the winnings made out to 14 bank accounts in the names of 10 different third parties, some of whom happened to be armed robbers and their immediate families (FATF 2002b).

Insurance Policies

Single premium insurance policies, for which the premium is paid in an upfront lump sum rather than in annual installments, have increased in popularity. Launderers or their clients purchase them and then redeem them at a discount, paying the required fees and penalties and receiving a "sanitized" check from the insurance company. Insurance policies can also be used as guarantees for loans from financial institutions. Many insurance products are sold through intermediaries; consequently, insurance companies themselves sometimes have no direct contact with the beneficiary.

Box 3.5 Other money-laundering methods

Structuring or "smurfing." This involves breaking down cash deposits into amounts below the reporting threshold of $10,000. Couriers ("smurfs") are used to make the deposits in several banks or to buy cashier's checks in small denominations.

Informal value transfer systems. These which include *hawalas,* an Arabic word for a particular international underground banking system. Handed cash in country A, a *hawaladar* can turn it into cash (or sometimes gold) in country B. The *hawala* includes the complete service from placement to integration. Similar services are provided under other names in other parts of the world, such as *fe chi'en* in China.

Wire and electronic funds transfers. These refer to a method through which banks transfer control of money by sending notification to another institution by cable (in the past) or electronically. Such transfers remain a primary tool at all stages of the laundering process, but particularly in layering operations. Funds can be transferred through several different banks in several jurisdictions in order to blur the trail to the source of the funds. Or transfers can be made from a large number of bank accounts, into which deposits have been made by "smurfing" to a principal collecting account, often located abroad in an offshore financial center.

Legitimate business ownership. Dirty money can be added to the cash revenues of a legitimate business enterprise, particularly those that are already cash intensive, such as restaurants, bars, and video rental stores. The extra money is simply added to the till. The cost for this laundering method is the tax paid on the income. With companies whose transactions are better documented, invoices can be manipulated to simulate legitimacy. A used car dealership, for example, may offer a customer a discount for paying cash, then report the original sale price on the invoice, thus "explaining" the existence of the extra illicit cash.

A slightly more sophisticated scheme may allow a criminal to profit twice in setting up a publicly traded front company with a legitimate commercial purpose—first from the laundered funds commingled with those generated by the business, and second by selling shares in this company to unwitting investors.

"Shell" corporations. These exist on paper but transact either no business or minimal business. A related concept, used mostly in the United States, is the special purpose

(box continues next page)

In addition, relatively complex cases involving single premium contracts have recently been discovered, involving slower procedures and less liquid transactions. These longer-term processes offer criminals a lower risk of detection—in essence, time itself provides the layering by separating chronologically the predicate crime from the eventual payoff. Evidence also suggests forays by money launderers, or those seeking to launder money, into the reinsurance industry, attractive because of its relative lack of regulation. Such transactions allow for more layering.

Securities

The securities sector is characterized by frequent and numerous transactions, and several mechanisms can be used to make proceeds appear as

Box 3.5 *(continued)*

vehicle. These are set up, usually offshore, complete with bank accounts in which money can reside during the layering phase. The shell corporation has many potential uses. One example is to buy real estate or other assets, then sell them for a nominal sum to one's own shell corporation, which can then pass the funds on to an innocent third party for the original purchase price.

Real estate transactions. These can cloak illicit sources of funds or serve as legitimate front businesses, particularly if they are cash intensive. Properties may be bought and sold under false names or by shell corporations and can readily serve as collateral in further layering transactions.

Purchase of goods. This practice can be particularly attractive for laundering, especially certain items. Gold is popular because it is a universally accepted store of value, provides anonymity, is easily changed in form, and holds possibilities of double invoicing, false shipments, and other fraudulent practices. Fine art and other valuable items such as rare stamps are attractive for laundering purposes because false certificates of sale can be produced, or phony reproductions of masterpieces purchased. Moreover, the objects are easily moved internationally or resold at market value to integrate the funds.

Credit card advance payments. A credit card holder may make a large payment with dirty money to the issuing bank, resulting in a negative balance due. The bank then pays out the balance with a check, which can be deposited into a personal account as apparently clean money. In recent years, increased bank scrutiny of these transactions has discouraged this money-laundering technique.

Currency exchange bureaus. These are not as heavily regulated as banks, and de facto, at least, may not be regulated at all, so they are sometimes used for laundering. Substantial foreign exchange transactions are said to be shifting from banks to these small enterprises. Two main laundering techniques are used. The first is to change large amounts of criminal proceeds in local currency into low-bulk European currency for physical smuggling out of the country, and the second is electronic funds transfer to offshore centers. In one reported case, a currency bureau reportedly exchanged the equivalent of more than $50 million through a foreign bank without registering these transactions in its official records.

---

legitimate earnings from the financial markets. In addition, securities transactions often are international. The sector most commonly is used during the layering and integration phases, since most law-abiding brokers do not accept cash transactions. However, this obstacle is not an issue for criminals operating within the financial sector itself, such as embezzlers, insider traders, or perpetrators of securities frauds, because their (usually noncash) funds are already present in the financial system. During the layering phase, a launderer can simply purchase securities with illicit funds transferred from one or more accounts, then use the proceeds from selling these securities as legitimate money.

Unlike regular securities, bearer securities (common in some European countries) do not have a registered owner, and when they change hands the transaction involves physically handing over the security, thus leaving no paper trail. The security's owner is simply the person who possesses it. Many but not all countries and jurisdictions have phased out the use of bearer shares because of their potential role in money laundering and tax evasion.

Another laundering mechanism is the completion of simultaneous "put" and "call" transactions (in essence, "side bets" on a stock's gain or loss) on behalf of the same client, who pays with dirty money. The broker pays out the winning transaction with clean money (minus a commission) and destroys the losing transaction to avoid suspicion. Technically, the client has only broken even with this deal, but profit is not the ultimate objective.

In its annual typologies reports on recent trends in money laundering, the Financial Action Task Force (FATF) reports that some countries have seen a significant shift in laundering activities from the traditional banking sector to the nonbank financial sector, as well as to nonfinancial businesses and professions.[3] Even where the nonbank financial sector is subject to anti–money laundering rules, organizations in these sectors are less willing to abide by them, a reluctance that likely accounts for the relative paucity of suspicious transaction reports originating from the nonfinancial sector. Legal and accounting professionals in particular cite privacy concerns, but FATF experts suggest that the lack of public pressure may also play a role (FATF 2002b).

Which Methods Are Used for Which Crimes?

A reasonable conjecture is that different methods are used for laundering the proceeds from different predicate crimes. The annual typologies reports of the FATF and a report published in 2000 by the Egmont Group of Financial Intelligence Units describe recent cases that illustrate methods of laundering and investigation. Given that these are simply reported cases, they do not necessarily reflect the relative importance of different techniques. With that qualification, the FATF and Egmont Group reports can be used to develop a matrix matching 11 predicate crimes with 20 money-laundering methods (table 3.1). There were 223 cases available for classification, and each case involved one or more offenses and methods of laundering, thus producing a total of 580 entries.

Three offense categories accounted for over 70 percent of entries: drugs (185), fraud (125), and other kinds of smuggling (92). The types of laundering methods were more evenly distributed—wire transfers were involved in 131 cases (22 percent), but no other single method was involved in more than 75 cases. For the three major offense categories, the observations were broadly distributed across methods.

While these findings offer some insights into the laundering methods used for different offenses, the results should not be overemphasized.

---

3. The report offers no systematic evidence to support this statement, and it is difficult to identify a current database that would allow any agency to do so. But the conjecture is plausible, and an analysis of a fuller sample of actual cases would shed some light on its accuracy.

Table 3.1 Frequency of predicate offenses and methods

Method	Drug trafficking	Blue-collar[a]	Smuggling (non-drug)	Counter-feiting	Bribery/corruption	Tax evasion	Fraud	Terrorism	Crime unknown	Total
Cash smuggling	6	1	1				1	1		10
Money orders, cashiers' checks	12	1	6			3	4	3	2	31
Structured deposits	10	5	1		2	2	2	2	2	26
Casinos/bookmakers		1					3			4
Currency exchange bureaus	13	1	5				2	4		25
Wire transfers	33	5	22	1	7	4	30	18	11	131
False invoices/receipts	5	2	6		1	4	4		3	25
Credit cards			1			1	1	2		5
Front company/organization	18		15	1	3	5	19	6	6	73
Purchase of high-value goods	14		9		2		5		4	34
Insurance policies	5		1					3		9
Alternative remittance systems	4	2	6					4		16
Real estate	13	2	5	1	2		5		3	31
Lawyers	11	2			1	2	10		3	29
Accountants/financial officers	11	5	4	1	3		10	1	1	36
Offshore accounts	8	2	4		3	3	7	1	3	31
Securities	10	2				1	8		1	22
Trusts	4		1		1		2		1	9
Shell corporations	8	1	5		2	2	12		3	33
Total	185	32	92	4	27	27	125	45	43	580

a. Includes prostitution, armed robbery, loan sharking, and illegal gambling.

Sources: FATF typologies reports, 1998–2004 (reports prior to the 1997–98 report do not feature case studies); Egmont Group (2000).

Neither the FATF nor the Egmont Group makes any claim to be offering a representative sample of cases. However, the information does have some value. For example, the data show that drug traffickers and other smugglers use a wide variety of methods for laundering the proceeds of their crimes. More weakly, they suggest that some methods are not much used, such as alternative banking systems and trusts and securities.[4]

Who Provides the Laundering Services?

The only information available as to who launders money comes from criminal and civil investigations, and the data represent the interaction of enforcement tactics with the underlying reality. Enforcement may aim primarily at operations that are more professional (because they are higher-value targets) or less professional (because they are easier to catch). Drug dealers' money launderers may get more attention because the dealers themselves are under more intense scrutiny. A substantial share of all reported US money-laundering cases involve drugs (chapter 5). Thus, the following observations about available cases are merely indicative.

The most obvious nexus between the criminal and financial realms would be persons inside the financial institutions themselves. Bank employees can be coerced or bribed not to file suspicious activity reports (SARs) or currency transaction reports (CTRs). Alternatively, the forms may be filled out, with the government's copy conveniently filed in the trash while the other copy remains in a drawer in case of an investigation.[5]

Lawyers are thought to be among the most common laundering agents or at least facilitators, though they have been at the center of few cases in the United States. A lawyer can use his or her own name to acquire bank accounts, credit cards, loan agreements, or other money-laundering tools on behalf of the client. Lawyers can also establish shell corporations, trusts, or partnerships. In the event of an investigation, lawyer-client confidentiality privileges can be invoked. In one case cited by the FATF in its 1997–98 typologies report, a lawyer charged a flat fee to launder money by setting up annuity packages for his clients to hide the laundering. He also arranged for credit cards in false names to be issued to his clients, who could use the cards to make ATM cash withdrawals. The card issuer knew only the identity of the lawyer and had no knowledge of the clients' identities.

Other professionals involved in money laundering include accountants, notaries, financial advisers, stockbrokers, insurance agents, and real estate

---

4. A Dutch study reports some details on a sample of cases involving money laundering (van Duyne 2003). The sample was dominated by drug cases and most involved relatively simple means of laundering.

5. Electronic filing, which would eliminate this option, is not currently required, at least not in the United States.

agents. A British report on serious and organized crime noted that in 2002, "purchasing property in the UK was the most popular method identified, involving roughly one in three serious and organized crime groups where the method was known" (National Criminal Intelligence Service 2003, 53).

Markets for Laundering Services

Since money laundering is a criminal service offered in return for payment, making laundering services more expensive would reduce their volume and thus the volume of predicate crime. Price might thus serve as a performance indicator. Unfortunately, law enforcement agencies do not systematically record price information acquired in the process of developing money-laundering cases, since that information is not necessary to obtain a conviction.[6]

Moreover, price is an ambiguous concept in this context. Apart from the fact that some laundering agents provide only partial services (for example, placement or layering), there are at least two possible interpretations of price: first, the fraction received by the launderer, including what he or she paid to other service providers, and second, the share of the original total amount that does not return to the owner's control. The latter share could include tax payments, as in the case of a retail proprietor who might charge only 5 percent for allowing the commingling of illegal funds with his or her store's receipts, but then might have to add another 5 percent for the sales tax that would be generated by these fraudulent receipts.[7]

The policy-relevant price is the second of these, i.e., the difference between the amount laundered and the amount eventually kept by the offender. Pushing offenders to use laundering methods that involve smaller payments to launderers but higher total costs (for example, because of taxes) to the predicate offender is indeed preferable to raising the revenues received by launderers as a group; after all, the difference may include payments to the public sector. Such substitution might occur if the government mounted more sting operations aimed at customers.

The difference is by no means only of theoretical interest. Take, for example, one case cited by the Egmont Group (2000) of high-priced laundering where most of the price did not accrue to the launderer. A credit manager at a car loan company was suspicious about one of his customers. "Ray" had just bought a luxury sports car worth about $55,000, financing the car through the credit company for $40,000, and paying the balance in cash.

---

6. The 2002 US *National Money Laundering Strategy* noted the importance of collecting such data.

7. It is possible, of course, that this laundering will generate income tax payments. This depends on the skill of the firm in generating false expenses. However, the sales tax is an unavoidable consequence of inflating gross retail revenues.

Records showed that Ray had taken out several loans over the past few years, all for the same amount of money and with a large portion as a cash deposit. In many cases the loans had been repaid early with cash. The national financial intelligence unit realized Ray was laundering for a long-established criminal organization, putting cash from the sale of drugs into the banking system. He would resell the newly bought cars, obtaining checks to deposit into a single bank account, in all totaling over $300,000. The losses made on the loan and the drop in the automobiles' resale values were the cost of obtaining "clean" money.

Information about the price of money-laundering services is scattered and anecdotal. In the money-laundering activity targeted by Operation Polar Cap, a coordinated law enforcement sting operation during the late 1980s, the drug trafficker would pay only 4.5 percent to the government sting launderer initially, but was willing to go to 5 percent if the laundering were done rapidly (Woolner 1994, 43). Later in the operation there were reports of much higher margins. Experienced investigators refer to a general price range of 7 to 15 percent for laundering for drug dealers, but some reports are inconsistent with such estimates. One *National Money Laundering Strategy* (US Treasury 2002, 12) reported a study that found commission rates varying between 4 and 8 percent but rising as high as 12 percent.

Other criminals pay much less for money-laundering services. For example, John Mathewson, who operated a Cayman Islands bank that laundered money for a number of white-collar offenders (e.g., Medicare fraudsters, recording pirates) and US tax evaders, charged a flat fee of $5,000 for an account, plus a $3,000 per annum management fee (Fields and Whitfield 2001). Mathewson, who provided a complete set of services, also kept 1 percent of the float that the clients' money earned when held overnight by other banks (US Senate 2001a, b).

The price paid for a particular money laundering service apparently is partly a function of the predicate crime and the volume of funds that needs to be laundered. Whereas legitimate financial transactions generate lower per-unit costs the larger they are, the opposite is true for money laundering—the risk of detection is a major cost, and that risk will rise with the quantity being laundered. On the other hand, a broker involved in Colombian black market peso operations stated in an interview that he charged less for larger volumes of money. He once garnered between $600,000 and $700,000 (5 to 6 percent) on a $12 million transaction that took two months to process.[8]

Table 3.2 provides information on a few cases for which some data on prices are available. The data are merely illustrative and so sparse that no inferences about price trends can be drawn.

---

8. Public Broadcast Service (PBS) interview. www.pbs.org/wgbh/pages/frontline/shows/drugs/interviews/david.html.

Table 3.2 Examples of money-laundering costs (in current dollars)

Name and date	Predicate offense	Amount laundered	Stages covered and techniques	Amount launderer received	Total cost of laundering to client	Comments
Name unknown, 1994	Drug trafficking	$633,900	Placement: Smurfing Layering: Transfers, offshore accounts, trusts Layering/integration: Real estate, truck parts All stages: Accountants	$63,390	10 percent commission	Cash handed off to accountant, who handled all stages of laundering.
Servicio Uno, date unknown	Drug trafficking	$3.3 million annually	All stages: Alternative remittance system	$165,000– $330,000 annually	5–10 percent commission	
Unknown	Armed robbery	$3.3 million	Placement/integration: Bookmaker No real layering necessary	Unknown	7 percent loss on bets	Launderer placed bets with bookmaker at high stakes and low odds, then received checks for winnings made out to clients.
"Henry," date unknown	Fraud	$850,000	Placement: Deposits in associates' accounts Layering: Wire trans-fers, notaries	All, minus costs (self-launderer)	$210,000, including real estate expenses and payoffs to associates	

(table continues next page)

Table 3.2 Examples of money-laundering costs (in current dollars) *(continued)*

Name and date	Predicate offense	Amount laundered	Stages covered and techniques	Amount launderer received	Total cost of laundering to client	Comments
German Cadavid, 1995	Drug trafficking	50–60 million pound sterling	Placement: Exchange business Layering: Structured wire transfers	Estimated $3–$4 million	7 percent commission	Owned money-transmitting service and exchange office serving local Dominicans.
Robert Hirsch, Richard Spence, Harvey Weinig, 1994	Drug trafficking	About $100 million	Placement: Cash shipments and large cash deposits Layering: Wire transfers	About $7 million, minus $1,000 to $6,000 to couriers per pickup	7 percent commission	Worked for Cali cartel. Deposits approved by rogue assistant manager at Citibank branch. Tried to steal $2.5 million from cartel.
Nilo Fernandez, 1993	None—Sting	$335,000	Placement: Cash shipments to Philippines Layering: Shell corporations	$56,000	16 percent commission	Fernandez was launderer for Dung Cong Wa, Vietnamese dealer in methamphetamines and stolen computer parts.
Stephen Saccoccia, 1993	Drug trafficking	$200–$750 million	Placement: Cashier's checks Layering: Wire transfers, false invoices	$20–$75 million	10 percent commission	First and only launderer for both Cali and Medellin cartels.

A large number of money laundering cases appear to involve opportunistic laundering rather than professional services. Where someone apart from the offender provides the service, he may provide it only to that offender, perhaps because they are related or connected through some other activity. Drug dealers appear to be more likely to purchase formal money-laundering services.

We began this study assuming that money-laundering services were provided by professional money launderers. Some would be engaged in other legitimate activities, but the assumption was that money laundering was a service that they provided to a number of clients, and that they were willing to provide it to those who could demonstrate financial capability and who seemed not to be working for the government. Such launderers exist, but in reported cases they are surprisingly rare.[9] A great deal of money seems to be self-laundered. For example, box 3.4 briefly describes laundering by Robert Maxwell, a flamboyant press lord in the United Kingdom. Other people may have aided him, but no one was an independent provider of laundering services. Terrorist financing cases also seem to involve people who belong very much to the cause rather than being mere commercial providers.

This is certainly not the first study to raise this question about self-laundering or money laundering integrated with the underlying crime. A decade ago, Australia's National Crime Authority stated: "Most money-laundering activity is carried out by the primary offender, not by 'professional' launderers, although the use of complicit individuals is often crucial to the success of the money laundering schemes" (Gilmore, 1999, 128, citing National Crime Authority, 1991, vii).

The question of whether there are large numbers of stand-alone money launderers is important for both policy and research purposes. The rationale for the current system is based in part on the claim that its design allows for apprehending and punishing actors who have provided a critical service for those who commit certain kinds of crimes, and who previously were beyond the reach of the law. For research purposes, the assumption of a substantial number of stand-alone launderers makes the market a useful heuristic device for analyzing the effects of laws and programs. As will be discussed in chapter 5, however, that assumption appears not to be well justified by the facts.

If money laundering is done mostly by predicate offenders or by non-specialized confederates, then the current regime accomplishes much less. A central point in a study by Mariano-Florentino Cuéllar (2003) is

---

9. The case of the Beacon Hill Service Corporation (Morgenthau 2004) is a conspicuous exception to this generalization. Beacon Hill was an unlicensed money-transferring business that allegedly provided money-laundering services to a wide range of clients over a period of almost a decade.

that in the enforcement of the AML regime there is no new set of offenders, just a new set of charges against the same offenders. Consequently, the new tools of the AML regime, while they might help increase the efficiency of law enforcement, would likely bring substantially more modest gains than has been posited.

For research, the market model may be strained. Price may not be well defined to most participants because the service is rarely purchased. Risk may also be hard to observe because it is derivative from participation in other elements of the crime. Assessing how interventions increase risks and prices for those transactions that do involve stand-alone launderers will have only modest value.

Classification of Offenses

Offenses can be classified into five categories for purposes of understanding the effects of specific money-laundering controls: drug distribution, other "blue-collar" crime, white-collar crime, bribery and corruption, and terrorism. The categories are more homogeneous with respect to the effects of interventions and the seriousness and distribution of the harm caused by particular offenses to society, but they also differ from each other in these dimensions. It can be conjectured, for example, that the response of white-collar offenders to increased scrutiny of, say, casinos, is likely to be different from the response of those who launder money on behalf of drug dealers. Similarly, the benefits from reducing white-collar crime by 1 percent might be seen as substantially less than those associated with a similar reduction in drug trafficking. The distribution of benefits from reducing either of the two types of offenses may also be quite different: those who are harmed by drug trafficking are disproportionately from poor and minority urban populations, while the costs of white-collar crime are borne far more broadly across society.

The five-part classification is offered here as a preliminary typology. Further research may show that some categories can be collapsed or that others may need to be expanded. For example, research might eventually demonstrate a need to distinguish between white-collar crimes in which the proximate victim is a corporation and those in which the victim is a set of individuals. It may indeed even be that the characteristic of the fruits of the crime matter; certainly cash is different from other forms of proceeds. At this stage, the classification is useful for conceptual purposes and for suggesting approaches to policy modeling.

Table 3.3 provides hypotheses about the differences among the five categories of offenses in four dimensions: reliance on cash, quantities of money involved, the severity of adverse effects, and whom they affect. The entries concerning the "severity of harm" and the "most affected populations" are judgments offered here not as authoritative but simply

Table 3.3 Taxonomy of predicate crimes for money laundering

Crime	Cash	Scale of operations	Severity of harm	Most affected population
Drug dealing	Exclusively	Very large	Severe	Urban minority groups
Other blue-collar	Mostly	Small to medium	Low to modest	?
White-collar	Mix	Mix	Low to modest	Broad
Bribery and corruption	Sometimes	Large	Severe	Developing countries
Terrorism	Mix	Small	Most severe	Broad

to identify dimensions that deserve consideration in policymaking and research.

Drug Distribution

Major drug traffickers face a unique problem, which is how to regularly and frequently manage large sums of cash, much of it in small bills. For example, in Operation Polar Cap in the mid-1980s, US agents acting as distributors associated with the Medellín cartel, handled some $1.5 million a week in currency. Few legitimate establishments—or even illegal ones, for that matter—operate with such large and steady cash flows.

This distinctive characteristic of drug distribution is particularly important because the current anti–money laundering regime initially was constructed primarily to control drug trafficking, an aspect of the regime that continues to affect public perceptions of the nature of the money-laundering problem.

Other Blue-Collar Crime

Other potential large-scale illegal markets that would seem at first glance likely candidates for generating a demand for money laundering include gambling and the smuggling of people. However, as seen in chapter 2, these crimes in fact generate relatively modest demand for money laundering simply because they have substantially lower revenues than drug markets. That is not a historical constant but an observation about the past two decades in industrial societies.

The amounts of money for any individual operation in these other areas appear to be much smaller than for drug distribution, in part because total and unit revenues are smaller and in part because what has to be laundered is net rather than gross revenues. For example, a bookmaker will receive from customers and agents only what they owe at the end of the accounting period (perhaps one or two weeks).

White-Collar Crime

The white-collar crime category includes a heterogeneous range of activities, such as embezzlement, fraud, and tax evasion. A distinctive feature of these crimes is that the money laundering is often an integral part of the offense itself, as illustrated in the Washington Teachers Union case (box 3.2). The Enron case demonstrates a more complex scheme in which shell corporations in the Cayman Islands served not only as questionable tax shelters but also as laundering mechanisms to obscure a trail of fraudulent behavior. Money-laundering services in such cases often are provided by the offenders themselves, since the offense requires skills similar to those involved in money laundering. Indeed, where there are false invoices and other elements of accounting fraud, such activities often constitute both the predicate as well as the laundering offense.

Bribery and Corruption

While bribery and corruption can be classified as white-collar crime, they are distinctive in terms of who benefits (public officials and those who benefit from their decisions), where they occur (primarily though not exclusively in poor countries), and the nature of their harm (reduced government credibility and quality of public services), as well as the almost inherently international character of the laundering—those corrupted would be well advised to keep the proceeds out of local banks unless the banks themselves were complicit or the amounts were small. Money laundering also is often embedded in the offense itself when the corruption is large-scale.

Terrorism

As has been frequently noted, the distinctive feature of terrorism is that it takes money both legitimately and criminally generated and converts it into criminal use. The sums of money involved are said to be modest—tens or hundreds of thousands of dollars rather than millions. Yet the harm is unique and enormous.

Table 3.3 summarizes the assessments of the relevant differences between the five types of offenses categorized in this chapter. There will be near consensus that terrorism poses a greater threat to social welfare than any of the other offenses. The harm associated with white-collar crime and non-drug, blue-collar crimes, on the other hand, may be considered by many to cause modest harms relative to the others. However, these two categories are very heterogeneous. For example, major environmental crimes (white-collar) could well strike some observers as just as harmful as selling cocaine.

The assessment of distributional consequences is intended as a reminder that benefits of interventions are far from uniform, since these offenses affect different parts of society. Indeed, there even are significant differences across nations; kleptocracy—corruption by high-level officials—is probably more important for sub-Saharan Africa than any of the other offenses.

Conclusions

This chapter has sketched only a few of the many dimensions of the money-laundering business. For example, it has addressed neither the manner in which laundering is distributed among nations, a matter of great political interest and controversy, nor the characteristics of those involved (such as their criminal histories and occupations), about which almost nothing is known. Rather, the focus has been on important characteristics that have been little studied in evaluating existing money-laundering controls.

Most striking is the variety of money-laundering methods and the variegated nature of what generates laundering. Much more is known about drug dealing, and it probably forms its own submarket, with more reliance on professional money launderers than other submarkets. So while it may be useful analytically to consider money laundering as a market, it is clearly a variegated set of markets at best.

Examining the variety of offenses and their adverse consequences suggests that the estimates of the total volume of money laundered, as set forth in chapter 2, have limited value, for a number of reasons. A reduction in the total amount of money laundering that represented a decline in gambling or corporate fraud but hid a smaller increase in terrorist finance would hardly be indicative of progress, given the much greater social harm caused by terrorism. Similarly, the methods that may prove most effective in reducing money laundering associated with cash smuggling for cocaine dealers may be much less useful in controlling money laundering by kleptocrats. So while there are certainly commonalities in many dimensions of money laundering across different offenses, it is also important to track performance of the AML regime for the individual categories of offenses.

4

The Anti–Money Laundering Regime

The global regime to control money laundering involves three dimensions: national and international building blocks, a firm legal and enforcement foundation, and close interaction between the public and private sectors in order to lower compliance costs and raise the probability of achieving its objectives. In principle, the global regime should have an agreed-upon international legal foundation with which national regimes are consistent in terms of laws and standards. The goal should be uniform enforcement and seamless cooperation across national jurisdictions. Cooperation and consultation with the private sector are important because they will contribute to lower costs, create a level playing field, and promote an accepted global public good from which the marginal benefit to each participant exceeds the cost, and where the incentive and scope for free riding are small.

In practice, this idealization of the global anti–money laundering (AML) regime is unattainable. The establishment of a robust AML regime is a challenge because of differences in institutions, perspectives, and priorities among countries as well as within them. As a result, compromises driven by the need to balance competing objectives are made at all levels in all jurisdictions.

This chapter summarizes the AML regime as it has evolved over some 30 years, and particularly since the mid-1980s.[1] It has two basic pillars, prevention and enforcement. The chapter summarizes the AML regime as it has evolved in the United States and includes a review of the *National*

---

1. See the glossary for thumbnail descriptions of many of the terms and institutions mentioned in this chapter.

Money Laundering Strategies of 1999–2003 in order to illustrate the structure and goals of the US AML regime. That regime is then briefly compared and contrasted with those in other countries in the context of multilateral efforts to establish a uniform, global AML regime. The chapter concludes with a short section on the costs of anti–money laundering efforts, which includes an estimate that a reasonable upper bound of the gross financial cost is $25 per capita.

Three principal conclusions come out of the review of the AML regime. First, the prevention pillar of the US regime has expanded to include a growing number of institutions and activities, while the enforcement pillar covers a growing number of crimes. Second, the past 15 to 20 years have seen the parallel development of a global AML regime alongside the US one, in part as a response to US pressure and leadership but also in response to the political and technological influences of globalization. Just as these forces have contributed to economic progress, they have provided opportunities for economic and financial mischief and have enhanced the scope for cross-border criminal activity.[2] Third, the national and global AML regimes as they exist today are imperfect because their construction has involved trade-offs between the actual and perceived benefits and costs of expanding them, between the cooptation of the private sector and privacy and human rights concerns, between national and international priorities, and between national and subnational priorities and structures.

Prevention and Enforcement

The prevention pillar of the AML regime is designed to deter criminals from using private individuals and institutions to launder the proceeds of their crimes. Enforcement is designed to punish criminals when, despite prevention efforts, they have facilitated the successful laundering of those proceeds.

The prevention pillar has four key elements: customer due diligence (CDD), reporting, regulation and supervision, and sanctions (figure 4.1, from bottom to top). CDD is intended to limit criminal access to the financial system and to other means of placing the proceeds of crime. Reporting requirements alert authorities to activities that may involve attempts to launder those proceeds. Regulations implement anti–money laundering laws and often specify detailed CDD and reporting requirements, while supervision ensures compliance with laws and regulations by financial institutions and nonfinancial businesses and activities. Finally, sanctions punish individuals and institutions that fail to implement the prevention regime, in particular with respect to CDD and reporting requirements.

---

2. Gilmore (1999), Levi (2002), and Wechsler (2001) provide additional background material on the global AML regime.

Figure 4.1 Pillars of the anti–money laundering regime

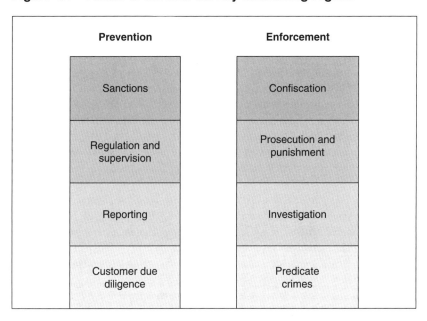

The enforcement pillar also has four key elements: a list of underlying offenses or predicate crimes, investigation, prosecution and punishment, and confiscation (figure 4.1). The list of predicate crimes establishes the legal basis for criminalizing money laundering. Various detection and investigative techniques are used to identify specific instances of money laundering and link each to predicate crimes. If justified by the investigation, the money launderer is prosecuted. If convicted, the money launderer is not only fined or sentenced to serve time, but the criminal proceeds that he was attempting to launder may also be confiscated or forfeited after having been initially blocked or seized.

Consider how this framework interacts with a hypothetical bread-and-butter money-laundering operation. A drug dealer, having collected $25,000 from the sale of illegal drugs, takes the money to a bank and seeks to open an account in order to deposit the money (placement) before wiring it to a bank in Colombia (layering), with the ultimate intention of bringing the funds back to the United States to invest in a legitimate business (integration). An effective AML regime requires the bank to conduct CDD before opening this account through a process sometimes referred to as "knowing your customer." What is the true name of the customer? Where does he live? What is his line of business? Can the bank be reasonably confident that the money that the customer wants to deposit is not derived from criminal activity?

Assume that the customer succeeds in passing these tests and is allowed to open an account. The bank is still required to submit a report to the authorities about the large cash deposit. An employee of the bank may also be suspicious of the fact that the customer is wiring a large amount of money to a bank in Colombia, and may decide that it is appropriate to submit a suspicious activity report (SAR) to the authorities.

If the bank fails to conduct CDD or to submit one or more reports about the cash deposit and the wiring of the funds to Colombia, contrary to regulations promulgated by the Federal Reserve and other banking supervisors, this failure may be uncovered during a supervisory examination or subsequent criminal investigation. As a consequence, the bank may be fined or otherwise sanctioned or penalized for not complying with the regulations.

Turning to the enforcement pillar of the AML regime, laundering (or the attempted laundering) of the proceeds from drug dealing can be prosecuted under US anti–money laundering law because drug dealing is a predicate crime or underlying offense for such a prosecution. The report of the bank about the large cash deposit or the suspicious transfer of the funds once they were deposited may lead to the detection of the drug dealing. Alternatively, law enforcement authorities may have had the depositor under observation as a suspected drug dealer and might use the bank reports as part of their investigation and prosecution of the underlying crime. Moreover, if it turns out that the bank deliberately assisted the criminal in laundering proceeds, or that a bank officer facilitated the laundering unbeknownst to and in violation of the bank's internal controls, then the bank or the officer could also be prosecuted for money laundering. Finally, it is possible that the funds never made it to Colombia, were seized, and subsequently confiscated as a result of a forfeiture proceeding.

In practice, the anti–money laundering regime rarely operates as in the simplified hypothetical example. The proceeds of the drug sales may be deposited in many separate branches of the bank, into the existing account of a legitimate business, or in amounts of less than $10,000 in order to avoid detection. They may take the form of a check rather than cash because they are the proceeds of a crime other than drug dealing, such as embezzlement. The depositor may be a lawyer acting on behalf of a shell corporation set up for a cigarette smuggler.

The examples of predicate crimes and methods of money laundering presented in chapter 3 suggest that the number of permutations and combinations of crimes and methods is very large. As a consequence, the prevention and enforcement pillars of the AML regime have been extended from banks to other types of financial and nonfinancial businesses and to individuals such as lawyers and accountants (known as "gatekeepers") who facilitate access to those institutions and businesses. However, the basic features of the AML regime remain the same. Prevention combines customer due diligence and reporting that is required by regulations under anti–money laundering laws. Supervision is employed and potential sanctions are available to ensure that the prevention pillar is firmly in place. Meanwhile, as criminals gather the proceeds of their predicate crimes, the investigation, prosecution and punishment, and confiscation elements of the enforcement pillar are employed to combat the underlying crime as well as to tighten the screws on the money-laundering process.

Current US Anti–Money Laundering Regime

The US anti–money laundering regime is central to the global regime because the central role of the US economy and financial system in the world today frequently results in the United States being the ultimate destination, or at least the conduit, for proceeds from crimes that may have been committed outside the country. Thus, the US AML regime is often, although not always, a model for other national regimes. The first column of table 4.1 chronologically lists the major developments in the US AML regime since 1970. Thumbnail descriptions of the major entries are in the glossary.

In many respects, the US prevention pillar is more elaborate and has evolved more than the enforcement pillar. Although the list of US predicate crimes that can give rise to money-laundering investigations and prosecutions has expanded substantially. In practice, there may be some tension between the two pillars, as when, for example, financial supervisory authorities are uncomfortable with the techniques of criminal investigative authorities.

Prevention

Table 4.2 summarizes the prevention pillar of the current US AML regime, including changes that have resulted since enactment in October 2001 of the USA PATRIOT Act and its subsequent implementation. The elements of the prevention pillar are listed across the top of the table, and three broad categories of economic actors (along with some subcategories) are listed down the side. The cells in the table indicate whether or to what extent the elements of the prevention pillar are applied to the various subcategories of economic activities.

Core Financial Institutions

The most stringent requirements apply to core financial institutions such as banks, securities firms, insurance companies, and various combinations of those institutions. All are required to have comprehensive AML compliance

Table 4.1 Evolution of the AML regime in the United States, Europe, and globally

Year	United States	Europe	Global
1970	Bank Secrecy Act (BSA) Racketeer Influenced and Corrupt Organizations Act (RICO)		
1977	Foreign Corrupt Practices Act (FCPA)		
1980		Measures Against the Transfer and Safe-keeping of Funds of Criminal Origin (Council of Europe)	Offshore Group of Banking Supervisors (OGBS) established
1986	Money Laundering Control Act (MLCA)	Drug Trafficking Offenses Act (United Kingdom)	Inter-American Drug Abuse Control Commission of the Organization of American States (OAS/CICAD) established ICPO–Interpol resolution on economic and financial crime
1988	Anti–Drug Abuse Act Money Laundering Prosecution Improvements Act		Statement of Principles (Basel Committee) UN (Vienna) Convention Against Illicit Traffic in Narcotic Drugs and Psychotropic Substances
1989			Financial Action Task Force (FATF) established
1990	Crime Control Act	Convention (Strasbourg) on Laundering, Search, Seizure and Confiscation of Proceeds from Crime (CoE)	FATF Forty Recommendations released Caribbean FATF established at Aruba meeting of Caricom
1991		First Money Laundering Directive (European Commission)	

Year			
1992	Annunzio-Wylie Money Laundering Act		Model Regulations Concerning Laundering Offenses Connected to Illicit Drug Trafficking and Other Serious Offenses released (OAS/CICAD)` International Organization of Securities Commissions (IOSCO) resolution on money laundering
1994	Money Laundering Suppression Act		OAS/CICAD declaration of Principles and Plan of Action at Summit of the Americas
1995	Regulation of funds transfers Revision of currency transaction report (CTR)	Europol created Europol Drugs Unit (EDU) established	Egmont Group of Financial Intelligence Units of the World established Communiqué of Summit of the Americas Ministerial Conference Concerning the Laundering of Proceeds and Instrumentalities of Crime (OAS/CICAD)
1996	Simplified suspicious activity report (SAR), tribal casinos regulated, exemptions to CTR reporting		FATF Forty Recommendations revised International Money Laundering Information Network (IMoLIN) established
1997	Proposed rules for money service businesses	Action Plan to Combat Organized Crime (European Union) CoE establishes the Select Committee of Experts on the Evaluation of Anti–Money Laundering Measures (PC-R-EV)	OECD Convention on Combating Bribery of Foreign Officials in International Business Transactions adopted
1998	Money Laundering and Financial Crimes Strategy Act SARs for casinos and card clubs	Joint Action on corruption in the private sector (European Union)	OECD report on Harmful Tax Practices Asia/Pacific Group on Money Laundering (APG) established UN Political Declaration and Action Plan against Money Laundering Model Regulations Concerning Laundering Offenses Connected to Illicit Drug Trafficking and Other Serious Offenses (OAS/CICAD)

(table continues next page)

Table 4.1 Evolution of the AML regime in the United States, Europe, and globally *(continued)*

Year	United States	Europe	Global
1999	Money service business regulation issued		Model Legislation on Laundering, Confiscation and International Co-Operation in Relation to the Proceeds of Crime (for civil law jurisdictions) released by the UN Office for Drug Control and Crime Prevention (UNDCCP)
	First National Money Laundering Strategy		OECD Convention on Combating Bribery of Foreign Officials in International Business Transactions entered into force
	Foreign Narcotics Kingpin Designation Act		Eastern and Southern Africa Anti–Money Laundering Group (ESAAMLG) established
			UN Convention for the Suppression of the Financing of Terrorism
2000		Recovering the Proceeds of Crime Report (United Kingdom)	Wolfsberg Global Anti–Money Laundering Guidelines for Private Banking (Wolfsberg Principles) issued
			FATF Report on Non-Cooperative Countries and Territories (NCCT)
			OECD list of 35 tax havens with harmful tax practices released
			Model Legislation on Money Laundering and Proceeds of Crime (for common law jurisdictions) (UNDCCP)
			Okinawa G-7 Summit endorses G-7 Finance Ministers' Report on Actions Against Abuse of the Global Financial System
			Financial Stability Forum Report of Working Group on Offshore Financial Centers
			Regional Task Force on Anti–Money Laundering in Latin America (GAFISUD) established
			UN (Palermo) Convention Against Transnational Organized Crime

2001	US PATRIOT Act: International Money-Laundering Abatement and Anti–Terrorist Financing Act (Title III)	Second Money Laundering Directive (European Union)	Report on Customer Due Diligence for Banks (Basel Committee) FATF Eight Special Recommendations on Terrorist Financing released
2002		Europol mandate expanded Proceeds of Crime Act (United Kingdom)	FATF Consultation Paper on Revisions to Forty Recommendations released FATF/IMF/World Bank Agreement on AML Pilot Project for Assessing Compliance with Anti–Money Laundering and Combating the Financing of Terrorism Standards Wolfsberg Statement on the Suppression of the Financing of Terrorism Wolfsberg Anti–Money Laundering Principles for Correspondent Banking International Association of Insurance Supervisors (IAIS) Anti–Money Laundering Guidance Notes for Insurance Supervisors and Insurance Entities
2003		Money Laundering Regulations revised (United Kingdom)	New FATF Forty Recommendations released UN Convention Against Corruption Wolfsberg Statement on Monitoring, Screening, and Searching

Note: See glossary for thumbnail descriptions of some elements.

Table 4.2 Prevention pillar of the US anti–money laundering regime

	Customer due diligence	Reporting requirements	Supervision	Sanction
Financial institutions				
Core financial institutions[a]	Yes	Yes	Yes	Yes
Other types of financial institutions[b]	Yes	Yes	Some	Limited
Nonfinancial businesses				
Casinos	Yes	Yes	Some	Yes
Dealers in precious metals and stones	Yes	Yes	No	Yes
Real estate agents	No	No	No	No
Other[c]	No	Some	No	No
Professions				
Lawyers and accountants	Limited	Limited	Very limited	Very limited
Trust and company services providers	Limited	Limited	Very limited	Very limited

a. Depository institutions, securities firms, insurance companies, and combinations of them.

b. For example, mutual funds commodity trading advisers, and investment advisers.

c. For example, travel agencies, and vehicle sellers.

programs and are traditionally subject to federal as well as state regulation and supervision.[3]

With respect to customer due diligence, these institutions must comply with extensive requirements in setting up new accounts and conducting transactions.[4] The assessment requirements are risk-based in the sense that the amount of information required depends on the institution's size, location, and customer base; the customer's size, location, and type of business; and the services offered to the customer. If the institution is unable to reach a satisfactory finding in the course of its due diligence, it is generally expected to decline to open the account or complete the transaction. The institution is required as well to retain records of its customer due diligence activities.

Turning to reporting requirements, institutions are required to submit suspicious activity reports (SARs) to the US Treasury Department's Financial Crimes Enforcement Network (FinCEN), cash transaction reports (CTRs) to the Internal Revenue Service (IRS), and Reports of International

---

3. Stand-alone US insurance companies are primarily supervised at the state level but are covered by federal AML laws and subject to federal AML regulations.

4. Current US AML regulations describe the CDD process for various institutions as a customer identification program (CIP). The information required for new customers includes name, address, date of birth, and taxpayer identification number (or passport number for a foreign customer). The information required for transactions includes the identity of those participating, addresses, legal capacity, and beneficial owner of the funds involved.

Transportation of Currency or Other Monetary Instruments (CMIRs) to the Customs Service.[5] Some types of activity may have a threshold below which it is not necessary to submit reports, such as suspicious transactions aggregating less than $5,000.[6] The normal threshold for CTRs and CMIRs is $10,000 and covers withdrawals as well as deposits.

One criticism of the US AML regime heard both in the United States and abroad is that these reporting requirements generate so much data as to cause an information overload, making it difficult for the recipient agencies to use the information efficiently in law enforcement and related investigatory activities.[7] Those who report the data contribute to the problem because their own procedures may be biased toward submitting unnecessary reports. No entity is penalized for excessive filing, and doing so can even provide implicit or explicit protection from criticism. The US AML regime and core financial institutions have also been criticized for applying more stringent CDD and reporting requirements to foreign than to domestic customers and transactions.

Core financial institutions such as banks are subject to substantial supervision that normally includes annual on-site examinations to ensure their compliance with a wide array of laws and regulations. A significant portion of the examination covers compliance with anti–money laundering and Bank Secrecy Act regulations, including reviewing other internal or external audits and testing institutions' procedures and processes.

If an institution is found to have fallen short of what is required or to be sloppy in implementing AML regulations, rules, and guidance procedures, it can be subject to informal or formal administrative actions by the regulator and, potentially, civil and criminal penalties. Experienced federal officials note that these examinations primarily serve to reinforce the prevention pillar of the overall AML regime, and rarely turn up direct evidence of actual money laundering.

The four elements of the prevention pillar of the US AML regime are applied comprehensively to US core financial institutions. It is not a zero-

---

5. US banks have been operating under a de facto order to report suspicious transactions since being required to do so by supervisors starting in the mid-1980s. The de jure requirement came into force in 1992 with the passage of the Annunzio-Wylie Money Laundering Act.

6. Agencies may also lower this limit in certain circumstances. For example, as a result of growing suspicions about check-cashing agencies in New York City, the limit was lowered to $1,000 for a period of time.

7. In mid-2004, the American Bankers Association (Byrne 2004) acknowledged that progress had been made in reducing the amount of data generated, but recommended that the threshold for banks to file CTRs for corporations and businesses be raised from $10,000 to $25,000.

tolerance regime, though, because, beyond the application of specified minimum elements, institutions are permitted and encouraged to employ risk-based procedures, depending on the nature of the institution and its business as well as the characteristics of its customers. Along with the use of proxy devices such as thresholds on reporting, a risk-based approach has the potential to let some prohibited customers and transactions slip through undetected.

Non-Core Financial Institutions

A broad range of other types of US financial institutions has been progressively incorporated into the US AML regime both prior to and as a result of the passage of the USA PATRIOT Act in October 2001. In effect, Congress delegated to the US Treasury many of the delicate decisions on where, as well as how, to draw the lines, reserving to itself the capacity to criticize Treasury decisions at a later date.[8] A major subcategory is money service businesses, which are now required to register with FinCEN if they offer such services as money orders, traveler's checks, money transmission, check cashing, or currency dealing or exchange. However, the catch-all category of other financial institutions also includes entities that may be engaged broadly in money management activities.[9] These US financial institutions are subject to CDD and reporting requirements that are essentially the same as those applied to core financial institutions.

A principal difference in the prevention pillar of the US AML regime as it applies to these institutions is that while they are subject to federal regulation, they are not subject to as systematic or comprehensive supervision as are the core financial institutions. For example, money service

8. The USA PATRIOT Act mandated the extension of CDD and associated reporting requirements to certain businesses, such as those engaged in fund transfers as well as all securities dealers and investment companies. It also authorized, but did not require, extension of the regime to persons engaged in real estate closings and settlements, futures commission merchants, commodity trading advisers, and trust companies. FinCEN has more discretion on whether and to what extent to subject this second group of businesses to the AML regime. To date, final rules have been issued for broker-dealers (securities firms), money service businesses, credit card operators, mutual funds, and futures commission merchants (FinCEN 2003a). Extension of the US AML regime also is being considered for life insurance companies, dealers in precious metals, stones, and jewels, commodity trading advisers, unregistered investment companies (hedge funds), investment advisers, travel agencies, sellers of vehicles, and real estate agents. An advance notice of proposed rule making has been issued for persons involved in real estate closings and settlements.

9. FATF's revised Forty Recommendations (2003c) for combating money laundering and terrorist financing finesses this problem by defining a financial institution as any person or entity that conducts business activities or operations in one or more of a list of 13 categories of activities, some with multiple subparts.

businesses providing any of the five services listed above are required to register at the federal level, while many businesses providing other types of financial services are not required to do so. Those other institutions, in fact, may be required to register at the state or local level, but they may not be formally licensed. Licensing normally requires some scrutiny of the background and other qualifications of the owners and managers. Even when the institutions are licensed, they generally are not subject to regular supervision or inspections. In principle, they can be sanctioned either criminally or civilly for not complying with the requirements of AML regulations, but in practice, the sanctions element of the prevention pillar as it applies to these financial institutions is more limited and may only come to light if suspected offenders are already under surveillance, or in the aftermath of an investigation. As a result, in constructing the AML regime, historical and institutional differences such as divisions of responsibility between the federal government and the states have to be taken into consideration.

Nonfinancial Businesses

The prevention pillar of the US AML regime is even less rigorous for nonfinancial businesses such as casinos, dealers in precious metals and stones, and real estate agents than it is for non-core financial institutions. With respect to customer due diligence, casinos are subject to "reasonable procedures" such as identity checks, record keeping, and determining whether customers are on lists of known or suspected terrorists. Casinos and card clubs with more than $1 million in gaming revenues are subject to SAR and CTR reporting requirements, with special thresholds. In principle, they are subject to federal regulation and some degree of state regulation and supervision, but the scope for effective and graduated sanctions is even more limited than for non-core financial institutions.[10]

Dealers in precious metals and stones as well as pawnbrokers are subject to general CDD and reporting requirements, but again, supervision of their compliance and any practical use of sanctions for enforcement are limited because businesses are licensed in state or local jurisdictions. Aside from withdrawing licenses as the result of criminal or civil proceedings against the business, the authorities have little leverage to supervise the CDD or reporting requirements or to sanction noncompliance.

Real estate agents provide a useful illustration of some of the issues involved in expanding the AML regime. The USA PATRIOT Act provided

---

10. Further complicating the process of applying the AML regime to nonfinancial businesses is the fact that they would prefer, if they are to be covered at all, that there be clear distinctions between what is required and permitted and what is not. Core financial institutions have similar preferences, but they are more experienced in living with regulatory ambiguities.

for potential inclusion in the US AML regime of "persons involved in real estate closings and settlements," which would include most agents. They were already subject to CDD with respect to name checks in the course of doing business—the issue was whether they should be subject to general CDD and reporting requirements under the AML regime. On April 29 and November 6, 2002, FinCEN temporarily exempted real estate agents from the regime, and on April 10, 2003, FinCEN called for assistance in determining and designing any necessary regulations. The resulting regime as applied to real estate agents and other participants in closings and settlements is likely to be less rigorous and comprehensive—and perhaps appropriately so—than that applied to casinos.

Publicly available responses that FinCEN had received as of June 9, 2003, to its request for assistance addressed four main points:

- Participants in real estate transactions are already covered because they are required to file CTRs, which can be designated SARs by the filer, and because they can be prosecuted for knowingly assisting or participating in money laundering committed by a client.

- There is little evidence of money laundering in this area of economic activity.

- The costs to those involved in the real estate industry (many are small businesses) imposed by requirements to establish full-fledged anti–money laundering programs would be high.

- Financial institutions are involved in most real estate transactions and should be responsible for AML aspects of those transactions.

The American Bar Association (ABA Task Force on Gatekeeper Regulation and the Profession 2003b, 5) made an additional point on the possibility of regulation in the area of real estate: "Not unlike the constitutional protection against compelled self-incrimination, the [legal] ethics rules [preserving the independence of the bar from government enforcement agencies] reflect an informed and time-tested decision to protect overarching principles critical to our system of justice, even if it means that government enforcement agencies must use their own devices (and not independent lawyers assisting private citizens) to advance certain investigative objectives (in this case, in the area of money laundering)."

The ABA's point illustrates an underlying feature of the AML regime, especially as its coverage expands. The public has an interest to deal with an identified problem. In response, the government in effect co-opts the private sector to perform or assist at the financial and even ethical expense of the private sector.

When FinCEN issues final AML regulations for CDD and reporting covering real estate—assuming that even happens—the scope to supervise compliance with regulations currently on the books will be very limited. In principle, FinCEN has such authority. It was one of the first national financial intelligence units in the world, and its role has subsequently been substantially expanded through such legislation as the USA PATRIOT Act to become the residual federal-level regulator and supervisor of various entities and activities for which there is no existing federal supervisor, such as trust companies. However, with a budget in fiscal year 2004 of $57 million and a staff of only 277 and a wide range of responsibilities, the unit lacks resources. Federal authority in this area is at most residual, because the basic authority lies with state and local jurisdictions. Sanctions available at the federal level to enforce uniform compliance are scarce.

Table 4.2 singles out three categories of nonfinancial businesses (casinos, dealers in precious metals, and real estate brokers) because they are specifically identified in the FATF's 2003 revision of its Forty Recommendations (FATF 2003c). Recommendation 20 also states: "Countries should consider applying the FATF Recommendations to businesses and professions, other than designated nonfinancial businesses and professions, that pose a money laundering or terrorist financing risk."

A reasonable question is what evidence is required to substantiate an assertion that a particular type of economic activity poses a risk of money laundering or the financing of terrorism. A description of a particular incident in a FATF typologies report would be insufficient evidence to convince many observers.

Other nonfinancial businesses covered to some degree by the US AML regime include travel agents as well as pawnbrokers, telegraph operators, and businesses involved in vehicle, boat, auto, and airplane sales. The regime does not currently cover other businesses sometimes involved in high-value transactions, such as stamp dealers. The line has to be drawn at some point, even if it is moved later.

Professions

FATF's 2003 revision of its Forty Recommendations called for extending the prevention pillar of the global AML regime to lawyers, notaries, other independent legal professionals, accountants, and trust and company service providers, insofar as they are engaged in specified activities.[11] The recom-

---

11. Recommendation 12d of FATF (2003c) calls for CDD by lawyers, notaries, other legal professionals, and accountants when they assist clients with such activities as buying and selling real estate, managing assets, managing accounts, organizing contributions to create, operate, or manage companies, legal persons, or arrangements, and buying and selling business. Recommendation 12f calls for trust and company service providers to use CDD when they act as a formation agent for a legal person, a director of a company, a trustee, or a nominee shareholder, or when they facilitate the process by providing, for example, a registered office or address. Lawyers are subject to reporting requirements when engaging with or for their client in financial transactions in these areas of activity, and countries also are "encouraged" to extend reporting requirements to the remaining professional activities of accountants and auditors (recommendation 16a).

mendations were an outgrowth of the so-called "Gatekeepers Initiative" agreed to at the G-8 Moscow Ministerial Conference in October 1999. The objective was to expand the scope of the prevention pillar by placing responsibility on professionals involved in facilitating financial transactions. However, there is a broad exemption where these professionals are subject to "professional secrecy or legal professional privilege." Trust and company service providers are required to report suspicious transactions for or on behalf of a client in the indicated areas (recommendation 15c).

The United States has no CDD or AML reporting requirements that apply to these professionals at present beyond CTR requirements and the penalties that professionals incur if they aid in money laundering. However, this type of sanction is part of the enforcement rather than the prevention pillar of the AML regime. US officials have told us that they can get the information they need from lawyers if they want it. On the other hand, in their critique of the levelness of the international playing field on anti–money laundering, Mark Pieth and Gemma Aiolfi (2003, 27) comment that "it would rather stretch the general meaning of the words self-regulation or 'risk-based approach'" to subject attorneys, notaries, and unregulated fiduciaries to this type of ad hoc regulation.

While supporting domestic and international AML efforts, US legal groups have resisted the application of AML requirements to lawyers as well as to trust and company service providers, which are often lawyers. For example, although lawyers are required to submit a CTR, legal groups argue that, on confidentiality grounds, they should decline to check the box indicating that the transaction may be suspicious. An ABA resolution in February 2002 urged "that the United States government seek to protect and uphold the attorney/client relationship, including the attorney/client privilege, in dealing with international money laundering" (ABA Task Force on Gatekeeper Regulation and the Profession 2003a, 2). In another resolution a year later the ABA stated that it "opposes any law or regulation that, while taking action to combat money laundering or terrorist financing, would compel lawyers to disclose confidential information to government officials or otherwise compromise the lawyer-client relationship or the independence of the bar" (ABA Task Force on Gatekeeper Regulation and the Profession 2003a, 1).

US lawyers also argue that they have their codes of ethics, are subject to disbarment by state or federal courts for misconduct, and are licensed by the states. Further, as one argument goes, federal involvement in lawyers' activities raises constitutional (states' rights) issues. In submissions to the FATF when it was considering revisions to its Forty Recommendations, lawyers argued that they should be subject to the AML regime only when acting as financial intermediaries. They noted similar views expressed by groups of legal professionals around the world, and in a Joint Statement to the FATF on April 3, 2003, they complained that research did not support the inclusion of any recommendations pertaining to lawyers in the Forty

Recommendations, and that consultation with them by FATF (on two separate occasions) had been inadequate (CCBE 2003).

As if reaching consensus on how to expand the AML regime to the legal profession were not difficult enough, efforts to regulate accountants and auditors in the United States and other countries further illustrate the difficulties in widening the AML net (box 4.1). Without specific CDD and SAR reporting requirements, the prospects for effective coverage of lawyers, accountants, or trust and company service providers within the prevention pillar of the US AML regime are thus extremely limited at this point. Moreover, the United States has no countrywide mechanism readily available to conduct supervision of these professions, so sanctions at present are left to the enforcement pillar, although recommendation 24b of the FATF (2003c) envisages supervision and sanctions that could involve self-regulatory as well as governmental organizations, as long as they can ensure compliance. For the moment, however, compliance with ethical standards offers no protection from prosecution for participation in money laundering. So although these groups of professionals were included in the new FATF Forty Recommendations with respect to CDD, reporting, supervision, and ensuring compliance, it remains to be seen whether and to what extent jurisdictions comply in the near term. Moreover, the recommendations themselves contain a large loophole exempting reporting on compliance when it conflicts with professional ethics regarding secrecy.

On the other hand, it is to be noted that in the related area of corporate governance, the American Bar Association in 2003 reluctantly adopted a resolution that permitted, but did not compel, disclosure of "confidential client information if the client is using the lawyer's services to commit a crime or fraud that would cause financial harm to others." However, this was a weak response to a crisis of confidence in the legal profession associated with an outbreak of major corporate scandals.

The USA PATRIOT Act (Section 314) calls for increased cooperation between financial institutions, regulatory authorities, and law enforcement authorities in operating the prevention pillar of the US AML regime. Such cooperation would recognize that information sharing improves information content. Public-private cooperation has been a formal part of the US AML regime since 1992, when the Annunzio-Wylie Money Laundering Act authorized the US Treasury to create a Bank Secrecy Act Advisory Committee with members of the government and representatives of the banking industry.[12]

The US banking industry has been critical of the framework that has evolved under the USA PATRIOT Act, commenting through the American Bankers Association to the US Treasury that its initial proposals amounted to a one-way street in which the government placed additional demands

---

12. The committee was not actually created until 1994.

Box 4.1   Accountants, auditors, and anti–money laundering regimes

The extent to which the global anti–money laundering regime ultimately will affect accountants and auditors is not yet clear, even in the United States. The nature of the duties carried out by these professionals puts them near the top of government lists in terms of those who can identify and report money-laundering activities. Not only are auditors and accountants regularly exposed to companies' financial records, but they also have expertise in the design, maintenance, and control of various internal operations.

In congressional testimony before the Committee on Banking and Financial Services, then Deputy Treasury Secretary Stuart Eizenstat (2000) stated: "We are considering how existing accounting standards on such subjects as illegal acts of clients . . . can incorporate money laundering safeguards." Although the USA PATRIOT Act of 2001 authorized the Treasury to extend existing anti–money laundering rules or enact new ones for auditors and accountants, US regulations have not yet incorporated these professions into the national AML regime.

Under the current US system, accountants and auditors generally play only a passive role in the detection of money laundering and are not directly involved in identifying illegal or suspicious transactions at any stage of their relationships with clients. While they must be aware of the possibility of encountering money laundering or suspicious transactions, they are not required to set up a program for their detection.

What responsibilities that accountants and auditors do have vary slightly according to which profession is involved. Accountants in charge of keeping companies' financial records are not required by any applicable accounting standards to detect money laundering.[1] Their responsibility is limited to reporting illegal acts that have both direct and material effect on clients' financial statements.[2] However, most of the time money laundering has only an indirect effect on financial statements, as in the case of a contingent liability such as fines in connection with crimes that have been committed. Furthermore, even if accountants happen to encounter possible money-laundering activities, current standards do not unequivocally require them to report actual or suspected transactions to the authorities. Their only obligation is to report to the board of the corporation involved.

Auditors have different requirements because they must certify the true representation of a company's activities through its records. Auditors must directly notify the government of illicit or suspected transactions in the event that management does not take satisfactory steps to address the matter. However, they are only required to report transactions that may have a direct negative effect on financial statements. Once a suspicious money-laundering activity that modifies the true representation of a company's activity is identified, it is the auditors' responsibility to assess the legitimacy of the transaction. If auditors find an illegal activity by a publicly traded company, they are required to report it to the Securities and Exchange Commission either through the corporate board or directly if the board is uncooperative. They must also provide an opinion on the financial statement.[3] Therefore, like accountants, auditors do not have to design their audit procedures to identify and track illegal activities, since they are simply required to be aware of the possibility that illegal activities may take place.

For the moment, the only stick-and-carrot mechanism available to the government is the standard of "willful blindness" that the government can use during a prosecution. In addition, the Supreme Court in 1984 in United States vs. Arthur Young & Co. held that "no confidential accountant-client privilege exists" (465 US 805, 818, 1984).

(box continues next page)

Box 4.1 *(continued)*

However, while there is no binding requirement on accountants or auditors to practice customer due diligence or to report suspicious transactions, they are encouraged to follow precautions and a risk-assessment approach when dealing with clients' activities. The issue is whether the government will impose more stringent requirements in the future. One possibility with regard to reporting suspicious activity would be to follow the example of other countries such as the United Kingdom, Switzerland, and Belgium, which require accountants to report all instances of suspected money-laundering activity by clients.

UK legislation covering accountants, auditors, and tax consultants is among the most comprehensive and follows the pattern applied to that country's financial industry. The UK Proceeds of Crime Act passed in 2002, along with associated money-laundering regulations that came into effect in March 2004, set a new and higher standard for accountants, auditors, and tax consultants. These professions are required to perform CDD and maintain evidence of client identification and transactions. In addition, they must set up anti–money laundering procedures, appoint a reporting officer to collect reports on all suspicious transactions, and submit those reports to the National Criminal Intelligence Service. The legislation authorizes criminal penalties for failure to abide by regulations or report suspicious activities.

Anti–money laundering regimes elsewhere in Europe are still in the process of developing procedures with respect to accountants and auditors. The European Federation of Accountants (FEE 1999) has proposed a monitored self-regulation regime controlled by accountant and auditor associations, consistent with the guidelines and principles in the money-laundering directive issued by the European Union. This position is also consistent with that of the 113-nation International Federation of Accountants, which argues: "Money laundering is far less likely to affect financial statements than are such types of fraud and misappropriations. Consequently, it is unlikely to be detected in a financial statement audit. Nevertheless, money-laundering activities may have indirect effects on an entity's financial statements and, thus, are of concern to external auditors" (IFAC 2002). Both the IFAC and FEE (2003) have expressed concern that extending the anti–money laundering regime to the accounting and auditing professions could increase the fees charged to clients and divert resources away from the principal duties and responsibilities of these professions.

---

1. See Private Securities Tort Reform Act of 1995 (Public Law No. 104–67, 109 Statute 737) and the corresponding SAS No. 54, Illegal Acts by Clients (American Institute of Certified Public Accountants, Professional Standards, vol. 1, AU sec. 317).
2. Securities Exchange Act of 1934 (15 U.S.C. sec. 78j, 1994).
3. SAS 54, Illegal Acts by Clients.

---

and requirements on financial institutions, rather than the type of network that they thought was the intent of Section 314.[13] Similar criticism can be found in a report by the Council on Foreign Relations (2004), which focuses principally on the financing of terrorism. A group of global financial institutions has established Regulatory DataCorp as a for-profit enterprise to

---

13. Byrne (2004) testified that administration of the USA PATRIOT Act's Section 314 "demand process" had been improved by implementation of procedural changes that reduced burdens on banks.

provide information to subscribers to aid them in their customer due diligence and to manage their legal, regulatory, and reputation risks. In private conversations, representatives of some of the sponsoring institutions have been critical of the degree of cooperation by the US government with this enterprise. Such public-private tension is inherent in attempts to establish and refine the AML regime.

A summary numerical description of the current US AML regime can be used to measure the extent of coverage by the prevention pillar of the seven categories of financial institutions, nonfinancial businesses, and professions listed in table 4.2. With full coverage receiving 4.0, a full point for each element of the pillar, coverage of the categories could be measured as follows:

- Coverage of core financial institutions would be scaled at close to 4.0, unless there was a small deduction for the risk-based nature of the CDD regime, the presence of thresholds in some reporting requirements, and the dispersed (nonfederal) supervision of insurance companies.

- Other types of financial institutions, on average, would be at 2.75, with credit of a full point each for the CDD and reporting elements, but half a point for supervision, and a quarter point for the limited scope of sanctions for noncompliance.

- Casinos would be at 2.0 overall, consisting of three-quarters of a point each for CDD and reporting because of exemptions and reporting thresholds, and a quarter point each for supervision and sanctions.

- Dealers in precious metals and stones would be at 1.50, because while they are almost at the same level in CDD and reporting requirements as casinos, they fall short in supervision and sanctions.

- Real estate agents would be at 0.50 because they are subject at least to CTR reporting requirements and the threat of the enforcement pillar.

- The two categories of professionals—lawyers, notaries and accountants, and trust and company service providers—might receive a slightly higher 0.75 because there is a somewhat more developed mechanism to police behavior and withdraw licenses to practice, at least after an offense has been detected and proved.

Although this numerical description of the scope of the prevention pillar suggests it is currently incomplete, such a description would have been very much lower before passage of the US Money Laundering Control Act in 1986. Core financial institutions would have registered about 2.0 on average because of some CDD and reporting requirements (for banks in particular), although the extent of the supervision and sanction mechanisms was limited. The Bank Secrecy Act of 1970 required banks and certain other financial institutions to retain records to facilitate subsequent tracing of financial transactions and to submit CTRs and CIMRs. The submission of SARs was not mandated until the Annunzio-Wylie Money Laundering Act in 1992 and not implemented until 1996.[14] Moreover, securities and insurance institutions were generally not covered, and neither were most other types of financial institutions. Broker-dealers unaffiliated with banks were not subject to SAR reporting requirements until passage of the USA PATRIOT Act in 2001, and the AML regime essentially did not apply at all to nonfinancial businesses, let alone professions.

Chapter 8 will return to the significance of how this pattern of regime expansion has evolved. For the moment, the description helps to illustrate the political, technical, and institutional compromises and trade-offs that are required to establish the prevention pillar of the US AML regime. At the same time, it tells us little about actual compliance.

Enforcement

The enforcement pillar of the US AML regime has expanded over the past 15 to 20 years, although less dramatically than the prevention pillar. The number of predicate crimes has increased during the period. New tools have been developed, and new mechanisms offer the promise of greater efficiency of the enforcement pillar, but their use has not been substantial.

Money laundering was not criminalized in the United States until passage of the Money Laundering Control Act (MLCA) in 1986.[15] Of course, money laundering existed before it became a criminal offense, and law enforcement authorities have long known to "follow the money" when investigating crimes that generate proceeds. Correspondingly, criminals worked hard to break or obscure the connection between their crimes and the proceeds from them. The Bank Secrecy Act of 1970 fully recognized the links between money and crime, including securities fraud, as well as the international dimensions of the phenomenon (Eldridge 1986).

---

14. The Annunzio-Wylie legislation was the first to require that banks and certain other financial institutions have AML programs, effectively mandating internal control procedures that were subject to outside scrutiny and supervision.

15. The MLCA defines money laundering as conducting or attempting to conduct a financial transaction "knowing that the property [or monetary instrument] involved in [the] financial transaction represents the proceeds of some form of unlawful activity with the intent to promote the carrying on of specified unlawful activity or knowing that the transaction is designed in whole or in part to conceal or disguise the nature, the location, the source, the ownership, or the control of the proceeds of specified unlawful activity or to avoid a transaction reporting requirement under State or Federal law" (Section 1956, laundering of monetary instruments).

Predicate Crimes

The list of predicate crimes or underlying offenses that could lead to a conviction for money laundering was relatively short in 1986, with the primary focus on drugs and drug-related criminal activity. The list has been expanded considerably in subsequent AML legislation, and includes more than 150 offenses covering almost everything that might be considered a serious crime, from environmental violations to health insurance fraud.

The US list of predicate crimes conspicuously does not include tax evasion. The ironically titled Bank Secrecy Act (because it was about breaking down bank secrecy) was prompted in part by tax evasion considerations in terms of identifying the parties with underlying financial interests, addressing concerns about tax havens and the role of financial services providers in facilitating access to them, and dealing with international flows of funds. Moreover, the Anti–Drug Abuse Act of 1988 made it a criminal offense to evade taxes on the proceeds of an unlawful activity. This provision was added to the enforcement pillar to allow the IRS to use its expertise to develop anti–money laundering cases. Thus, US enforcement of anti–money laundering de facto is closely tied to the enforcement of tax evasion,[16] even though the crime of tax evasion per se does not normally lead to money-laundering charges, except to the extent that the criminals have evaded paying taxes on the proceeds of their crimes.[17]

Although the absence of tax evasion from the list of predicate offenses is not a particular enforcement problem for the United States, and it conveniently sidesteps domestic political sensitivities concerning privacy and how US tax laws are enforced, the omission adversely affects global cooperation. A former high-level Latin American official commented to one of the authors that if the United States wants other countries to cooperate more on countering the financing of terrorism and money laundering, it should cooperate more aggressively in dealing with Latin Americans who evade taxes on investments in the United States.

The United States has been somewhat responsive to these concerns, which was one reason for US support of a European initiative to address harmful tax competition. The Organization for Economic Cooperation and Development (OECD 1998) released a report on the subject, laying out principles for the identification of harmful tax competition, which was directed primarily at tax havens and their low tax rates, solicitation of

---

16. For example, in July 2003, a stockbroker (Adam Klein) pleaded guilty to money laundering and admitted that he had also evaded taxes on the proceeds of the underlying crime.

17. *Barrons* (October 13, 2003, F5) reports some new links between the tax enforcement and AML regimes. Multiple payments of cash equivalents adding up to more than $10,000 to fund managers require the filing of a form 8300 that used to go only to the tax authorities but now is reviewed by AML authorities as well. The investor is also notified of these reports, in contrast with SARs or CTRs.

investment funds, and reluctance or inability to provide information to the tax authorities of other countries.[18]

The OECD report stirred a furor not only among those it targeted—so-called tax havens, many of which saw one of their principal sources of foreign exchange earnings under attack—but also within some OECD countries whose governments indirectly sponsored the report. Tax evasion and the international exchange of tax information is politically explosive in many countries, not just the United States.[19] The report led to designating 35 jurisdictions as having harmful tax practices, principally offshore financial centers (OECD 2000). Thirty of these jurisdictions subsequently made a commitment to increase transparency and exchanges of information, so that by December 2003 only five—Andorra, Liechtenstein, Liberia, Monaco, and the Marshall Islands—remained "uncooperative tax havens."

The US Treasury under Secretary Paul O'Neill, during the Bush administration, initially was quite critical of the OECD tax haven initiative. The US eventually agreed with its G-7 colleagues on a joint statement of support in June 2002: "We agree that the administration and enforcement of tax laws depend increasingly on transparency and effective international exchange of information. We call on all countries to permit access to, and exchange, bank and other information for tax purposes; OECD countries should lead by example." However, the OECD initiative has been weakened by less progress than had been expected with respect to intra-OECD, in particular intra-European, tax cooperation.

Treatment of offenses abroad is another feature of the predicate crime element of the enforcement pillar of the US AML regime. Although many domestic crimes qualify as predicate offenses under US AML law, only a subset of crimes committed abroad can lead to money-laundering prosecutions in the United States. This reduces the scope for the United States to cooperate in the global AML regime, since nonrecognition under US law of a money-laundering offense abroad impedes the law enforcement process in other countries. For example, until passage of the USA PATRIOT Act in 2001, foreign corruption was not a predicate crime for a money-laundering offense in the United States. In addition, trafficking in human beings, counterfeiting

---

18. The principles involved the combination of (1) low or no taxes (or withholding) with a lack of transparency, (2) ineffective information exchange, and (3) facilitation of tax evasion by applying different tax regimes to foreign rather than domestic investors, such as by not requiring a physical presence or substantial activities in the jurisdiction (OECD 1998). The third criterion was later set aside at the insistence of the United States on grounds that it is difficult to articulate clearly.

19. US opposition is based primarily on privacy concerns, along with the view that tax competition leads to lower taxes. In the context of countering terrorism financing and money laundering, the two views have led to recommendations to promote the international exchange of information, but to not allow under any circumstances that such information be used for tax purposes (Rahn and de Rugy 2003).

of currency, and forgery can be predicate offenses for money-laundering charges if committed in the United States, but not if committed abroad.[20]

Investigation

Turning to the investigation element of the enforcement pillar, reporting through such mechanisms as SARs is one of the links between the AML prevention and enforcement pillars. However, consistent with complaints about the US government's failure to open a two-way street with the private sector, critics often view SARs as a black hole with little if any feedback as to their relative effect (James 2002).

One feature of the investigative element that has received better marks is the explicit authorization via the 1988 US Anti–Drug Abuse Act to use sting operations to obtain evidence to convict money launderers, which has proved to be an important enforcement tool. For example, Operation Highbind in 1993 and 1994 enabled FBI and Immigration and Naturalization Service agents to pose as drug dealers with dirty money and meet with members of Chinese-American fraternal organizations that functioned in part as laundering rings investing criminal proceeds in illegal gambling enterprises.

Federal agents will often masquerade not as customers but as providers of money-laundering services. Such was the case in Operation Juno in 1996, when IRS and Drug Enforcement Administration (DEA) agents ran a stock brokerage that laundered $14.5 million in drug profits through the black market peso exchange.[21] One of the most prominent money-laundering sting operations was Operation Dinero, when DEA agents opened an offshore bank to provide services to the Cali drug cartel.[22] Over the course of six months, they laundered $52 million, recovered nine tons of cocaine, and uncovered ties between the cartel and Italian organized crime.

Prosecution and Punishment

Little is known about how prosecutors make resource allocation and prosecutorial decisions in money laundering or other cases. Mariano-Florentino

---

20. Seven of the 20 categories of crimes explicitly cited by the FATF for coverage under national AML legislation are not considered for this purpose to be crimes in the United States if the offense is committed outside the country. The other four categories are sexual exploitation, counterfeiting of products, environmental crime, and insider trading and market manipulation. The last is a particularly sensitive area because the US approach in this area differs substantially from that of many other jurisdictions in that it is not grounded on a definition of the underlying offense.

21. See www.usdoj.gov/dea/major/juno.htm (accessed November 12, 2003).

22. See www.usdoj.gov/dea/major/dinero.htm (accessed November 12, 2003).

Cuéllar (2003) is critical of the failure of the law enforcement community to use the AML enforcement pillar more actively to disrupt the financial infrastructure of criminal activities. Sentencing guidelines, which may or may not be followed closely, govern subsequent punishments (see chapter 5).

R. E. Bell (2001), writing from a British perspective, lays out a useful two-by-two taxonomy of prosecutorial approaches involving the nature of the offense and the prosecution. He asserts that most common are prosecutions in which the charge of money laundering is linked with the charge for the underlying offense, of which money laundering was an integral part. Less common are prosecutions in which the money laundering was outsourced, but the prosecution of the money launderer is integrated with the prosecution of the person who committed the crime. Integrated money laundering in stand-alone prosecutions, according to Bell, is reserved for big international cases where the crime is committed in another jurisdiction. Least common are cases involving outsourced laundering in stand-alone prosecutions, because they are the most difficult and resource intensive to develop. Unfortunately, there are no data publicly available to test these plausible assertions about relative incidence.

Confiscation

Confiscation of the proceeds of crime through seizure and forfeiting procedures is a powerful element of the US enforcement pillar. However, criminal forfeiture was outlawed by Congress in 1790 and not reintroduced until passage in 1970 of two major pieces of legislation directed at combating organized crime: the Racketeer Influenced and Corrupt Organization (RICO) and the Continuing Criminal Enterprise (CCE) Acts (Truman 1995).

Not only does confiscation serve as a deterrent to criminal activity and deprive criminal organizations of resources, but it also helps to fund law enforcement activities. Such tied funding violates recommended best practices in public finance, since the revenue side of government finance should be separated from the expenditure side. Moreover, confiscation and forfeiture can create odd incentives. In a number of states, including Indiana, Missouri, North Carolina, Washington, West Virginia, and Wisconsin, forfeited property under state law goes to education, but when the property is seized and confiscated in collaboration with the federal authorities, the state law enforcement authorities can keep what is returned by the federal authorities for their own use, which is 80 percent of the total amount confiscated.

Such arrangements may distort law enforcement in the direction of pursing cases that have larger expected value in the forfeiture dimension, which may not be the same as those with larger expected value on the scale of other enforcement priorities, such as addressing the most heinous crimes. As Rep. Bob Barr (R-Georgia) said in 1999, "In many jurisdictions, it [confiscation] has become a monetary tail wagging the law enforcement dog".

Senator John Kerry (1997, 176), reflecting on his experience as chairman and ranking member of the Senate Subcommittee on Terrorism, Narcotics, and International Operations, warned against the "dark and dangerous underside" of asset seizure in which defendants buy lighter sentences by bargaining with hidden property. Nevertheless, the tool is widely used in the United States at the federal as well as the state and local levels.

As noted, one important aspect of the confiscation element is the sharing of the proceeds with other jurisdictions. A longstanding program for the equitable sharing of forfeited property with other federal, state and local jurisdictions is governed by published guidelines.[23] In addition, since US ratification of the 1988 UN Drug Convention, the United States has had a program of equitable sharing of forfeited assets with foreign governments that cooperate and assist in investigations. From 1989 to March 2002, the international program shared 44 percent ($171.5 million) of eligible forfeited assets with 26 foreign governments (US Treasury 2002, 61).

A final noteworthy aspect of the enforcement pillar is related to one of the reasons behind asset sharing, which is to encourage cooperation and the sharing of information; this is important not only between governments and levels of government but within a given level of government. A significant step forward in this area was the establishment in 1990 of FinCEN in the US Treasury Department as a central repository of information, with the additional mandate to analyze the information from such sources as SARs.

US National Money-Laundering Strategies

The US Congress passed the Money Laundering and Financial Crimes Act in 1998 in part to improve coordination of the nation's anti–money laundering efforts. The act mandated the Secretary of the Treasury, in consultation with the Attorney General, to develop an annual National Money Laundering Strategy (NMLS) for presentation to Congress over the five years from 1999 to 2003 in February of each year.

The intention of the reports was to cover research-based goals, objectives, and priorities; coordinated prevention measures; detection and prosecution initiatives; and proposals for partnerships with the private sector and cooperation between federal, state, and local officials.[24] The Treasury also was required to submit an evaluation of the effectiveness of US AML policies, an additional task that the US Treasury argued was fulfilled by the

---

23. The program began in October 1986 with an amendment to the Tariff Act of 1930.

24. The act also mandated identification of "high-intensity financial crimes areas" as part of a stepped-up enforcement effort on which the NMLS was to report. Most of the progress in this area reflected efforts that were already under way in 1998.

NMLS itself (GAO 2003a, 67). The 1999 NMLS was completed and delivered on September 23, 1999.[25]

In many respects, the legislation requiring the NMLS reports reflected the same concerns as those behind the National Drug Control Strategy, an annual report mandated since 1988. Many agencies are involved in dealing with the same problem and need to find meaningful progress indicators. A review of the five NMLS reports—using the framework for the AML regime that involves three broad types of AML goals, the two-pillar regime, application of the market model to money laundering, and evolution of the regime—illuminates the structure and goals of the US AML regime as well as some of the trade-offs and constraints it has faced.

Each NMLS included on average 55 action items (from a high of 66 in 1999 to a low of 48 in 2003) grouped under three to six major objectives. The action items covered a wide range of issues and were much too numerous to constitute a particularly pointed strategy or even to be completed in a period as short as a year. It was difficult to identify the highest-priority items because they were all presented with roughly equal emphasis. The apparent aim of the NMLS was to present a broad strategy rather than specify precise and well-defined objectives. One consequence of this approach was that many items were implicitly carried over from one year to the next, even while new items were added identifying new initiatives or reflecting changing circumstances. The most notable example was a shift in emphasis to countering terrorist financing following the attacks of September 11, 2001.

The NMLS was thus largely an annual report on major aspects of ongoing AML initiatives by various agencies of the US government. Little effort was made explicitly to follow up on issues raised in the previous year's report, even though the Money Laundering and Financial Crimes Act required just such follow-up. The result was a pattern of promises but with limited public disclosure of results. For example, an interagency report on US policy toward foreign government officials (kleptocrats) who use the international financial system to convert public assets to personal use was completed in November 2000, but the results were neither published nor mentioned in the next year's NMLS.[26] Another example was a study completed in 2001 by the Customs Service, summarized briefly in the 2002 NMLS but not released, on percentage commissions charged to launder money in narcotics cases, based on undercover cases. Despite a stated intention of posting the entire study—which included such important information as the annual costs of compliance with the Bank Secrecy Act—

---

25. As is frequently the case with mandated reports to Congress, only one (the 2000 NMLS) arrived roughly on time (March). The 2001 report was released on September 12; the 2002 report in July; the 2003 report in November.

26. In the interests of full disclosure, Edwin Truman was involved with this project. One innovation in the 2000 NMLS that generally was carried forward was the identification of responsible officials (by position) or groups of officials for each action item.

only a summary of a related report prepared by FinCEN and Deloitte & Touche on the costs of SAR preparation was ever posted (FinCEN 2002).

There were some exceptions in terms of adequate follow-up of previous proposals. In the 2002 NMLS, an important action item from 2001, to study the use of the Internet to raise and move funds to terrorist groups, resulted in a thorough report entitled *Terrorist Financing Online*, included in the 2003 NMLS (US Treasury 2003, appendix H) with supporting analysis of actual and potential policy responses. (See box 4.2 for a more general discussion of money laundering and electronic finance.)

Notwithstanding their shortcomings, the five NMLS reports provide useful illustrative material on the objectives, structure, and evolution of the US AML regime. Table 4.3 presents the distribution of action items in the five strategies across the three broad goals of the US AML regime to reduce predicate crime, promote the integrity of the financial system, and address the global, "public bads" of terrorism, corruption, and failed states (chapter 1). For the five-year period of the strategies, about 65 percent of the action items concerned predicate crime and about the same percentage involved integrity of the financial system. The pattern was quite uniform until the final year, when the share of items focused on crime fell off and those focused on the financial system rose. The three global "public bads" generally received much less attention—even in the post–September 11 period covered by the 2002 and 2003 NMLS reports, less than 30 percent of the action items addressed this AML regime objective. The few action items classified as addressing failed states, for example, were aimed at countries that failed to adopt or live up to international AML standards.

Table 4.4 shows the distribution of the same action items across the elements of the prevention and enforcement pillars of the US AML regime. Each of the four elements in each of the two pillars was addressed to some extent over the five-year period, but in general prevention received more emphasis than enforcement.

Within the prevention pillar, the reporting element (e.g., extension of SAR requirements) generally received the most emphasis, but not in all years. Customer due diligence was the next most frequently addressed element, but in the 2003 NMLS the largest number of action items matched up with the supervision element, in part because of enhanced efforts to combat terrorist financing.

Within the enforcement pillar, the investigation element received the most attention in every year, accounting for about 40 percent of all action items over the period as a whole. Prosecution and punishment were emphasized substantially less but were second, followed by confiscation and augmentation of the list of predicate crimes.

The element of identification of predicate crimes received relatively more attention in the 1999 and 2000 NMLS reports, when the Clinton administration sought to expand the enforcement scope of the AML regime by passing new legislation, an effort that failed in both years. The 2001 NMLS, the

Box 4.2 Electronic finance and money laundering

Electronic finance has opened a new frontier for the global anti–money laundering regime, as well as for the criminals it aims to apprehend. The interaction of technical change with finance and business can take the form of electronic banking, Internet payment systems, or electronic debit cards such as smartcards. The lightly regulated Internet, which combines considerable anonymity with a global scope and electronic speed, is a major concern with respect to money-laundering techniques and the financing of terrorism. Such mechanisms open up opportunities for new types of crime such as cyber fraud that can drain funds from a bank account in Pittsburgh and transfer them to an account in Dubai.

Although such impersonal interactions suggest new ways to disguise the movement of funds, the basic challenges they present in terms of prevention and enforcement are fairly familiar. The opportunities provided by electronic finance to move and launder substantial amounts without interacting with the core financial system are severely limited. For example, drug dealers cannot deposit actual cash in an electronic bank, as the cash first has to be physically deposited in an institution. Electronic cash has to be uploaded to a smartcard from an account in some type of financial institution located somewhere that can be required to keep records of such transactions.

Consequently, the elements of the AML prevention pillar as they are applied to institutions in the core financial system can be brought to bear on electronic finance. The surface anonymity of the interactions may make customer due diligence and reporting suspicious transactions more difficult, but banks and other institutions in the core financial system have the same anti–money laundering obligations relative to their electronic customers as they do relative to their flesh and blood customers. Moreover, in a number of major jurisdictions, those obligations can be and have been imposed on the virtual institutions of electronic finance.

The elements of the enforcement pillar also are available to investigate and prosecute crimes involving electronic finance. Such investigations may involve different skills, but in some cases trails may actually be easier to follow through the Internet, for example, because Internet messages normally leave records behind. Techniques are available to disguise Internet tracks by passing messages through sites called "anonymizers," but deciphering disguises and following leads that go cold is not new to 21st century law enforcement. A more significant challenge, as with other aspects of the global AML regime, is to improve international cooperation associated with different priorities, procedures, laws, and regulations.

As noted in the 2003 *National Money Laundering Strategy,* the Internet poses unique additional challenges with respect to the specific area of terrorist financing (US Treasury 2003, appendix H). However, most of those challenges are not associated with the actual movement of funds, aside from the familiar fact that the amounts are small and the terrorist act occurs after the funds have been used. The principal additional challenges come from the fact that terrorists use the Internet both to communicate and to raise funds through such institutions as charities.

In sum, while electronic finance may be a new frontier for the global anti–money laundering regime, the frontier is located not in another part of the universe but in the same world where ground rules of economics and finance apply. To be effective, the global regime must build on what it already has started to do, which is to address the challenges posed by electronic finance on an ongoing basis.

Table 4.3 Distribution of US *National Money Laundering Strategy* action items across AML goals, 1999–2003
(percent of all action items)

Goal	1999	2000	2001	2002	2003	Five-year total[a]
Reducing predicate crime	67	90	83	78	10	66
Promoting integrity of financial system	65	57	63	48	81	63
Reducing global "public bads"	7	6	2	28	24	13
Memorandum:						
Total number of action items	66	58	41	50	48	263

a. Number of action items affecting each anti–money laundering goal as a percentage of total number of action items over five years.

Note: Some action items addressed more than one anti–money laundering goal.

Source: *National Money Laundering Strategies* (US Treasury 1999–2003).

first strategy issued by the Bush administration, which was drafted before September 11 and coincidentally issued the next day, included only one item that matched up with the predicate crimes element, a general commitment to submit a "money laundering bill which will address [unspecified] deficiencies" in the then current statutes.

It took the tragedy of September 11—an example of how the AML regime has been shaped by events—for the Bush administration to embrace the Clinton administration's legislative proposals and move them through the Congress. Most were subsequently incorporated into the USA PATRIOT Act.[27] For example, as proposed by the Clinton administration and at the urging of other OECD countries, the post–September 11 legislation made foreign official corruption an offense that can be prosecuted in the United States; criminalized bulk cash smuggling across the US border; and provided the executive branch with additional authority to crack down on foreign jurisdictions, institutions, and classes of transactions thought to pose a serious money-laundering threat.

We also classified the 263 action items in the five NMLS reports on the basis of whether they could implicitly or explicitly be fit into an analytic framework of a market for money-laundering services. An example would be whether the item was intended to tighten the supply of those services

---

27. The incorporation into the USA PATRIOT Act of Title III (International Money Laundering Abatement and Anti–Terrorist Financing Act of 2001) was largely at the insistence of Democratic Senate leaders, with support from influential Republican senators. The Republican House leadership initially argued for stand-alone AML legislation, which would have met substantial resistance in the House. The final legislation incorporated not only proposals to strengthen and expand the US AML regime, but also important provisions on correspondent banking and private banking. This substantially expanded the US AML regime in directions that had not yet been accepted globally.

Table 4.4 **Distribution of US** *National Money Laundering Strategy* **action items across AML prevention and enforcement elements, 1999–2003** (percent of all action items)

	1999	2000	2001	2002	2003	Five-year total[a]
Prevention						
Customer due diligence	5	28	12	12	10	13
Reporting	26	50	46	38	16	35
Supervision	8	3	5	2	20	8
Regulation and sanctions	5	0	2	2	4	3
General[b]	18	5	24	28	44	22
Total[c]	*55*	*74*	*76*	*70*	*81*	*68*
Enforcement						
Predicate crimes	6	9	2	0	2	4
Investigation	55	45	32	30	28	40
Prosecution and punishment	11	16	12	8	22	14
Confiscation	5	3	12	10	2	6
General[b]	0	3	15	12	31	11
Total[c]	*62*	*64*	*61*	*52*	*69*	*60*
Memorandum:						
Total number of action items	66	58	41	50	48	263

a. Number of action items affecting each pillar/element as a percentage of total number of action items over five years.
b. Items related to the specified pillar but not to any particular element or elements.
c. Excluding items that may involve more than one element of the pillar.

Note: Some action items are classified in more than one pillar or more than one element of the pillar.

Source: National Money Laundering Strategies (US Treasury, 1999–2003).

by limiting certain types of laundering channels, or to reduce the demand for money-laundering services by increasing the probability of confiscation. On average, only about a third of the action items in each area could be interpreted in this manner.

Almost a quarter of the annual action items in the five strategies called for further study or research with regard to money laundering and the AML regime. The incidence was considerably higher in the 2000 and 2001 NMLS reports, more than 30 percent, and about average in the 1999 NMLS, but substantially below average in the 2002 and 2003 reports. Note that the sharp break in this tendency is not between the Clinton and Bush administrations but with the two strategies prepared after September 11.

One carryover from the Clinton to the Bush administration was an effort to review the federal government financial resources devoted to anti–money laundering at the federal level, with a view to eventually ensuring the appropriate and effective allocation of resources. The 2000 NMLS included such a review along with a "rough cut" set of estimates, but the initiative apparently did not reach fruition because in the 2001 NMLS a new action item was included to review the costs and resources devoted to anti–money laundering efforts, this time to allow for more informed budget allocations. A high-level interagency working group was formed to accomplish this task. The 2002 NMLS, which, as noted, was the only one of the five strategies systematically to follow up the action items in the previous report, stated that analytical disagreements between agencies prevented fuller development of the material submitted. Nevertheless, the work was to continue during 2002 and incorporated the element of resources devoted to stopping the financing of terrorist entities. The effort apparently has not been successful to date, since the 2003 NMLS did not mention its continuation.

Such limited follow-up and disclosure not only hindered the overall success of the NMLS but also undercut the effectiveness of the interagency cooperation that the NMLS approach was intended to encourage. Such cooperation would have been strengthened through public commitments to build on the progress that had been achieved, and with more consistent identification of those to hold responsible for that progress. For example, despite numerous statements of good intentions to develop comprehensive databases on money-laundering cases, as called for in the 2001 NMLS, the NMLS of the following year (US Treasury 2002, 10) reported that "the cost involved in taking any one system used by a federal law enforcement agency as the relevant model outweighed the potential benefit, since different investigative agencies have different goals, missions and performance measures." The 2003 NMLS, in turn, made no mention at all of developing uniform databases, leaving one to assume that the idea was abandoned as attention shifted to countering terrorist financing.

Touching on another important area of cooperation, more than 10 percent of the action items in the five NMLS reports called for consultation with the private sector, with no significant difference in the incidence of such items between the first two and the last three strategies. Action items in the NMLS for 1999, 2000, and 2003 explicitly although briefly recognized privacy concerns.

A prominent element of the first three NMLS reports was interagency and intra-agency studies of the role of "gatekeeper" professions (lawyers, accountants, auditors) in efforts to combat money laundering, including ways to better inform them of their responsibilities, and how, or even whether, to best incorporate coverage of their activities within the AML regime prevention pillar. By the 2001 NMLS, incorporation of these professional categories was directed toward formulating the US position on the revision of the FATF Forty Recommendations in this area. The 2001 NMLS (p. ix) quoted President Bush on the relevance of the professions to the AML regime: "We will aggressively enforce our money laundering laws with accountability and coordination at the Federal, State and international levels. Our goal is to disrupt and dismantle large-scale criminal enterprises and prosecute professional money launderers, including corrupt lawyers, bankers, and accountants." Although this statement does not explicitly recommend extending the prevention pillar to cover lawyers and accountants, it certainly is consistent with such a reading. Nevertheless, to date those professionals have resisted being included in the prevention pillar of the US regime.

Also prominent in the first two NMLS reports was a focus on taxation, particularly in terms of promoting effective fiscal enforcement, addressing harmful tax competition problems that had been flagged in the 1998 OECD study, examining tax havens, and considering expansion of the list of US predicate crimes to "selected tax crimes." This topic was not included in the 2001 and 2003 strategies, but surfaced in the 2002 NMLS as a call for improving the international exchange of tax information. Raising taxation issues illustrates how the early NMLS process was responding to international concerns about harmful tax practices, including criticism of the US AML regime for not treating foreign tax evasion as a predicate crime with respect to US money-laundering prosecutions or legal assistance.

The taxation issue also illustrates the influence of domestic politics on the AML regime. Although the positions of the Clinton and Bush administrations on the basic issue of harmful tax practices were not substantively different—both favored enhancing information exchange and enforcing international financial standards—the accompanying rhetoric was quite different. The Clinton administration was more receptive to concerns of other countries about low- or zero-tax jurisdictions in the context of tax competition, while the Bush administration, with its antitax orientation, was much less receptive, particularly with respect to the treatment of certain Caribbean jurisdictions. The privacy issue resonated more within the Bush administration, notwithstanding the fact that it was mentioned at least as often in the first two NMLS reports prepared in the Clinton administration as in the last three NMLS prepared in the Bush administration.

A review of the National Money Laundering Strategies illustrates several important points. First, it confirms the relevance of the three broad types of goals for the AML regime: reducing predicate crime, maintaining the integrity of the financial system, and combating global "public bads." Second, it supports the view of the AML regime as having prevention and enforcement pillars with multiple elements. Third, it provides limited but weak support for the market model of the AML regime. Fourth, more broadly speaking, it provides evidence that the AML regime is not an abstraction—its evolution reflects shifting priorities, compromises, and trade-offs. We return in chapter 8 to the future of the US NMLS and our recommendations for it.

The Global Anti–Money Laundering Regime

Globalization in the form of an increase in the volume and speed of flows of international as well as national goods, funds, and information has played a major part in conditioning the evolution of the global AML regime. Lawrence Summers, then Deputy Secretary of the US Treasury, told the Financial Action Task Force plenary on June 26, 1996: "At the very moment that the world economy is expanding and integrating, creating vast new opportunities for business, so the technology and capacity at the disposal of criminals is greater than before."

Four years later, at a meeting of the IMF's International Monetary and Financial Committee, Summers, by then secretary of the US Treasury, ratcheted up his rhetoric several notches. "Abuse of the global financial system is a clear case of a 'global public bad'—indeed, it is the dark side of international capital mobility," he said. "The international community has begun to take action against financial system abuse, including the public release of three lists of uncooperative or problematic jurisdictions [with respect to money laundering, practitioners of harmful tax practices, and lax financial supervision], and has called on the international financial institutions to join this effort. Assisting this effort should be seen as an integral part of the international financial institutions' mandate to protect the integrity of the international financial system. Money laundering activities have the potential to cause serious macroeconomic distortions, misallocate capital and resources, increase the risks to a country's financial sector, and hurt the credibility [or] integrity of the international financial system."

Summers was by no means alone in his assessment. Prior to the 2000 G-7 summit in Japan, the G-7 finance ministers stated in a report entitled "Actions Against Abuse of the Global Financial System": "Financial crime is increasingly a key concern in today's open and global financial world, which is characterized by the high mobility of funds and the rapid development of new payment tools." The actual G-7 summit statement on the topic read: "To secure the benefits of the globalised financial system, we need to ensure that its credibility and integrity are not undermined by money laundering, harmful tax competition, and poor regulatory standards."[28]

These statements illustrate two points about the interaction of money laundering with the globalization phenomenon and the stability of the financial system. First, globalization, and the deregulation that helps promote it, assists money launderers in their criminal activities. Second, the global spread of criminal activity, and the associated phenomenon of money laundering that fuels that process and facilitates the amassing of substantial financial resources, undercut public support for globalization. Vigorous efforts to deal with these problems are understandably limited by considerations of privacy and human rights, and by concerns about the arbitrary use of state power. However, these concerns can also constrain the capacity of governments to deal expeditiously and effectively with money laundering and other criminal activities, which in turn further undercuts support for globalization. The global "public bads" linked to money laun-

---

28. See Wechsler (2001) for a description of the Summers strategy on these issues.

dering are reckoned by some to outweigh the global "public goods" associated with globalization.

Differences between the US AML regime and those of other nations and regions also continue to impede multilateral efforts to achieve a uniform global regime. While the current global regime has been shaped and prodded to a considerable extent by US developments and initiatives, different forces have at times affected the structure and evolution of other national regimes. For example, the principal concern that prompted establishment of the Australian AML regime in 1990 was tax evasion rather than drugs. In the United Kingdom, concerns about drugs and terrorism dominated in the 1980s, even though comprehensive money-laundering regulations including customer due diligence and reporting requirements for the financial sector did not go into effect until 1994. (Table 4.1 provides a chronological list of the major developments in US, European, and global or multilateral anti–money laundering regimes. The glossary provides thumbnail descriptions of the major entries.)

Despite differences across regimes, and notwithstanding the enormous complications posed by globalization itself to combating criminal activity, the prevention and enforcement pillars of the global anti–money laundering regime have evolved rapidly over the past 15 years. At the very least, as William Gilmore (1999, 204) concluded, while "the strategy will not eradicate international drug trafficking or international organized crime, it will . . . create an increasingly hostile and inhospitable environment for the money launderer and others involved in highly lucrative forms of criminal behavior and afford new elements of protection to economic and political systems. To achieve this is to achieve something of real and lasting value."

Prevention

Customer due diligence is an area where the US prodded other jurisdictions to adopt a parallel component in their AML regimes. The 1986 US MLCA legislation required the chairman of the Federal Reserve Board, who was then Paul Volcker, to consult with his fellow Group of Ten (G-10) central bank governors at the Bank for International Settlements (BIS) about money laundering and bank efforts to control the activity. The legislation pointed out that money laundering is a global phenomenon and that if one country's banks and financial institutions are required to implement AML measures—increasing their costs and turning away their customers—then the same standards should be applied globally to reduce regulatory arbitrage and level the playing field.

The initial reaction of Volcker's central bank colleagues was horror—they maintained that central bankers and bank supervisors should be concerned more about the safety and soundness of individual banks than about the stability of the banking system. Under this view, banking supervisors should not become involved in law enforcement, which is the responsibility of the judiciary and the police. Calmer heads prevailed, but this episode illustrates the tension between the prevention and enforcement pillars of AML regimes.

The principal result of the US initiative was that the Basel Committee on Banking Supervision in 1988 issued a statement of principles regarding the obligations of banks to know their customers, avoid suspicious transactions, and cooperate with law enforcement authorities. An associated working paper acknowledged that differences in roles and responsibilities of national bank supervisory agencies in the suppression of money laundering at the time reflected "the role of banking supervision, the primary function of which is to maintain the overall financial stability and soundness of banks rather than to ensure that individual transactions conducted by bank customers are legitimate" (Basel Committee on Banking Supervision 1988, paragraph 3). However, the report added that "despite the limits in some countries on their specific responsibility, all members of the [Basel] Committee firmly believe that supervisors cannot be indifferent to the use made of banks by criminals."

The involvement of the Basel Committee in the anti–money laundering campaign marked a significant step not only because it recognized the risks of regulatory arbitrage and the need for a level global playing field, but because it involved the setting of international standards. Following the Basel Committee's lead, the International Organization of Securities Commissions (IOSCO) issued a resolution on money laundering in 1992. In 2002, the International Association of Insurance Supervisors (IAIS) issued Anti–Money Laundering Guidance Notes for Insurance Supervisors and Insurance Entities.

Switzerland is an example of a national AML regime that evolved quite differently than the US regime. The Swiss trace their concern with money laundering to adoption of a code of conduct by the Swiss Bankers Association in 1977 in the wake of the Chiasso banking scandals, which began as simple fraud in the early 1960s and ended up as major financial and embarrassment for Credit Suisse and much of the rest of the Swiss banking system. The Swiss approach places heavy emphasis on deep knowledge of customers, which is well justified in a banking system principally oriented toward private banking and investment management rather than retail banking.

In addition, in Switzerland as in Germany and France, suspicious activity reports are commonly based more on strong evidence than on hunches, and they more often lead to criminal investigations than in other countries. The Swiss (Pieth and Aiolfi 2003) argue that their AML regime is more rigorous than the US AML regime; US observers such as former treasury official William Wechsler (2001) think they have a point.

The Swiss system also relies heavily on the integrity and responsibility of financial institutions to ensure compliance with national AML laws and regulations. In contrast, the US and UK AML regimes operate in financial systems where retail transactions are at least as important as wholesale transactions and asset management relationships.[29] Pieth and Aiolfi (2003) have characterized the US and UK AML regimes as emphasizing the collection and submission of data to national authorities as part of an "early warning system" that may produce little more than information overload.

Financial Action Task Force

At the Paris Economic Summit of the Group of Seven (G-7) in 1989, France and the United States proposed an initiative that led to establishment of the Financial Action Task Force on Money Laundering (FATF) as a temporary body housed at the OECD but separate from that organization. However, establishing the FATF involved an agreement that it would not address tax issues.

The principal initial motivation for the establishment of the FATF was to combat drug abuse and the financial power of drug traffickers and other organized crime groups whose activities are facilitated by money laundering. Public concern about illegal drugs in the United States had reached extraordinary levels in 1989. The FATF delegations include supervisors, officials from finance ministries, and representatives of ministries charged with law enforcement (in the US case, the Justice Department). This interdisciplinary character has contributed to an impressive amount of intragovernmental cooperation as a positive by-product. The FATF's initial five-year mandate was to assess the results of cooperative efforts and suggest additional preventive steps. That mandate was extended in 1994 and 1999 and extended for a record further eight years on May 24, 2004.

In 1990, FATF promulgated its initial "Forty Recommendations" that provided a general AML framework, starting with ratification and implementation of the 1988 Vienna Convention, outlining the roles of national legal and financial systems and regulators in combating money laundering, and setting forth certain principles of international cooperation.[30] The Forty Recommendations were revised slightly in 1996 and then revised comprehensively in 2003 based on analysis, in light of FATF's review of trends in money laundering, of how far the recommendations should be extended to cover the financial and nonfinancial sectors as well as various

29. So important are retail transactions to the UK financial system that the AML regime there is sensitive to the charge that the regime itself may impede access to retail financial services. For example, the UK CDD regulations contain a subsection providing guidance about application of the regulations to limit the risk of financial exclusion.

30. In 1991, the European Community adopted its first directive on money laundering that sought to establish minimum standards throughout what is now known as the European Union. Stessens (2000) maintains that the action was motivated in part by other global attempts to address the money-laundering phenomenon, and also by concerns that money launderers or criminals would take advantage of the increasingly free flow of capital and financial services throughout the European Union. The need to establish a level playing field in Europe also was a concern. Gilmore (1999) stresses the particular challenge that human rights concerns have posed to establishing an AML regime in Europe.

"gatekeeper" professions through such methods as due diligence, reporting, regulation and supervision, and international cooperation.

A detailed report prepared in October 2001 by the Basel Committee Working Group on Cross-Border Banking and the Offshore Group of Banking Supervisors on Customer Due Diligence for Banks expanded on the obligations of banks to know their customers and upgrade record keeping to include more extensive due diligence for higher-risk accounts, ongoing monitoring, and proactive account management. The report (Basel Committee on Banking Supervision 2001) became the basis for recommendations 5 through 12 of the 2003 FATF Forty Recommendations on customer due diligence for the full set of financial, nonfinancial, and professional categories listed in table 4.2.

Neither the US AML regime nor the regimes of many other major countries today fully conform to the FATF recommendations in this area. For example, the United Kingdom does not apply the regime to insurance companies because UK authorities to date have judged the risk of money laundering through general insurance business as low (IMF 2003d, 108). The United Kingdom has applied its CDD and reporting requirements to lawyers under its Proceeds of Crime Act of 2002, although compliance has been limited. A 2004 survey by Coleman Parkes Research of companies selling high-value goods, such as car dealers or estate agents, found that two-thirds of such UK businesses do not comply with anti–money laundering regulations with respect to CDD and reporting requirements.

Canada was ahead of other jurisdictions in applying AML regulations to lawyers, but repealed the regulations after they were successfully challenged in a number of provincial courts on the grounds that they eroded the right of Canadians to independent counsel and to confidentiality with lawyers. Canada now leaves to the provinces the responsibility for the supervision of lawyers.

In contrast, the Australian minister for justice and customs announced in December 2003 his government's intention to fully comply with the 2003 FATF Forty Recommendations in order to ensure that Australia's anti–money laundering system "continues to model best practice."[31] At the same time, the government released a full set of consultation documents based on the new recommendations.

With respect to reporting requirements, some countries' AML regimes differ from those of the United States. For example, most other jurisdictions use suspicious transaction reports (STRs), which differ from suspicious activity reports (SARs) in that there has to be an actual transaction involved. A SAR can be about a transaction that may merely have been dis-

---

31. Press release at www.ag.gov.au/www/justiceministerhome.nsf.

cussed or attempted but not consummated. This may make the STRs more useful because they are more focused, but the distinction, as in the earlier comparison with Switzerland, illustrates differences in AML regimes. In Australia, any overseas remittance is entered into a database for scrutiny, a feature of the AML regime that relies on that country's relatively recent abolition of most formal capital controls. In addition, many non-US jurisdictions do not require CTRs or CIMRs or the equivalent, except to the extent that the underlying activity or transaction might be captured in an SAR/STR.[32]

In the area of supervision and sanctioning of noncompliance, recommendation 29 of the 2003 FATF Forty Recommendations calls for supervisors to have "adequate powers to monitor and ensure compliance by financial institutions" and explicitly includes the authority to conduct inspections to ensure compliance.[33] Some jurisdictions do not allow on-site examinations of financial institutions except under special circumstances, relying instead on the audit process. This in turn means that such jurisdictions may be more amenable to including accountants in their role as auditors as participants in the preventive aspects of the AML regime (box 4.1).

A particular challenge to the global AML regime is the existence of informal funds transfer (IFT) systems, such as *hawalas*, that operate on the unregulated side of the international financial system. Although *hawalas* are found throughout both the developed and developing world, their widespread use in the Middle East and South Asia prompted increased attention after September 11, 2001, despite the fact that those terrorists do not appear to have used an IFT mechanism to fund that operation.

Some argue that *hawalas* or other forms of IFT do not pose a unique money-laundering threat because other mechanisms provide the same opportunities (Passas 2000). Others stress that IFT systems often provide low-cost,

---

32. Recommendation 19 of the 2003 FATF Forty Recommendations calls upon countries only to "consider" adopting cash-reporting measures. SAR/STR may also be subject to different minimum reporting requirements in different jurisdictions (for example, 15,000 euros in the European Union and generally $10,000 in the United States, roughly 50 percent lower) and differ with respect to type of financial and nonfinancial business required to submit reports.

33. Recommendation 24b applies to nonfinancial businesses and professions, and sets a lower standard for "effective systems for monitoring and ensuring their compliance with requirements to combat money laundering and terrorist financing," including a potential role for self-regulatory organizations in this area. Countries with dual (federal-state) or only local-level approaches to the regulation and supervision of financial and nonfinancial businesses and professions will find it more difficult to meet this standard. For example, the regulation and supervision of the insurance industry in the United States is largely at the state level although it was reported in the *New York Times* (December 26, 2003) that some large insurance companies are pushing for establishment of a federal regulator to level the playing field in US insurance regulation and to influence federal legislation and regulations that affect insurance firms, including elements of the USA PATRIOT Act.

safe, and convenient services that are not otherwise available to the public (Buencamino and Gorbunov 2002). Still others stress that IFT systems thrive where the formal banking system is weak or nonexistent, or where there are significant distortions or controls in the payments or foreign exchange systems. Mohammed El Qorchi, Samuel Maimbo, and John Wilson (2003) have noted the potential adverse statistical, fiscal, and balance-of-payments implications of such operations.

What is clear is that bringing IFT mechanisms into the global AML regime presents complex problems for both recipient and remitting countries because of the very incentives that have allowed these systems to survive and thrive for generations. Regulations alone will not suffice—*hawalas* are essentially illegal in Pakistan and India, yet they thrive in those countries. High-cost regulations requiring registration, transparency, record keeping, and reporting are not likely to be fully effective because the institutions that can incur the costs will not be able to pass them on to their customers, who will continue to demand low-cost financial services. Reasonably effective incorporation of IFT systems into the global AML regime requires balancing many considerations within individual countries and the international financial system as a whole.

The repeated references in this chapter to the FATF evidence its key role as a standard setter in developing the global AML regime, particularly the prevention pillar. The FATF has limited membership (33 nations or jurisdictions)[34] and operates by consensus—potential constraints that it has addressed by maintaining high standards for its members, and by directly or indirectly sponsoring a number of regional clones, a move that reflects its recognition of the economic and political implications of globalization. The Caribbean Financial Action Task Force (CFATF) was established in 1996, the Asia-Pacific Group on Money Laundering (APG) in 1998, the Eastern and Southern Africa Anti–Money Laundering Group (ESAAMLG) in 1999, and the Financial Action Task Force on Money Laundering in Latin America (GAFISUD) in 2000. In addition, the Council of Foreign Ministers of the Commonwealth of Independent States (CIS), the former Soviet Union, announced in March 2004 that it was considering setting up a regional task force on money laundering. Conspicuous in their absence from the regional list are the Middle East and Central Asia, although by the fall of 2004 plans were under way to create a Middle East–North Africa FATF.

---

34. Current FATF members are Argentina, Australia, Austria, Belgium, Brazil, Canada, Denmark, the European Commission, Finland, France, Germany, Greece, the Gulf Cooperation Council, Hong Kong, Iceland, Ireland, Italy, Japan, Luxembourg, Mexico, the Netherlands, New Zealand, Norway, Portugal, Russia, Singapore, South Africa, Spain, Sweden, Switzerland, Turkey, the United Kingdom, and the United States.

The FATF is without significant enforcement power over jurisdictions that do not live up to its standards. It sponsors self-evaluations and peer reviews of its members, thus exercising global-level supervision, but has limited scope to sanction noncompliance. As of June 2003, even the United States was in full compliance with only 19 of the relevant 28 former FATF recommendations based on a self-assessment of its AML regime. Its short-falls concerned measures applied to insurance companies and money exchange and transmission operations. Since passage of the USA PATRIOT Act, efforts have been under way to correct these problems.

Starting with the Seychelles in 1996, the FATF also has periodically issued statements critical of the actions or inactions by non-FATF jurisdictions.[35] The FATF's success in forcing the Seychelles government to impose rules on its financial businesses inspired a more comprehensive effort to identify other countries and territories in the world whose regimes to prevent, detect, and punish money laundering did not meet internationally recognized standards (box 4.3). This "name and shame" initiative was launched officially in 2000 with the publication of 25 criteria, based on the Forty Recommendations, for identifying noncooperative countries and territories falling short in their AML regimes (FATF 2000). While most jurisdictions on the list were small, it included some major nations such as Egypt, Indonesia, Nigeria, the Philippines, and Russia.

As of July 2004, six countries remained on the list. One of them, Nauru, a Pacific island with a population of 12,600, has been subject since November 2001 to countermeasures that include the application of old FATF recommendation 21 (see footnote 35) as well as enhanced surveillance and reporting of financial and other relevant actions involving that jurisdiction.[36] The countermeasures require financial institutions to report transactions or attempted transactions that involve the jurisdiction or entities known to be incorporated in the jurisdiction. More recently, such measures were applied to Myanmar/Burma.

Liechtenstein, which was on the initial list, is credited with having accomplished one of the most rapid and impressive reconstructions of its AML regime, but it is left with the historical residue of more than 80,000 shell corporations, some with known unsavory links (including Saddam Hussein).

---

35. Regarding the Seychelles, the FATF invoked old recommendation 21 to scrutinize closely business relations and transactions with persons, companies, and financial institutions from countries that do not or insufficiently apply the Forty Recommendations. This aim was to force the Seychelles to repeal its Economic Development Act, which was designed, in the words of US Treasury official Ronald Noble, then president of the FATF, "to attract capital by permitting international criminal enterprises to shelter both themselves and their illicitly gained wealth from pursuit by legal authorities." In the same year, the FATF also applied recommendation 21 to one of its own members to induce Turkey to pass adequate AML legislation.

36. See chapter 7 for a more detailed account of the Nauru case.

Box 4.3   The FATF Non-Cooperative Countries and Territories Initiative

The Financial Action Task Force (FATF) undertook an initiative in 1999 to identify jurisdictions that had inadequate AML regimes and were not cooperating sufficiently with the global AML effort. The FATF issued its first report (FATF 2000) the next year on the basis of 25 assessment criteria applied to four areas: (i) financial regulations, including customer identification, excessive financial secrecy provisions, and lack of a suspicious transactions reporting system; (ii) other regulatory impediments, including registration requirements for certain types of businesses and their beneficial owners; (iii) obstacles to international cooperation, including administrative and judicial constraints; and (iv) inadequate budgetary outlays for anti–money laundering activities and the lack of a financial intelligence unit (FIU) or similar entity.

During two rounds in 2000 and 2001, the FATF reviewed 46 countries or territories as part of what has been called its "name and shame" process. The 15 territories included dependent territories such as Bermuda and autonomous territories such as Aruba. In 2002, the FATF suspended new reviews while cooperating with the IMF and World Bank on their reviews of compliance with global AML standards, but FATF continues to monitor jurisdictions that it previously reviewed. On the first or second round of its reviews, the FATF "passed" 23 and "failed" 23 jurisdictions. Of the latter group, 17 later "passed" as the result of subsequent reviews. The AML regimes of six jurisdictions have not yet been passed by the FATF: Cook Islands, Indonesia, Myanmar/Burma, Nauru, Nigeria, and the Philippines.

As part of this process, the FATF has threatened to endorse the application of countermeasures on jurisdictions that do not make adequate progress to improve their AML regimes. Under the original FATF recommendation 21, these countermeasures were envisaged as being applied to jurisdictions with serious deficiencies in their AML regimes. The measures may include more stringent customer due diligence requirements, enhanced reporting requirements, limits on establishing financial institutions in FATF countries, and warnings to nonfinancial-sector businesses with respect to dealings with entities in those jurisdictions. The threat of countermeasures was applied to Nauru, the Philippines, and Russia in 2001, Nigeria and Ukraine in 2002, and Myanmar/Burma in 2003. In the cases of the Philippines, Nigeria, and Ukraine, the threat was later lifted because those countries made some progress in improving their AML regimes. In the case of Russia, sufficient progress was made that it was admitted to the FATF as a full member. The countermeasures were applied to Nauru and Burma/Myanmar.

The FATF has also conducted mutual assessment reviews of the AML regimes of its members, which currently number 33. Two members are regional institutions: the European Commission and the Gulf Cooperation Council. Except for Russia, none of the other 31 members has "failed" a FATF assessment. Thus, the 30 other FATF jurisdictions, including Hong Kong, which is an autonomous territory of China, can be said to have "passed" their mutual assessment FATF reviews.

If Liechtenstein is to move on to clean up this residue, it will require the cooperation of other jurisdictions.

The FATF, International Monetary Fund (IMF), and World Bank agreed in the fall of 2002 on a one-year pilot project to assess compliance with measures to combat money laundering and the financing of terrorism. The project in effect transferred most of the peer reviews and evaluations of FATF members and nonmembers to the other two organizations as a step toward a global supervision system.[37] Drawing largely on national experts, the IMF and World Bank organized overall assessments in cooperation with the FATF and FATF-style regional bodies.

Guidelines also were established for the use of independent experts with regard to criminal law enforcement matters and nonprudentially regulated financial activities of such professionals as lawyers, accountants, and real estate dealers. Their portions of the reports were printed in italics. This was done out of concern about so-called mission creep in the IFIs and out of concern that greater focus on this area would distract them from their core missions.

Participation in an IMF/World Bank review is entirely voluntary, and the country being reviewed itself decides whether the resulting report is published, a procedure that has the potential to negate the "name and shame" mechanism used to press countries with shortcomings.[38] The IMF and World Bank have no powers to sanction, and limited scope to promote compliance through their lending and technical assistance programs.

Under the 2002–03 pilot project, 41 reviews have been conducted (IMF 2004a, 2004c), 33 of them by the IMF and/or World Bank with the help of independent experts, and the remainder done by regional FATFs. As of April 2004, IMF/World Bank reports on 15 of the 19 country reviews that had been completed had been published in whole or in part.[39]

Notwithstanding the drawbacks to IMF/World Bank monitoring of compliance with international standards on combating money laundering and terrorism financing, the G-7 and the FATF called for continuation of the assessment program on a permanent basis, and the executive boards of the IMF and the World Bank agreed in March 2004. They also agreed to fully integrate the treatment of criminal law enforcement and nonprudentially regulated financial activities into a single assessment document, dropping the italics.

Offshore Financial Centers

Following a recommendation of a working group of the Financial Stability Forum (FSF 2000), the IMF also reluctantly undertook a program in 2000 to assess 44 jurisdictions identified as offshore financial centers (OFCs). Part of the IMF's reluctance to become involved in this area related to the fact that

---

37. The IMF had already accepted FATF's standards to combat money laundering and terrorism financing as one of its 12 internationally recognized standards and codes.

38. The country reviews are conducted as part of the Reports on Observance of Standards and Codes (ROSCs), which in turn are part of the IMF's more comprehensive Financial Sector Assessment Program (FSAP) that sometimes involves an in-depth Financial System Stability Assessment (FSSA). ROSCs discuss compliance in a general context, while full assessments also include detailed ratings of compliance.

39. The reviews for Bangladesh, Honduras, Israel, and Tanzania had not been published.

nearly half of the jurisdictions were not Fund members. Several were dependencies of members, such as Montserrat, which is an overseas territory of the United Kingdom. In addition, some Fund members perceived the assessment task as being only loosely related to the institution's core responsibility to ensure macroeconomic and financial stability. Their concern was that the program could take resources and focus away from the Fund's principal tasks. After the assessment program was up and running, and perhaps in response to those sentiments, program director Barry Johnson stated: "First, let me be clear that the IMF does not chase criminals. We help jurisdictions set up the necessary legal and financial infrastructure, provide technical assistance to draft laws and regulations, work with the authorities to develop the required expertise and set up the financial intelligence units needed to gather information from the financial services industry, and ensure that there are trained staff to implement laws and regulations" (*IMF Survey*, February 16, 2004, 39).

As of November 2003, the IMF had conducted some type of assessment of 40 of the 44 offshore financial centers. The program is regarded as generally successful based on a review by the IMF (2003c) and the Financial Stability Forum (FSF 2004). It is difficult to reach an independent judgment because by mid-2004 reports had been published for only 16 assessments, with publication of another 10 in prospect. The IMF (2003c) review of the program reached four broad conclusions. First, the supervisory deficiencies in offshore financial centers are similar to those in the most other jurisdictions where the IMF has conducted assessments. Second, the wealthier the jurisdiction, the closer it comes to meeting high supervisory standards. Third, the offshore financial center assessments have led to improvements in many supervisory and regulatory systems in the jurisdictions evaluated. Fourth, there is lax supervision and regulation of the nonbanking sector, which is par for the course as AML regimes are established and implemented.

One concern of the offshore financial centers themselves had been that they would lose legitimate business and associated revenues as a result of the assessment process.[40] Figure 4.2 suggests that such concerns may have been misplaced at least with respect to business in 10 offshore financial centers. The share of total cross-border financial assets accounted for by the five jurisdictions normally identified as traditional offshore centers—the Bahamas, Bahrain, Cayman Islands, Luxembourg, and the Netherlands Antilles—has been essentially unchanged for a decade, including since 1999, when OFCs began to receive increased attention. By contrast, the shares of the other jurisdictions in the 10 OFCs—Japan, the United Kingdom, the United States, Hong Kong, and Singapore—have been in a rather steady decline.

Of course, these data are only suggestive. Illegitimate business is probably only a small portion of total business in these centers. Offshore finance

---

40. See Suss, Williams, and Mendis (2002) for a discussion of the economic motivation for becoming an offshore financial center and an early assessment of the impact of FSF and FATF initiatives on such jurisdictions in the Caribbean.

Figure 4.2 Share of cross-border assets of offshore financial centers, 1992–2003 (percent)

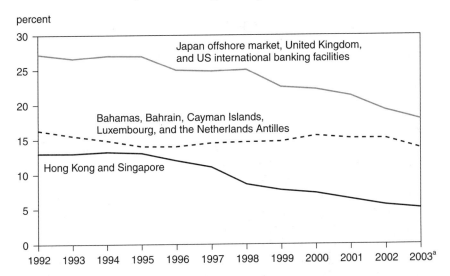

percent

Japan offshore market, United Kingdom, and US international banking facilities

Bahamas, Bahrain, Cayman Islands, Luxembourg, and the Netherlands Antilles

Hong Kong and Singapore

Note: Offshore financial centers' cross-border assets are equal to external positions of banks in individual reporting countries minus local positions in foreign currency of banks in those countries.
a. Data are for the third quarter of 2003.
Source: BIS (2004).

could have attracted more legitimate business to some of these jurisdictions, or the program and associated improvements related to global standards may have had no effect on financial flows. Moreover, smaller offshore financial centers may have lost more business. Esther Suss, Oral Williams, and Chandima Mendis (2002) report that the number of licensed banks in Antigua and Barbuda declined from 58 in 1997 to 21 at the end of 2001 as a result of the attention focused on their offshore financial center activities by the FSF, and because of concerns raised by the FATF's Non-Cooperative Countries and Territories Initiative in 2000.

Enforcement

The enforcement pillar of the global AML regime relies heavily on a number of regional and United Nations conventions (table 4.1). Particularly important are the 1988 UN Convention Against Illicit Traffic in Narcotic Drugs and Psychotropic Substances (Vienna), the 1999 OECD Convention on Combating Bribery of Foreign Officials in International Business Transactions the 2000 UN Convention Against Transnational Organized Crime (Palermo), and the 2003 UN Convention Against Corruption.

While these conventions and agreements have succeeded on paper in establishing a common AML framework, in practice there are important differences.

An initial European Commission directive on money laundering issued in 1991 was principally concerned with laundering of drug proceeds and applied only to the financial sector. A second directive in 2001 widened the focus to all "serious offenses" and required members to bring within the coverage of the AML regime auditors, accountants, tax advisers, notaries, other legal professionals, real estate agents, casinos, and dealers in high-valued goods. In June 2004, the European Commission proposed a third AML directive incorporating terrorism into the AML framework and conforming the EU AML regime to the 2003 FATF Forty Recommendations.

There are two basic approaches to criminalizing money-laundering predicate offenses. Under the US approach (used in Japan as well), specific crimes are listed, which has the advantage of pinpointing those types of activities of substantial concern.

The alternative approach, found in most other jurisdictions, criminalizes money laundering in connection with all offenses involving proceeds from the crimes or in connection with all "serious offenses," conventionally defined in terms of a punishment threshold such as a maximum or a minimum imprisonment. This approach has the advantage of capturing what is regarded as serious by the local authorities,[41] but it may exclude categories important to other authorities, thereby undermining the quid pro quo mutual reinforcement of national AML regimes. In general, law enforcement has every reason to support adding concerns ranging from narcotics to terrorism to the AML agenda.

Legislative implementation of enforcement measures around the world has been spotty. For example, according to the IMF/World Bank 2004 assessment report on the Czech Republic's AML regime, that country's definition of money laundering as an offense generally meets the international standard, but the implementing criminal code fails to cover the acquisition, possession, or use of assets with the knowledge that such assets originate from a criminal activity, and sets a higher burden of proof than is consistent with the international standard. Similarly, as of 1993, Greece was a party to various international agreements but had not yet enacted any implementing legislation, and France, Luxembourg, Portugal, and Spain had criminalized money laundering only in connection with drug offenses.

The 2003 FATF Forty Recommendations sought to resolve this dilemma by linking the two approaches. It establishes a definition of "serious

---

41. Even using a definition of a "serious crime" that specifies either a maximum or minimum does not guarantee uniformity of treatment. Some serious crimes are not "caught" by either test, and in other cases the activity is not a crime.

offenses"[42] and also specifically designates 20 broad categories of predicate offenses for money laundering that include corruption, bribery, market manipulation, and environmental crimes.

However, the designated predicate money-laundering crimes in the 2003 FATF Forty Recommendations do not include tax evasion, consistent with the FATF's mandate to avoid tax evasion. As discussed earlier, this omission not only reveals a lack of uniformity in the global AML regime but can also hinder cooperation. Some countries such as France include tax evasion as a money-laundering offense in their national legislation, but undercut the inclusion because the offense is not reportable by financial institutions.

An Oxfam global report on tax havens in 2000 claimed that developing countries as a group may be forgoing $50 billion in annual tax revenues as a result of tax competition and the use of tax havens. The report does not provide background on how the estimate was derived, so it is impossible to evaluate the figure. However, the figure itself conveys the criticism that the playing field in international finance as regards tax issues is uneven. In August 2003, Secretary-General Kofi Annan issued a report to the UN General Assembly calling for increased international cooperation on tax issues involving money laundering, transnational crime, international terrorism, tax evasion, and tax incentives for investment by competing countries.

With respect to the investigation element of enforcement, some jurisdictions such as the United Kingdom do not condone sting operations. Recommendation 27 of FATF (2003c) endorses investigative techniques such as "controlled delivery, undercover operations and other relevant techniques," but not explicitly sting operations. Jurisdictions also differ in their standards and procedures to enforce due process, human rights, and privacy. The US Casablanca undercover operation in 1998 was regarded as a resounding success in the United States, but the operation and its aftermath created tensions with Mexico. In February 2004, four bankers convicted in Mexican courts in connection with the operation were released when the US sting operation was declared unconstitutional under Mexican law.

Approaches to the structure of the AML regime as well as prosecutions for money-laundering offenses differ across jurisdictions depending in part on fundamental legal principles, such as whether they are based on common law or civil law. For example, under civil law principles it is more difficult to establish criminal liability for legal persons. Common law principles are generally credited with supporting better economic performance (Caprio and Honohan 2001), but the better protection they afford property rights

---

42. The FATF definition requires a maximum penalty of more than one year of imprisonment or a minimum of more than six months.

tends to get in the way of a tight AML regime in which everything is regulated. These differences and impediments generally are not regarded as insurmountable, but they complicate the establishment of a uniform global AML regime.

Finally, in the area of confiscation, national practices again differ. For example, the 2003 FATF Forty Recommendation 3, citing the Vienna and Palermo UN Conventions, carefully calls upon countries to adopt confiscation measures, outlines the desirable content (identification and freezing of property, preserving the state's ability to recover the property, and investigation), and suggests that countries consider measures to allow confiscation without a criminal conviction, or through procedures that shift the burden of proof to the defender to demonstrate the lawful origin of the property. Cross-country practices are far from uniform in this area, which tends to impede international cooperation by, inter alia, limiting the scope to share assets that might be seized.

On the other hand, most countries have financial intelligence units (FIUs) to combat money laundering, and the 2003 FATF Forty Recommendations include nine (26 through 34) that primarily relate to enforcement issues, including the establishment of FIUs, along with six (35 through 40) that relate to international cooperation on anti–money laundering. The powers of such national FIUs differ, however. For example, the Czech FIU cannot share information with its foreign counterparts in the absence of treaties or conventions. In addition, where an FIU is situated within governmental structures may affect its ability to coordinate information flows and interact with those who are conducting criminal investigations.

The Egmont Group of Financial Intelligence Units established in 1995 now includes more than 80 entities that coordinate their work on money-laundering issues. The aim is to support national programs through the exchange of information (under closely specified conditions), enhance expertise, and foster better communication. Although such organizations as the Egmont Group are not centrally involved in international enforcement— which continues to be handled through traditional police and justice channels governed largely by bilateral and multilateral treaties, conventions, and arrangements (such as mutual legal assistance treaties in criminal matters in the case of the United States)—they represent a significant recognition that enforcement is an important dimension of the global AML regime.

In Europe, the mandate of the Europol Drugs Unit (EDU) established early in 1995 to coordinate actions on drug crimes was eventually expanded to cover criminal activities associated with money laundering. Later in 1995, Europol itself was created and it absorbed the EDU in 1999. The European Union has been faced with more intense coordination and enforcement issues as it has developed and deepened the single market, with a greater need for common rules and areawide enforcement actions.

At the global level, the international police coordination organization Interpol established a Financial and High Tech (FHT) Crimes Sub-Directorate under its Specialized Crimes Directorate in September 2001. The FHT investigates funds derived from criminal activities, as well as currency counterfeiting and intellectual property rights offenses. It focuses on providing expertise to law enforcement agencies and increasing interjurisdictional communication and cooperation (Interpol 2003).

National and global AML regimes initially exist only in agreements and laws. They are effective only if there is compliance and implementation. For example, in early February 2004, the European Commission notified France, Greece, Italy, Luxembourg, Portugal, and Sweden that they had failed to implement changes in their national laws mandated by the 2001 EC Money Laundering Directive.[43] On the other side of the world, the story is told that the government of Vietnam is unconvinced that it needs to apply CDD to its banks if it owns them.

The World Bank (2003a) makes the case for how money laundering adversely affects developing countries because they are often small and more susceptible to disruption. But it acknowledges that the magnitude of these consequences is difficult to establish because the impact cannot be precisely quantified either in general or for a specific country. In developing countries with limited governmental resources, and where anti–money laundering may, correctly or incorrectly, be regarded as a luxury good, one option for strengthening the global AML regime is to provide technical and financial assistance bilaterally or through international financial institutions.

Costs of the US Anti–Money Laundering Regime

In principle, the gross financial costs of the AML regime should be weighed against the benefits of efforts to prevent and combat money laundering, to which we turn in chapters 5 through 7. Systematic quantitative information on the costs of the AML regime is scarce, so this section draws on scraps of US and British information in order to make a ballpark estimate of the gross financial costs of the US AML regime. That estimate for 2003 is on the order of $7 billion, or about $25 per capita.

An anti–money laundering regime imposes both direct and indirect as well as financial and nonfinancial costs that take three forms: (1) costs incurred by the government or public sector in establishing and administering the regime, (2) costs incurred by the private sector in carrying out the requirements of government, and (3) costs borne by the general public. Were it not for these costs, the standard of zero tolerance for money laundering could be applied to measuring the success of the AML regime in achieving all of its goals. In other words, any dollar of proceeds of crime or

---

43. The European Union also could have made a major contribution to the global AML regime by limiting the largest new euro note to €100, comparable to the largest US note of $100; instead the largest note is €500.

some other form of those proceeds that was laundered would be proof that the system was flawed.

In addition to the gross financial costs of prevention and enforcement, the potential for information overload, in practice, should also be considered. The government may collect so much information because it perceives the costs of doing so as being negligible, but this approach runs the risk that the massive amount of irrelevant information might drown out information that is of value.[44] The result may be a point on a "Laffer curve" for AML information beyond which additional filings reduce the investigative capability of the government. Pieth and Aiolfi (2003) as well as several reports by the government itself have voiced concern about the collection of excessive information by the US AML regime. The General Accounting Office (GAO 1996) argued specifically that too many CTRs were being filed, imposing unnecessary costs on both the private and public sectors, and undercutting the usefulness of the reporting system. Seven years later, FinCEN (2003a) set a goal to reduce the number of CTRs (now numbering over 12 million annually) by 30 percent. Although the stated aim was to reduce the submission of CTRs with little or no value to law enforcement, and which thus imposed costs for industry, an implicit motivation was to lower costs and increase the effectiveness of CTRs for the US government.

Evidence on the issue of information overload in the United Kingdom comes from KPMG (2003, 16): "The nature of the process at ECB [Economic Crime Branch of the National Crime Intelligence Service], exacerbated by the significant number of poor quality SARs provided by disclosing entities, has led to significant delays in disseminating SARs which have not been fast-tracked." Michael Gold and Michael Levi (1994) reached a similar conclusion.

Problems of incidence and interpretation also are involved. Consider each of the three areas in which the AML regime imposes costs: the government, private-sector institutions, and the general public. The government incurs direct costs through prevention and enforcement, such as operating the SAR and similar databases and investigating specific transactions.

The government uses laws and regulations to shift some of its costs onto financial and nonfinancial institutions and, potentially, independent professions.[45] Banks incur direct costs when they are required to set up inter-

---

44. Generalizations in this area are difficult in the absence of carefully assembled data. For example, it is possible that the costs of compliance are unknown. The government may bear only a small share of those unknown costs. It may not be in a position to judge costs and benefits for either the private or public sector. It may be unaware of the issue, though that would be unlikely in the often contentious environment of US financial regulations. Finally, the government may not recognize that one of the costs of the AML regime is the less efficient use of any information because of the costs of searching for it.

45. Reinicke (1998) refers to this process of increasingly assigning and delegating information and analysis responsibilities to the private sector as "horizontal subsidiarity."

nal control systems to detect money laundering or systems to generate the data sought by the government. Costs borne by financial and other institutions and businesses may be shifted to customers. Of course, the individual institutions consider the costs net of any direct or indirect financial benefits. Representatives of a number of the institutions interviewed for this study emphasized that they integrate the requirements of the AML regime into their overall risk management systems, and that they see reputation or "image" advantages and other gains from running "squeaky clean" operations.

Also relevant are distinctions between the institution's long- and short-run costs as well as the general level of competition it is facing. Nevertheless, to the extent that the net effective financial costs are positive, the price of the services provided by individual financial institutions and businesses go up; if the institutions use a cost-plus-markup approach to pricing decisions, the general public pays some of the costs. For example, banks raise the price of services to the customer, either directly via monthly fees or indirectly via higher minimum balance requirements to recoup some or all of their net AML costs. A potential indirect effect of this cost shifting is that these price increases may exclude some customers from access to standard banking services such as electronic deposits or check cashing.

Customers also bear opportunity and transaction costs, since they must provide additional documentation to satisfy the regulations and may experience as a consequence delays and other types of transaction costs. A less tangible b}t often no less important cost to some customers is the increased intrusion, or loss of "privacy." Intrusiveness also can contribute to a will-not-pay or will-not-play posture on the part of customers who either defy the rules or withdraw from participation in the financial system. Either way, the overall effectiveness of the AML regime may be weakened because of a loss of information. Similar compliance problems can arise if AML requirements are perceived to be applied unevenly among customers (e.g., more harshly to individuals than to corporations).

Costs to the Government

No systematic estimates are available for the costs of the various elements that make up the AML regime in the United States or any other country.[46] Moreover, developing such estimates poses complex conceptual challenges. For example, the government's costs to operate SAR and CTR databases can be estimated, but those costs are a small part of total government AML costs and do not include the enforcement costs associated with inves-

---

46. The best analyses are by the UK authorities, and we rely on them quite heavily. Although the 2000 *National Money Laundering Strategy* initiated a tally of resources that the US government devotes to combating money laundering, the findings were never made public.

Figure 4.3   Trends in US federal prevention and enforcement real outlays, fiscal 1985–2004 (in millions of 1995 dollars)

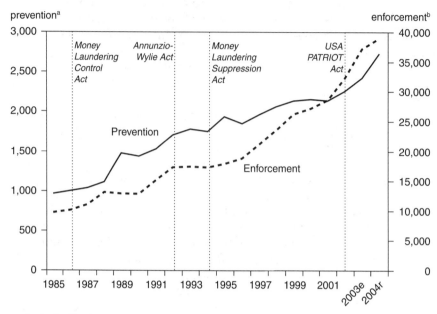

e = budget estimate
r = budget request

a. Includes outlays for US Treasury and non-Treasury agencies involved in the prevention process. US Treasury agencies are the Office of Comptroller of Currency and the Office of Thrift Supervision. Non-Treasury agencies are the Commodities Futures Trading Commission, Federal Reserve System, National Credit Union Administration, Federal Deposit Insurance Corporation, and Securities and Exchange Commission.
b. Includes outlays in Function 750 (Administration of Justice: federal law enforcement, federal litigative, judicial, correctional activities and criminal justice assistance) of the US federal budget. FinCEN is also included in Function 750.
Source: US Federal Budget, *Annual Report: Budget Review* (fiscal 1985 to 2004). Board of Governors of the Federal Reserve System, fiscal 1985 to 2004.

tigative and regulatory activities employing these databases. Those latter costs are difficult to estimate, in particular the marginal costs, because few investigations focus solely on money laundering. Rather, the AML regime generates data that government agencies use along with other investigative materials in pursuing criminal investigations and developing prosecutions.

Despite such constraints, it is possible to put together ballpark estimates of total US annual (fiscal year) federal outlays for all types of prevention (principally by financial regulators) and enforcement activities, using as a starting point the "750" account of the federal budget covering the administration of justice. Figure 4.3 displays the trends in real (1995) dollars from 1985 (prior to enactment of the 1986 Money Laundering Control Act) to

2004. The data include expenditures associated with the AML regime as well as expenditures associated with other regulatory or law enforcement activities. In real terms, the average annual increase over the period was 6.1 percent for total prevention expenditures, 7.4 percent for enforcement expenditures (almost an order of magnitude larger than prevention), and 7.3 percent for the combined total.

Not a great deal can be said about expenditures on the actual AML regime, although one can ask whether the passage of the four major pieces of AML legislation in the years indicated in figure 4.3 by the vertical lines had a marked impact on our proxies for aggregate prevention and enforcement expenditures.

Over the period measured, the average three-year increase in prevention expenditures was about 13 percent and in enforcement expenditures about 26 percent. These averages can be compared with the three years surrounding the passage of the four pieces of US AML legislation from one year prior to passage, as the base, until two years after passage. For prevention, the comparison reveals that the only above-average increase was surrounding the passage of the MLCA in 1986, and the excess was less than 10 percent; for the other three dates the increase was the same as or less than the average. For enforcement, a similar above-average increase occurred from the base in 1985 to 1988, but the increase from 2000 to 2003 (surrounding the passage of the USA PATRIOT Act) was substantially larger, about 20 percent more than average. Thus, there may have been marked increases in expenditures by the federal government associated with these four major adjustments to the US AML regime, but they appear to have been largely washed out in the aggregate data by other factors affecting regulatory and supervisory expenditures.

A rough rule of thumb is that perhaps 2 to 3 percent of total US government regulatory and enforcement expenditures at present might be attributable to the AML regime.[47] On this basis, the federal government in fiscal year 2003 may have spent something like $1.5 billion on the AML regime, which would be 0.014 percent of nominal GDP in 2003.[48] For the public sec-

---

47. The costs of AML regime prevention and enforcement are combined with data on other aspects of regulation and law enforcement that have nothing to do with money laundering. This is easiest to appreciate on the law enforcement side, which includes activities (such as Secret Service protection) that have negligible or zero money-laundering components. US government officials generally opt for the lower estimate (2 percent), which is consistent with the "rough cut" estimate of the federal budgetary costs of the US AML regime of $1 billion in fiscal year 2001 presented in the 2000 NMLS (appendix 6). The higher estimate (3 percent) is consistent with the data assembled for this study, which included expenditures by the Federal Reserve System that were excluded from the 2000 NMLS estimates.

48. Suskind (2004) reports that US Treasury Secretary Paul O'Neill subsequently decided that the $1 billion estimate for budget expenditures in fiscal year 2001 should have been closer to $700 million. We were unable to find the basis for his revision, and, as noted, the original estimate excluded costs incurred by the Federal Reserve System.

tor as a whole, including state and local expenditures, the total may have been twice as large, about $3 billion as an upper-bound estimate.[49]

Costs to Private-Sector Institutions

Estimates of AML regime costs to private-sector institutions are similarly elusive. In the case of large banks it is possible to separate out the costs of units explicitly set up to comply with AML regulations and reduce a bank's vulnerability to it. However, internal costs associated with filling out forms and examining customer records for AML compliance cannot be readily separated from other reporting requirements related to the Bank Secrecy Act. Interviews with officials in a number of large financial institutions suggest that it is these dispersed costs that are the principal expense.

The literature on the costs of bank regulation is small, but a review by Gregory Elliehausen (1998) of what is available helps to obtain some sense of the order of magnitude of costs for banks and, by extension, other financial institutions and nonfinancial businesses subject to AML regulations. Elliehausen distinguishes four concepts of costs: opportunity costs when regulation prevents an institution from engaging in a profitable activity; operating costs, divided between start-up and ongoing costs; total costs of the activity, even if not required by law or regulation; and incremental costs specifically associated with the required activity.

Most useful for purposes here are estimates cited by Elliehausen drawing on the work of the accounting firm Grant Thornton (1992, 1993) for the Independent Bankers Association of America. Elliehausen is relatively comfortable with the methodology in these studies, which provide estimates of ongoing operating costs of complying with Bank Secrecy Act regulations as of 1991, including a large component of AML regulations as well as other matters. One Grant Thornton study estimates that compliance with the Bank Secrecy Act accounted for 0.2 percent of individual banks' noninterest expenses, while the other said 0.5 percent. This range translates into between $240 million and $600 million for the entire banking system. Using the larger number and scaling it by the growth of nominal GDP between 1991 and 2003 produces a figure of about $1 billion. A ballpark upper-end estimate of the costs of AML regime compliance for banks would be $1.5 billion in 2003, recognizing that AML requirements have increased over that

---

49. We did not find even roughly comparable data on the AML prevention and enforcement expenditures by state and local governments, so we were forced to rely on some ready reckoning. Government consumption expenditures at the state and local levels are about 1.7 times those at the federal level, which might suggest applying a larger multiplier to estimated federal expenditures to come up with total government expenditures on anti–money laundering. However, a disproportionate amount of the AML activity is at the federal level, which suggests doubling the estimate for the federal government should produce a reasonable upper-bound estimate of total government financial costs of the US AML regime.

period. The figure might reasonably be doubled to obtain an upper-end guesstimate of $3 billion for all private-sector institutions.[50]

Studies by KPMG (2003) and Pricewaterhouse Coopers (2003) for the UK National Criminal Intelligence Service and the Financial Services Authority (FSA), respectively, provide a partial cross-check for these estimates. The KPMG study provides a "rough estimate" of the current cost of the UK SARs regime for reporting entities of £90 million. If we scale this figure by the size of the US economy relative to the size of the UK economy and convert it from pounds sterling to dollars, the corresponding estimate is $1.1 billion. Since reporting of SARs is an important but only one element of the AML regime, this rough estimate suggests that a figure of $3 billion for the entire US regime is not unreasonable as an upper-bound estimate.

The Pricewaterhouse Coopers study for the FSA reports on the one-time compliance costs of extending customer due diligence to existing customers who had not previously been subjected to CDD because they were customers of the institutions prior to the introduction of those requirements in the United Kingdom in 1994. The study suggests that the costs for banks are slightly more than half those for all major financial institutions.[51] Pricewaterhouse Coopers also compares the costs of the two proposed approaches with the overall AML compliance costs in the United Kingdom. Using the arithmetic outlined above, the comparable total for compliance costs to financial institutions in the United States would be about $2.1 billion, which is in the same ballpark as our estimate of $3 billion.[52] A 2002 study by Celent Communications, a Boston financial-research organization, reportedly concluded that AML spending by US financial institutions in the wake of the passage of the USA PATRIOT Act would total $10.9 billion over 2003–2005, or about $3.5 billion a year. Allowing for the fact that some of these would be one-time costs and Celent might have had an institutional interest in generating a larger rather than a

---

50. Excluding real estate from the "finance, insurance, and real estate" category of US GDP by industry, depository institutions account for about 40 percent of the rest of the category, which also includes nondepository institutions, security and commodity brokers, and insurance. On the other hand, the AML prevention regime is currently applied with much greater force to depository institutions, which suggests that doubling the estimate for banks should produce a reasonable upper-bound estimate.

51. Pricewaterhouse Coopers examined two approaches to implementing the AML regime. The finding cited in the text combines estimates of the costs of the more expensive approach with estimates of the costs for six major banks that are already implementing something close to the more expensive approach.

52. The May 9, 2003, *Federal Register* (page 25108) notice of the incremental paperwork burden associated with revisions to the US CDD regulations applied to 22,057 US financial institutions covered by the USA PATRIOT Act. Each institution was expected to incur 11 hours per respondent on average. Assuming that these hours would be divided equally among tellers, bookkeepers, and financial officers on the basis of mean hourly earnings as reported by the US Bureau of Labor Statistics, augmented by 30 percent for benefits, the total cost of this adjustment to the US AML regime was a modest $5.7 million.

smaller estimate, the Celent estimate would appear to be in the same ball-park as the aforementioned estimates.[53] Recall, however, that these are estimates of gross financial costs and do not take into account any financial or nonfinancial benefits of complying with the AML regime.

The two studies for the UK authorities also looked at AML costs to the government. The KPMG study of the SAR regime estimates these costs at only about 12 percent of the costs to reporting institutions. However, that figure should not undercut our guesstimate of the rough equality between the overall costs of the US AML regime to the government and private-sector institutions. Many government costs with respect to prevention, such as drafting regulations and conducting examinations, are unrelated to the actual management of information flows. The United States is also far more active than the United Kingdom in prosecutions (chapter 5). Moreover, our estimate of total US federal prevention costs (figure 4.3) is only about one-fifth of the total prevention plus enforcement costs.[54]

Elliehausen's summary of the research in this area establishes a strong case for the presence of economies of scale with respect to the costs of AML compliance, where assets or some more refined definition of a bank's output measure scale.[55] Fixed costs of compliance reflect such items as computer systems, which account for a large component of start-up costs for AML regimes.[56] However, variable costs may also be lumpy for small institutions; ongoing compliance involves larger proportions of labor costs, but special skills (human capital) are involved. To the extent that a large component of the costs imposed on firms are fixed costs, it is understandable that there is resistance by casinos, the real estate industry, lawyers, and accountants to expanding the AML regime into their lines of business.[57] The AML regime

---

53. Celent Communications was cited in *Business Week* (December 1, 2003, 102) as the source for an estimate that more than 13,000 US financial institutions had yet to implement basic watch lists to screen new customers. The firm argued that many small institutions would rather pay a fine than install costly new technology for customer screening.

54. The Pricewaterhouse Coopers study estimates that the cost to the UK government of the expanded retrospective CDD would be a minuscule amount (0.3 percentage points) of the total cost to firms. This low figure is understandable because the change in the AML regime applies principally to the reporters and the cost to the government only involves receiving additional reports but not any subsequent action using the reports.

55. Pricewaterhouse Coopers (2003, 88) reports that large banks benefit from economies of scale in outsourcing some aspects of customer due diligence to credit bureaus.

56. KPMG (2003, 48) estimates that the capital costs of the UK SAR regime are roughly two-thirds of annual compliance costs. On the other hand, Celent (www.celent.net/japanese/PressReleases/20020927/AntiMoneyLaundering.htm [accessed March 8, 2004]) reported that hardware costs were only 6 percent of the estimated total of three-year AML regime expenditures by US financial institutions.

57. HM Treasury (2002) estimates that the cost of extending the UK AML regime to lawyers, accountants, and real estate dealers, converted into dollars and scaled to US GDP, is $2.1 billion. However, it should be noted that the US AML regime does not as yet apply extensively to these professions.

imposes additional one-time costs for continuing in business, as well as subsequent costs resulting from frequent changes in regulations.

A report to Congress on the use of currency transaction reports illustrates some of the complexities of AML regime costs for banks, and presumably for other reporters as well. A survey by FinCEN (2002) of the reasons why banks did not take advantage of the potential exemptions from CTR reporting detected little difference between the responses of so-called megabanks, each with more than $32 billion in assets, and all other financial institutions. Among the more prominent reasons for not using the exemption was that it is not cost effective to change systems once they are in place, suggesting a large role for fixed costs. Other reasons included the additional due diligence costs involved and fear of regulatory action if an exemption were to turn out to be wrong. The survey findings suggest some of the reasons for the potential information overload in the reporting element in the US prevention pillar.

Costs to the General Public

Notwithstanding the economic and social benefits of the AML regime, the general public incurs costs from the increased regulation in the form of reduced efficiency and higher charges. While there is little to go on to estimate out-of-pocket or opportunity costs of the AML regime, comprehensive cross-country research by the World Bank (2004) shows that more regulation in general is associated with lower labor productivity, greater use of the informal economy, increased corruption, and higher costs. There is no reason to believe that such effects of regulation would be any different in the case of the AML regime—the only question is the magnitude of the adverse effects. A topic for future research might be to adapt the World Bank's survey approach in connection with estimating AML regime costs to the general public.

The Pricewaterhouse Coopers report (2003, 75) on expanded CDD in the United Kingdom stated that "a new regulation, which makes it more expensive to enter a market, might be expected to soften the level of competition, to the potential detriment of consumers." In addition, Elliehausen (1998) argues that the policy implications of economies of scale in the costs of regulation are that they inhibit entry of new firms into banking, limit interinstitutional competition, undermine deregulation efforts across the financial sector, and reduce incentives for financial innovation because regulatory costs are relatively high at low levels of output that are associated with the early phase of regulation.

Pricewaterhouse Coopers provides some quantitative insight into the costs of the AML regime to the UK general public. The report estimates a cost per customer of between 7 and 12 percent of the overall cost of implementing the one-time adjustment in the UK AML regime with respect to

CDD, depending on which approach would be chosen. The estimate is based on the customer's time required, the opportunity cost of that time, and any materials. In addition, there may be other transaction costs associated with routine business operations.

What might be a plausible upper-end estimate of the out-of-pocket costs of the AML regime to the US general public? A rough guess is that private-sector institutions are able to shift up to a third of their gross financial costs to consumers, perhaps something on the order of $1 billion per year on the basis of the earlier guesstimate of the $3 billion annual cost of the AML regime to those institutions as a group. We have no empirical basis for this figure, but in the context of our estimate of the costs of the overall AML regime, these costs are not additional to those borne by those institutions. Perhaps a similar figure of $1 billion, which amounts to one-third of the estimated gross costs to financial and nonfinancial institutions and businesses, is reasonable as an upper-end estimate of current additional costs of the AML regime to the US general public. It may be on the high side given the Pricewaterhouse Coopers estimate cited in the previous paragraph, but that estimate appears to be based on a rather narrow conceptual base.

In addition to the general costs of regulation to the public, certain aspects of the AML regime may impose a disproportionate burden on poorer households. For example, requirements to present multiple forms of identification to establish a bank account have created problems in low-income (legal and illegal) immigrant communities. Indeed, as noted above, the United Kingdom provides an exception it its requirements for CDD in part so as not to make access to the financial system too difficult for low-income and immigrant groups. In the United States, the risk-based approach to customer due diligence raises social concerns about possible profiling by country of origin or by race. Moreover, increased regulation in the formal economy is likely to increase reliance on the informal economy. When it comes to money laundering, this means reliance on informal means of transferring funds across borders, which is particularly relevant for legal as well as illegal immigrant workers who transmit a large portion of their earnings back to their countries of origin.[58] One consequence of customers lacking low-cost access to the traditional banking system is a less effective AML regime, because their exclusion makes tracing money that much more difficult. The larger the flow of legitimate funds through unregulated channels, the harder it is to find money laundering through the same mechanisms.

In summary, adding together our crude estimates of the gross financial costs of the US AML regime to the government, private-sector institutions, and the general public produces a rough upper-bound total of $7 billion. The figure includes $3 billion for the government, $3 billion for private-sector institutions (of which $1 billion might be shifted to the general pub-

---

58. A task force report by the Inter-American Dialogue (2004) estimates total remittances to Latin America in 2002 were $32 billion.

lic), and $1 billion in additional costs for the private sector. Assuming this figure is in the ballpark, it represents about 0.06 percent of US GDP in 2003, or about $25 per capita.

The costs of a given AML regime differ across countries. The United States and some other wealthy industrial countries can establish a comprehensive AML regime at modest cost relative to GDP because they have efficient banks and other institutions with sophisticated internal control systems that make it relatively easy to add AML dimensions. Institutions in poorer nations may have more difficulty in complying with requirements such as the FATF's Forty Recommendations. Similarly, large institutions may enjoy competitive advantages within wealthy nations to the extent that setting up an effective AML system within an institution has substantial fixed costs. Interviews with officials of financial institutions suggest that these are very much second-order issues, but too little is known about them to dismiss them summarily.

Much more attention deserves to be given to the costs of the AML regime, but it would seem that the biggest issue is not necessarily the financial costs. Of course, views may differ with respect to nonfinancial costs, such as intrusions on privacy. In the wake of September 11, the judgment was that additional nonfinancial costs should be absorbed, and the advocates of increased prevention and enforcement received new powers. More recently, the pendulum may have swung back some, but in the United States this is a familiar story in terms of the AML regime, where it has not been at all uncommon over the years for any given piece of legislation actually to relax provisions mandated in previous legislation. The principal example is the Money Laundering Suppression Act of 1994, which authorized the liberalization of regulations for the granting of exemptions for cash transaction reports. As noted by FinCEN (2002), the relaxation of those particular regulations has been only a partial success. The legislation authorized the Treasury to designate a single agency to receive SARs at the same time it extended the AML regime to money transmission businesses and to casinos. In other words, relaxing the regulations was part of the political quid pro quo for expanding coverage of the AML regime.

Even if the estimated total financial cost of the US AML regime is considered to be small—as stated, $7 billion is a mere 0.06 percent of 2003 GDP—the cost needs to be justified, particularly if the prevention pillar is to be expanded or the enforcement pillar strengthened. This suggests a need for better data and fresh approaches to the analysis of these issues in the years ahead.

5

Combating Predicate Crimes Involved in Money Laundering

How successful have the anti–money laundering (AML) regimes of the United States and other countries been in controlling crime, particularly "predicate" offenses that give rise to money-laundering activities? While previous chapters have primarily focused on describing the phenomenon of money laundering and the structure of regimes to combat it, this chapter moves to assessing those regimes, starting with a look at implementation of the enforcement pillar in the United States and other industrialized nations. The emphasis is on intermediate measures of performance such as the number of suspicious activity reports, prosecutions, convictions and incarcerations, seizures, and forfeitures. A model of the market for money-laundering services is used to link interventions to outcomes, although conceptual and empirical complexities limit the utility of the model, particularly in generating performance measures. The chapter ends with some indicative calculations that suggest that enforcement efforts have yet to make money laundering a particularly risky business in the United States.

Enforcement and Predicate Crimes

Until September 11, 2001, the primary emphasis of money-laundering enforcement in the United States and elsewhere was on reducing predicate offenses—initially the sale of illegal drugs, but more recently a wide array of crimes. Critical to the prevention pillar of those efforts is the flow of required reports that are intended to generate investigative information. More important are the number and characteristics of criminal prosecutions and convictions for money laundering, and the application of associated penalties such as seizures and forfeitures.

Suspicious Activity Reports

In the United States, SARs have replaced currency transaction reports as the primary source of information from financial institutions and other reporting sources (such as casinos and currency exchange bureaus) to assist anti–money laundering efforts. Although CTRs still play a role—more than 13 million of them were filed in 2001 and 1.5 million were at some point identified in the course of a criminal investigation (FinCEN 2002)—SARs at this point are viewed by professionals in the enforcement field as more informative.

According to the US Financial Crime Enforcement Network (FinCEN 2003b), the number of SARs filed in the United States increased from 52,000 in 1996 to 288,000 in 2003 (figure 5.1). Little information is available on the underlying suspected activity, as 48 percent of SARs filed between April 1, 1996, and June 30, 2003, were characterized only as "violations of the Bank Secrecy Act (BSA)/Structuring/Money Laundering," which is not very informative. The only other large category was check fraud, which accounted for 12 percent of the filed reports.

The number of SARs related to terrorism predictably increased sharply following September 11. Whereas in September 2001, 27 SARs mentioned possible terrorism, another 1,342 were filed in the following six months. However, this number had decreased again within another year. In the six months beginning October 2002, only 290 terrorism SARs were filed.

An encouraging trend has emerged with regard to the party initiating terrorism-related SARs. In the six months after September 2001, 85 percent of these SARs were filed due to apparent matches with the names of individuals or entities provided to institutions by government agencies. But from October 2002 to March 2003, most such SARs were a result of due diligence processes of financial institutions themselves, independent of any government-published lists. Several banks created internal watch lists to alert tellers and other employees to customers' previous suspicious behavior.

Though 69 financial institutions have filed SARs related to terrorism, over half of the reports from October 2002 to March 2003 came from just three banks. Sixty-eight terrorism SARs (23.4 percent) were reported directly to law enforcement authorities, meaning that the violation was ongoing and required immediate attention.

The number of SARs filed, like most other criminal justice outputs, is an inherently ambiguous indicator of changes in enforcement. A rise in the number of SARs may reflect either an increase in money laundering or increased stringency of the AML regime. The rate of increase in recent years is so large that, with a caveat as to quality, there is good reason to believe that it is the stringency of the regime that has intensified. There are

Figure 5.1　Suspicious activity reports filed, 1996–2003

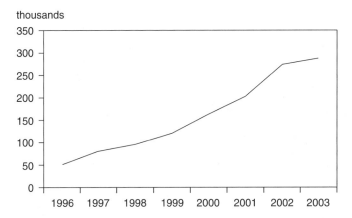

thousands

Source: Financial Crime Enforcement Network (FinCEN 2004).

no events that would explain a comparable increase in the incidence of money laundering.

SARs are of variable quality. An enforcement official described one bank as encouraging the filing of SARs with a low threshold but providing minimal information about the transaction—in other words, the purpose was to protect the bank against charges of violating reporting requirements, with little focus on assisting the government. If banks and other regulated firms feel a greater need to protect themselves against government sanctions by filing reports, the increase in numbers may not indicate improved diligence. Moreover, the increase may be weakening the effectiveness of the regime in the process by lowering the signal-to-noise ratio. On the other hand, another bank was described as having invested in training its staff to file reports only when there was indeed reasonable suspicion and to make the reports informative. Such discrepancies in efforts point to the need to examine not merely the number of filings but the extent to which they have resulted in detection and punishment of money-laundering offenses.

For the 6½-year period ending October 31, 2002, 940,000 SARs produced 70,000 direct referrals to federal law enforcement agencies, of which almost half were to the FBI. Unfortunately, there is no information on how many resulted in or contributed to cases.

The US General Accounting Office (GAO) has periodically attempted to ascertain the results of the SAR filings in terms of prosecutions and convictions. An early study (GAO 1998) found that state officials reported "limited or no investigative actions" from materials supplied by FinCEN. Even today, the extent to which information provided by SARs has helped to make criminal cases is unclear. Another GAO study (2002) that examined

> **Box 5.1 Detecting money laundering through failures to file suspicious activity reports**
>
> Two relatively small US banks were fined in 2002 for failure to file suspicious activity reports (SARs). In September, the US Financial Crime Enforcement Network (FinCEN) imposed a $100,000 civil penalty against the Great Eastern Bank of Florida, which had total deposits of $55 million. Great Eastern failed to alert authorities about the questionable activities of at least 20 different customers. Among the unreported activities were structured deposits, transfers immediately following large deposits, and the deposit of large numbers of sequentially ordered money orders and travelers' checks. In some cases, when Great Eastern did file SARs, the reports lacked the relevant information that would have provided assistance in an investigation. FinCEN determined that Great Eastern's violations were willful because the bank had been on notice to improve its compliance with the anti–money laundering (AML) rules after the Federal Deposit Insurance Corporation (FDIC) repeatedly found material deficiencies in the bank's AML program.
>
> Later that year, Broadway National Bank (BNB) of New York City pled guilty to charges of failing to file SARs, failing to have an anti–money laundering program in place, and permitting the structuring of transactions. According to convicted money launderer Joseph Vershish, the laxness of the BNB staff was well known among those of his profession. Management did not question the origins of cash or ask to know their customers' business locations, and would readily authorize transfers just a few days after large or structured deposits. Security guards would even warn "smurfs" (couriers) of the presence of government agents. The bank's biggest client was convicted drug dealer Alfred Dauber, who alone laundered millions of dollars through BNB. The bank paid a $4 million fine, a significant but not crippling amount for a bank with $89 million in total deposits. Since 1998, BNB has been operating under a cease-and-desist order by the Office of the Comptroller of Currency and has established and implemented an effective AML program, according to that agency.

all SARs involving credit cards during a two-year period from October 1, 1999, to September 30, 2001, found 499 such filings, of which 70 were referred to law enforcement agencies (39 federal, 31 state or local). But the GAO noted that FinCEN was unable to report whether any of these referrals resulted in criminal prosecutions.

The requirement itself to file SARs can indirectly generate useful information. Box 5.1 describes two instances in which it was the failure to file by two small banks that provided information that led to penalties against them.

Prosecutions and Convictions

Available data on money-laundering charges in the United States—which come from judicial sources for the federal level and from surveys of inmates in federal and state prisons—cover the number of persons charged, convicted, and imprisoned in federal courts.[1] Charges can be brought against

---

1. Judicial data on state court convictions are not available, although the inmate survey presented in more detail below reinforces a general impression that there are few convictions in state court on such charges.

Table 5.1 Defendants charged with money laundering, 1994–2001

Year	Money laundering as any charge	Money laundering as primary or secondary charge	Percent with money laundering as primary or secondary charge
1994	1,907	1,341	70
1995	2,138	1,487	70
1996	1,994	1,457	73
1997	2,376	1,619	68
1998	2,719	1,831	67
1999	2,656	1,885	71
2000	2,503	1,771	71
2001	2,110	1,480	70

Source: Bureau of Justice Statistics (2003).

both the customer who seeks to have money laundered and the provider of the service, although the data do not distinguish between these two types of offenders.

Federal Prosecutions and Convictions

Data on prosecutions and convictions in federal cases are available from the Administrative Office of the Courts (AOC) and the US Sentencing Commission. The data sets are different because the US Sentencing Commission data reflect only those who were sentenced in a given year,[2] while the AOC data reflect all matters related to a criminal charge that were conducted in a given year. For example, some of those convicted in 1999 were not sentenced until 2000. The analysis presented here refers primarily to the AOC findings (Bureau of Justice Statistics 2003), although US Sentencing Commission data are also used to provide some additional insights.

Table 5.1 shows that the total number of defendants charged with money laundering rose from 1994 to 1998 and then fell sharply through 2001. Slightly more than 2,100 persons were charged with money laundering offenses in 2001, compared with more than 2,700 in 1998. Only 22 businesses were criminally convicted in 2001, and for about 30 percent of those charged with money laundering, the offense was not one of the two most serious charges. Table 5.2 shows the number of convictions for which money laundering was the lead offense, which is not necessarily the offense with the highest statutory penalty but normally the one that generated the investigation. In the vast majority of these cases (81 to 88 percent, depending on the year), those charged were convicted.

What predicate crimes generate money-laundering convictions? In this respect, there is a significant difference between those charged with money

2. These data were accessed online at the National Archive of Criminal Justice Data of the Inter-University Consortium for Political and Social Research, www.icpsr.umich.edu/NACJD/index.html.

Table 5.2 Adjudications and convictions in cases with money laundering as the most serious offense, 1994–2001

Year	Adjudications	Convictions	Percent convicted
1994	1,159	933	81
1995	1,073	906	84
1996	1,241	1,080	87
1997	1,245	1,108	89
1998	1,370	1,199	88
1999	1,571	1,371	87
2000	1,527	1,329	87
2001	1,420	1,243	88

Source: Bureau of Justice Statistics (2003).

laundering as the lead offense and those for whom it was a secondary offense. For about 60 percent of the first group (which constitutes two-thirds of the total), a property offense (embezzlement or fraud) was the predicate crime and for only one in six was the predicate crime a drug offense. However, among the smaller group whose lead charge was not money laundering, about 90 percent were charged with drug trafficking. That is probably the consequence of differences in maximum statutory sentences. Drug offenders face longer sentences than those convicted of money laundering, so drug-money launderers are more likely to be charged with the drug offense if they had any involvement beyond pure money laundering.

The vast majority (84 percent) of those charged with money laundering in 2001 were charged under Title 18 sections 1956 and 1957, which cover the transfer or transportation of criminally derived money or property with the intent to conceal or disguise its illicit nature or origin. The other 16 percent were charged under sections of Title 31 that address monetary reporting/recording offenses such as cash smuggling, structured transactions, and failure to file required reports.

US Sentencing Commission data in table 5.3 provide another view on the same matter, since they include other charges that resulted in convictions. Crimes identified in these data are different from the predicate crimes, in that they may involve an individual who laundered money from a fraud committed by someone else but was also convicted of embezzlement in his or her own right.[3] Of the 1,543 defendants sentenced under one or more money-laundering statutes in 2000, 828 were also convicted of one or more other criminal offenses, and 715 were sentenced only for money laundering. Of the latter, 125 individuals were also charged either with a conspiracy, which might have included a crime other than money laundering, or with being the principal offender. Thus, nearly half of those convicted may have been involved only in the laundering and not in other aspects of the crimes,

---

3. Data are not available to compare predicate offenses and these other charges.

Table 5.3 Other offenses for which convicted federal money launderers were sentenced, 1995, 2000
(numbers in parentheses indicate percent of total cases)

Offense	1995	2000
Number of cases involving money-laundering statutes[a]	1,155	1,543
Also charged with drug trafficking	351 (30)	467 (30)
Also charged with fraud	151 (13)	258 (17)
Also charged with smuggling (non-drug)	32 (3)	59 (4)
Also charged with racketeering	31 (3)	37 (2)
Also charged with embezzlement	22 (2)	25 (2)
Also charged with tax evasion	15 (1)	23 (2)
Charged with no other crimes	568 (49)	715 (46)
Percent of drug cases also charged with money laundering	2	2
Percent of fraud cases also charged with money laundering	2	1
Percent of smuggling cases also charged with money laundering	1	2
Percent of racketeering cases also charged with money laundering	4	4
Percent of embezzlement cases also charged with money laundering	1	1
Percent of tax evasion cases also charged with money laundering	3	6

a. Includes Title 18 sections 1956 and 1957 (money laundering), and Title 31 sections 5316 (cash smuggling), 5324 (structuring transactions to evade reporting requirements), and 5313 (failure to file currency transaction report).

Source: US Sentencing Commission (2003).

although there is no way to know whether they were customers or providers of money laundering. More than two-thirds of these "pure" money launderers were sentenced under Title 18 statutes as opposed to Title 31.

Table 5.3 shows that for both 1995 and 2000, 30 percent of all defendants convicted of money laundering were also convicted of drug offenses. Of 255 cases in 2000 where a Title 31 offense was one of the charges, 223 (87 percent) had no non–money laundering charges, while 218 (85 percent) had nothing besides Title 31 charges.

Interestingly, of all persons convicted of drug offenses in federal court, only 2 percent were also convicted of money laundering. This figure was not much different from that for those convicted of fraud who were also convicted of money laundering (2 percent in 1995 and 1 percent in 2000). The dominance of drugs among secondary charges for money laundering reflects the dominance of drug offenses in the federal criminal justice system. About 60 percent of federal prison inmates have been convicted of drug offenses.

Money-laundering sentences averaged about 36 months, substantially less than the average of approximately 48 months for all those convicted in federal court (Bureau of Justice Statistics 2003). Seventeen percent of those sentenced under the guidelines were given longer sentences because they had leadership roles. About 20 percent of the cases involved more than $1 million in funds (US Treasury 2002, 5). The mean sentence for cash/monetary instrument smuggling (Title 31) was 19.6 months; for structuring transactions, 13.4 months; and for failure to report currency transactions, 8.5 months. These figures are consistent with the conjecture that most of these cases are pure money laundering, usually with a low-level offender who does nothing else but some illegal legwork for the "predicate criminal"; once again though it must be emphasized that the role may be delivering the funds to the launderer rather than providing the actual service.

Inmate Survey

The federal court data reviewed above have significant limitations because not every successful money-laundering investigation results in a conviction for money laundering, as opposed to some other offense. For example, the prosecutor may drop the money-laundering charge in return for a plea to another charge related to the predicate offense itself. The fact that money-laundering charges usually result from investigations that began with another crime (Joseph 2001) reinforces the concern about the comprehensiveness of the figures. Fortunately, some other data throw light on how many money launderers are in prison, regardless of the offense associated with the inmate's conviction.

Approximately every five years, the Bureau of Justice Statistics interviews a large sample (about 18,000 in 1997) of inmates in both federal and state prisons. The questionnaire includes items on their criminal activities, not restricted to those for which they were convicted. These data provide an important supplement to the administrative data. Questions in the most recent (1997) survey concerning money laundering have been analyzed by Jonathan Caulkins and Eric Sevigny (of Carnegie-Mellon University and the University of Pittsburgh, respectively), who reported the relevant results of their work in personal communication with the authors. Note that although these data are not directly comparable to any year of court data, since most of those incarcerated in 1997 were convicted in an earlier year, table 5.3 showed little change in the pattern of convictions from 1995 to 2000.

Among federal prison inmates, 3,030 (2.8 percent of the total population) reported that they were serving time for a money-laundering conviction. Two-thirds of those had some drug involvement and another 18 percent reported forgery/fraud convictions.[4] Including those who said that they laundered drug money but were not convicted on that charge, federal prisons in 1997 contained an estimated 4,416 money launderers (5 percent of

---

4. Some of the discrepancies between the inmate survey and the court data may reflect the longer sentences of drug offenders; thus the prison population of money launderers will be richer in drug-money launderers than the population entering prison.

the total population). Among those who said that they laundered drug money, only about one-sixth (467) were estimated to have had no other involvement with drugs.

None of the state prison inmates reported that they were currently serving time for a money-laundering offense. However, an estimated 6,368 state prison inmates (0.6 percent of the total population) self-reported that they did launder money, and in every case they reported that the money involved came from drug offenses. This finding that only drug offenders have laundered money is an artifact of the questionnaire, since only inmates reporting drug convictions were asked about money-laundering activities. Only about 100 reported that they were money launderers exclusively; the others said they were also drug dealers. Again, this response may be a consequence of the way the questions were asked.

Many persons who launder money are in prison for other offenses, particularly for drug offenses. Thus, though there appears to be a negligible number of state-level convictions for money laundering, the self-reported inmate data suggest there are actually more money launderers in state prison than in federal prison; money laundering may have been a minor part of their drug-dealing activities and they may have been customers rather than providers of money-laundering services.

In the federal system, the court statistics (both from the AOC and the US Sentencing Commission) do not suggest a dominant role for drugs. However, the inmate survey suggests that most of those in prison on money-laundering charges were in fact involved in drug dealing. There do not appear to be many stand-alone money launderers in the prison system.

Financial Penalties

Given the nature of money laundering as an offense, prosecution of it, unlike prosecution of a violent crime, can be expected to generate substantial financial penalties. The government may seize the laundered money and other assets of those charged and seek forfeiture upon their conviction. In some cases, these seizures and forfeitures can generate very substantial amounts—a prominent case involving a Bank of New York official in 1999 resulted in criminal forfeitures of $8.1 million (US Treasury 2002, A-15). In 2001, the only year for which comprehensive data are available, total seizures and forfeitures were $627 million (US Treasury 2002).

The federal government also levies other financial penalties. Figure 5.2 shows a substantial increase in the total amounts of fines and restitution, from $100 million in 1996 to $665 million in 2001. The data, provided by the US Sentencing Commission, reflect the growth in the size of the average penalty rather than the number.

**Figure 5.2   Total fines and restitution for money
laundering in the United States, 1990–2001**

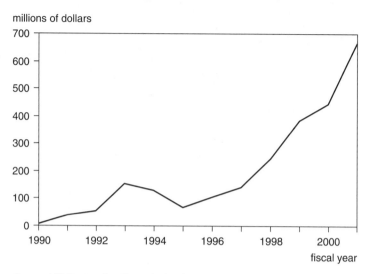

millions of dollars

Source: US Sentencing Commission (2003).

   The relevant metric to assess these figures is the total volume of funds
laundered. Choosing an estimated total figure toward the lower end of the
usual range, such as $300 billion, implies that the current level of penal-
ties—seizures, forfeitures, fines, and restitutions—is almost trivial, only
four-tenths of 1 percent. However, if the total figure is only a few tens of
billions—or at least if the forms of money laundering of greatest social concern are only a few tens of billions—then the level of penalties might be
1 to 3 percent, perhaps enough to have a modest deterrent effect on those
tempted to commit the predicate crimes.

Enforcement in the United Kingdom
and Other Nations

We treat the United Kingdom separately not so much because of its importance in the international financial system but because it has been more
advanced than any other nation, including the United States, in the analysis of its own AML regime. A study of the country's system for suspicious
activity reports, funded by the British government (KPMG 2003), found an
extraordinary increase in the number of SAR filings since 2000: from 20,000
in 2000 to a projected 100,000 in 2003. According to the study, the increase
reflects the extension of AML requirements to lawyers and real estate
agents. At least 6 percent of a sample of SARs disseminated by the UK
National Crime Intelligence Service resulted in "a positive law enforce-

ment outcome (i.e., prosecution, confiscation, cash seizure, etc.)," while another 5 percent were still being used in an active investigation.[5] The study also noted, however, that there was little feedback from law enforcement agencies to the filing institutions.

In England and Wales, there were only 357 prosecutions for violation of money-laundering statutes in the 12 years from 1987–98 (KPMG 2003).[6] Though the UK Financial Services Authority has made AML a major priority, the sense of strategy in criminal investigations and prosecutions is lacking. That view was reinforced by a recent review of the AML regime in the United Kingdom by the International Monetary Fund, which found that enforcement was limited even though the structure and laws for it were in place (IMF 2003d).[7] The report went on to state: "Cases are generally considered for enforcement only when there is little chance that they will be seriously contested or complicated. . . . The Crown Prosecution does not prosecute any matters other than narcotic money laundering." In 2000 and the first half of 2001, the report continued, there were only 18 "skilled-person" visits to financial institutions focusing on AML issues (IMF 2003d, 100, 102).

Finally, the IMF noted many financial and professional entities effectively out of the sight of regulators. Money service businesses in the UK had always been subject to the AML regime, but until November 2001 no regulatory agency had responsibility for assuring compliance. Even now, the UK Financial Services Authority has been mandated to provide only a "light touch" supervisory regime for money service businesses.

A report by the Performance and Innovation Unit (2000) of the UK Cabinet Office on the use of confiscation orders also found that the system performed poorly. For non-drug crimes in 1998, for example, only 136 confiscations were ordered and 6 million pounds collected—less than half of what was ordered to be confiscated. For drug cases the numbers were larger, but only 10 million pounds were collected in a market estimated to total some billions of pounds in revenues.

Other Nations

The US Department of State (2003) provides the numbers of suspicious activity reports filed in other nations as reported by financial intelligence units in those countries. Table 5.4 shows the number of SARs for seven

---

5. Given that the researchers were unable to track the ultimate use of most of the sample of SARs, this is the least favorable presentation of the data. By the most favorable analysis, one-third of SARs resulted in a law enforcement success, mostly as intelligence rather than as evidence for prosecution.

6. Data were not available for Scotland and Northern Ireland.

7. The United Kingdom was one of the first jurisdictions to permit publication of the detailed findings of the IMF/World Bank review team.

Table 5.4 Suspicious activity reports by country, 1994–2002

Year	Australia SARs	Australia SARs/1,000 population	Belgium SARs	Belgium SARs/1,000 population	France SARs	France SARs/1,000 population	Japan SARs	Japan SARs/1,000 population	Netherlands SARs[a]	Netherlands SARs/1,000 population	Switzerland SARs	Switzerland SARs/1,000 population	United Kingdom SARs	United Kingdom SARs/1,000 population	United States SARs	United States SARs/1,000 population
1994	—	—	942	0.09	—	—	6	—	3,541	0.23	—	—	15,000	0.26	—	—
1995	—	—	3,106	0.31	—	—	4	—	3,001	0.19	—	—	13,700	0.24	—	—
1996	—	—	4,480	0.44	—	—	5	—	2,574	0.17	—	—	16,120	0.28	52,069	0.20
1997	5,772	0.31	7,136	0.70	—	—	9	—	3,800	0.24	—	—	14,140	0.25	81,197	0.30
1998	6,877	0.37	8,754	0.86	—	—	13	0.0001	3,993	0.25	160	0.02	14,120	0.24	96,521	0.36
1999	6,541	0.35	7,995	0.79	1,665	0.03	1,059	0.01	10,803	0.68	303	0.04	14,500	0.25	120,505	0.44
2000	7,085	0.37	9,885	0.97	2,537	0.04	7,242	0.06	11,023	0.69	311	0.04	18,400	0.31	162,720	0.59
2001	7,247	0.37	10,902	1.06	—	—	12,372	0.10	20,282	1.27	417	0.06	—	—	203,528	0.73
2002	—	—	—	—	—	—	18,768	0.14	25,000	1.56	—	—	—	—	224,232[b]	0.80

— = not available

a. Financial institutions in the Netherlands are required to report "unusual" transactions to the Dutch Financial Intelligence Unit, which then forwards the "suspicious" reports to law enforcement officials.

b. Includes only the first 10 months of 2002.

Sources: SARs: Financial intelligence units in Australia (Australian Transaction Report and Analysis Center—AUSTRAC); Belgium (Belgian Financial Intelligence Processing Unit—CTIF-CFI); France (Unit for Processing Information and Action against Illegal Financial Flows—TRACFin), Japan (Japan Financial Intelligence Office—JAFIO), the Netherlands (Office for the Disclosure of Unusual Transactions—MOT); Switzerland (Money Laundering Reporting Office—MROS); the United Kingdom (National Criminal Intelligence Service—NCIS), and the United States (FinCEN). Population: CIA *World Factbook, 1992–2001;* UK National Statistics Online, 1987–1991.

nations and the United States from 1994–2001. The numbers have such a range as to suggest that very different processes generate them in different nations. For example, Mexico reported 500,000 SARs in 2002, while Argentina reports only 200, yet no one would assert that the Mexican banking system is three orders of magnitude more aggressive in this respect or that money laundering is so much rarer an event in Argentina.[8]

Nations do indeed differ in their approach to the reporting of suspicious activities. For example, in Switzerland the emphasis is on the customer rather than the transaction, and great discretion is given to the reporting institution, in sharp contrast to the United States (Pieth and Aiolfi 2003). The Netherlands saw an 81 percent increase in 2002 over the previous year in the number of "subjective unusual transaction reports," largely due to the increase in the reporting of international money transfers. Suspicious transaction reports in that country rose 25 percent over the same one-year period, from roughly 20,000 to around 25,000. Unlike in other nations, Dutch financial institutions (as well as casinos and credit card companies) are required to file "subjective unusual transaction reports" rather than SARs with their financial intelligence unit, the Meldpunt Ongebruikelijke Transacties (MOT—Office for the Disclosure of Unusual Transactions). The MOT in turn decides whether to forward these cases in the form of suspicious transaction reports to law enforcement authorities. The strategy appears to be designed to encourage institutions to file a report if they have any doubt at all about a transaction, and let MOT sort the wheat from the chaff. In 2000, a Suspicious Transactions Intranet went into operation in the Netherlands, allowing police to view all such reports since 1997.

In February 2000, Japan expanded the scope of predicate offenses to include all serious crimes. It also overhauled its suspicious transaction reporting system by creating a financial intelligence unit to analyze and disseminate SARs, cooperate with law enforcement officials, and exchange information with units in other jurisdictions. Previously, the Ministry of Finance received the reports but was not required to take any of the aforementioned actions. With these changes, the number of SARs in Japan rose from 13 in 1998 to nearly 19,000 in 2002, more than 12,000 of which were deemed useful in law enforcement investigations.[9]

---

8. These countries are not included in table 5.4 but are cited in US State Department (2003).

9. The latter figure has to be taken with some skepticism, since both the share of all SARs and the total number useful to law enforcement seem extraordinarily large. The actual figure suggests a reporting system that, though new, is effective at identifying only questionable transactions, and an enforcement system that is unusually energetic in pursuing these reports. On the other hand, a 2004 report on Japan by the IMF/World Bank (IMF 2004b) noted "the effective application of legal powers appears to be limited, as evidenced by the low numbers of investigations and prosecutions, which may be due, inter alia, to the limited resources allocated and to the insufficient level of coordination among the different agencies involved in anti–money laundering and combating the financing of terrorism."

In Australia (population of 20 million), where every international transaction must be reported, the country's financial intelligence unit—the Australian Transaction Report and Analysis Center (AUSTRAC)—reported 7 million such transactions in 2001, among them 1.7 million deemed by AUSTRAC as "significant," a broader notion of "suspicious" than that used in the United States. Actual SARs in 2001 numbered only 7,000.

Data on money-laundering convictions and sentences are available for only a few countries. Petrus van Duyne (2003) reports that over 1993–2000 the Dutch police identified 159 criminal cases involving more than $500,000 (about 1 million guilders at the time), an average of about 20 cases annually; the population of the Netherlands is about 15 million.[10] Arie Freiberg and Richard Fox (2000) report that Australia's money laundering control efforts generate only about 20 convictions on such charges annually, and a German criminologist, Michael Kilchling (personal communication), reports a similarly small figure for Germany.

In summary, it appears that no other nation prosecutes money-laundering offenses as aggressively as the United States, which is a recurrent complaint of US officials involved in international money-laundering matters. Even with the creation of systems that generate large numbers of reports, there is little evidence of substantial criminal investigations that are consistently pursuing substantial cases against violators. The Netherlands, which has relatively sophisticated capability in criminal intelligence and investigation of organized crime, may be an exception, but even there the numbers for major cases remain small compared with the United States.

What might explain this apparent difference in anti–money laundering efforts between the United States and other wealthy nations with sophisticated financial and judicial systems? First, drug trafficking, central to the creation of the AML regime, has been a more significant problem in the United States than in any other industrial nation. Second, the United States launched a successful prosecutory campaign against the Mafia in the 1970s and 1980s that developed many of the legal tools and much of the organizational expertise for money-laundering prosecutions. Only in a very few other nations (notably Italy) has organized crime prosecution been prominent. Finally, the United States has a more aggressive law enforcement culture generally than do most other nations.

These differences between the United States and the rest of the world could be either exacerbated or reduced by the new concern with terrorist financing. While Western European nations have been generally responsive to the new terrorist threat and have collaborated with US agencies, the issue remains more prominent in the United States, which arguably has suffered from terrorism more directly than most other nations, with the most recent tragic exception of Spain in March 2004. However, a 2002 Eurobarometer

---

10. A comparable number of cases in the United States on a per capita basis would be 400, rather than the actual figure of about 2,000.

poll suggested similarly high levels of concern about terrorism in the European Union and the United States, with 82 percent of Western Europeans fearing a terrorism incident (European Commission 2003, table 1.13).

Outcome Measures and Analytic Frameworks

The intermediate performance measures mentioned so far in this chapter do not provide a basis for assessing the effectiveness of the AML regime. Considering the many ways and means to launder the proceeds of crime in the United States and globally, it can be reasonably assumed that no AML regime, consistent with smooth operation and low costs for the economy and financial system, can make laundering impossible. Zero tolerance may be a strategy, but the elimination of money laundering is not feasible, and subtler outcome measures are needed. This section deals with the problem of finding such measures of the effectiveness of the AML in reducing crimes other than terrorism and bribery/kleptocracy, since the bulk of AML activities have been devoted to such criminal activities as drugs, other illegal markets, and white-collar crimes.

Two broad mechanisms of the AML regime help reduce crime. First, customer due diligence and other elements of the prevention pillar can make it more difficult for offenders either to carry out the crime (for example, pay their suppliers) or obtain its full benefits. In this respect, the controls have a prospective effect. Second, suspicious activity reports and other back-end activities (such as those associated with reporting) can generate evidence of a crime, and SARs can also become evidence for investigations that have other origins. In this sense, SARs act retrospectively in that they not only increase the risk of criminal sanction but also provide the basis for seizure of criminal proceeds.

In terms of crime control, the AML regime may generate two other benefits. First, it produces a form of condign punishment. Seizure of funds and incarceration of those who conspire to make the profits legitimate generates revenue for the government and punishes senior offenders. In some instances the only way to apprehend the principal offenders, who separate themselves from the predicate offenses, is to convict them of money-laundering offenses associated with predicate crimes that have been committed by others.[11] Such cases show that the law with respect to a wide range of predicate crimes applies to everyone. Second, AML systems may improve the efficiency of law enforcement, an effect distinct from reducing

---

11. In a 1997 speech, then US Treasury Secretary Robert Rubin described money laundering as "the 'Achilles heel,' as it gives us a way to attack the leaders of criminal organizations. While the drug kingpins and other bosses of organized crime may be able to separate themselves from street-level criminal activity, they cannot separate themselves from the profits of that activity." www.usdoj.gov/criminal/press/VIcount.htm.

predicate crime. Even if they do not necessarily result in the government apprehending more offenders, the existence and tools of the AML system may permit the same number of offenders to be captured and convicted at lower cost.

Market Model

A starting point for an assessment of the relationship between the AML regime and the reduction in predicate crime is to view money laundering as a market, with customers for, and suppliers of, money-laundering services. Specific AML interventions can then be linked to predicate crime reductions by how they affect the money-laundering market, particularly the price of services and, thus, the returns from crime, as illustrated by the analysis in chapter 4 of the five US National Money Laundering Strategies.

For example, if money laundering is more difficult (expensive), then drug dealers will face higher costs and charge higher prices for their services, thus reducing the consumption of drugs. Assume that prior to the creation of an AML regime, a high-level drug dealer charged his customers (themselves lower-level dealers) $10,000 per kilogram of cocaine and received $10 million annually in gross revenues. As a consequence of the barriers imposed by the AML regime, assume he now has to pay 10 percent of the proceeds to the money launderer and hence receives only $9 million. Assuming competition between drug dealers, which seems a reasonable characterization of such a market, the $10 million previously just compensated the dealer for risks (legal and otherwise) and other costs. In the face of reduced net returns, the dealer will raise prices to customers, and thus increase the retail price of cocaine, making the reduction in cocaine consumption a function of the elasticity of demand.

While combating drugs has been particularly prominent in the development of the AML regime, the same logic applies to other income-generating offenses such as fraud and gambling. By creating a probability of detection and punishment, the AML regime makes money laundering more risky for both customers and providers. It raises the price of the service and/or the costs of searching for the service (customers finding suppliers), which in turn reduces the return from the predicate crime and thus the quantity of these offenses.

What determines the demand for, and supply of, money-laundering services? The demand for money-laundering services can be thought of as a function of the following:

- *The volume of criminal revenues.* Since scrutiny of sources of criminal earnings for low earners is limited, and because low earners do not need to transform (launder) the money they make, it is probably only criminal incomes of more than perhaps $50,000 annually that create a need for concealing the source.

- *The price of these particular money-laundering services relative to other methods of obtaining the benefit of the unimpeded use of these funds.* At very high prices, potential customers may be content to keep the money in mattresses (metaphorically) or transfer it in small and inconvenient bundles of cash across borders to locations with less stringent controls. Those offenders may be worse off than they would be with untrammeled access to money-laundering services, but they can continue to function, albeit at a lower level.

- *Other costs of laundering money, such as the time it takes to find a supplier and the risk of the search.* Both are influenced by the intensity of enforcement of the AML regime. Money-laundering customers face a risk of legal and financial penalties if they transact with unreliable suppliers. Some potential penalties are derivative of supplier-oriented risk; the launderer can mitigate the penalty by turning in the customer who has committed the predicate offense. In addition, the continuing presence of sting operations, in which the government simulates the behavior of a launderer, poses a separate risk to the customer. That risk may be manifested in the time it takes for customers to find a provider to whom they assign a low probability of being a government agent.

The supply of money-laundering services is determined primarily by the stringency of the AML regime. Absent the prevention pillar of the AML regime and with only a rudimentary enforcement pillar associated with tracing the proceeds of crime back to their source, the cost of laundering those proceeds would surely be low, but not zero. Prior to the 1970 Bank Secrecy Act, criminals could deposit the cash proceeds (no matter how large) from their crimes in local banks with no questions asked by the bank (placement), move them around the world (layering), and enjoy them at their leisure (integration).[12] Criminals and their banks were subject to ex post investigation, but in the absence of authorities having seizure and confiscation powers, and once the proceeds were safely outside the jurisdiction, risks would be minimal. Meyer Lansky, a well-known associate of the US mafia in its heyday, is only the most prominent of criminals who earned money by finding ways to launder earnings from gambling and other illegal markets so as to reduce the risk of the money being traced to its criminal source. He might be charged as an accomplice in the criminal act, but the actual money laundering was not an offense.

Today, it is reasonable to assume that money launderers face no costs other than those posed by law enforcement such as seizure of assets and incarceration. The time involved in actually laundering funds is minimal.

---

12. Banks may have nonetheless preferred not to deal with criminal offenders, since a revelation that a particular bank provided services to a major drug dealer might well lead to some social condemnation, even during a time when there were no formal rules prohibiting such dealings.

Some of the price charged for money-laundering services may reflect skill in the methods used for hiding the origins of money, but one can assume that such skills are in ready supply and that enough of those with the skills can be persuaded to commit this crime for an appropriately high fee. Consequently, incarcerating, say, a few hundred launderers will not reduce the pool of competent labor substantially, though it may raise the price that has to be paid to obtain that labor, redistributing criminal income and inducing entry by new participants.

The effective cost of money-laundering services is not fully reflected in the price charged. In addition to search time, the effective cost includes reliability in a number of dimensions such as integrity (delivering the specified amount of money), timeliness (delivering the money when promised), and scope (having a variety of methods of delivery to different locations). Quality among suppliers may be differentiated, reflecting an institution's or an individual's capacity to deliver services reliably, a particularly important consideration in the criminal world. Thus, an observed reduction in prices may reflect a shift from higher- to lower-quality money-laundering services.

Multiple Markets

An important analytic complexity is that there may be more than one market for money-laundering services, depending on the predicate offense and the amount that needs to be protected. For example, as was illustrated in chapter 3, laundering $1 million in drug revenues from the United States to Mexico may require a higher percentage payment than laundering the same amount in a bankruptcy fraud, simply because the launderer of drug moneys incurs risks of more serious penalties from law enforcement as well as greater potential physical risks (violent retaliation for failure to protect assets). If the transaction involves actual cash, it may also be more expensive (per dollar) to launder large sums than small, for the same reasons. For noncash operations, the relationship between size and cost may go the other way.

Launderers may also "specialize," either in terms of the kinds of funds they accept or the kinds of institutions with which they transact. Money laundering is also differentiated by phase; some launderers may not provide full-service operations. For example, a simple currency exchange bureau may only move money out of the United States (placement), but not provide for the layering of the money so that it can no longer be traced, or bring it back into the United States where the funds can be freely used with no questions asked (integration). Black market peso brokers, on the other hand, often serve both the supply and the demand ends of the market. They first export the narco-dollars to Colombia (or arrange to purchase them for resale in the United States), then exchange them for pesos for the cartels' domestic use, and lastly provide dollars to Colombian importers who wish to avoid the costs and bureaucracy of obtaining dollars legally. Thus, the proceeds of drug sales in the United States may resurface, cleaned, in the accounts of US companies that sell their products to Colombian businesses.

One segment of the market for money-laundering services may consist of launderers employing a variety of methods for servicing customers, depending on the latter's specific needs. In this conventional market, the providers have multiple and independent customers and recruit agents (for example, bank officials and casino employees) to ensure that they can provide a range of services. Customers, who know other customers with whom they share information, shift among launderers depending on the price and quality of service. For example, there is anecdotal evidence that drug dealers, circumspect though they may be, do share information about money launderers.

Another segment of the market consists of almost accidental customer-agent relationships. Customers do not find professional money launderers whose principal activity is providing those services, but rather seek out corrupt employees of financial intermediaries who service only one or a small number of clients as a by-product of their legitimate occupations. Search costs are high for both sides, reflecting the risks of disclosing need or availability and the lack of any organizing focal point for the search. For example, in its *1997–1998 Report on Money Laundering Typologies*, the Financial Action Task Force (FATF 1998) referred to a financier who allowed a single drug trafficker to use his company to establish a source of funds. The trafficker gave cash to the financial officer to deposit in a company account, and the funds were then transferred to Monaco for the ostensible purpose of buying Goya paintings. The paintings were fakes and, moreover, were never shipped, and the drug trafficker was the beneficiary of the payments for the fake Goyas, receiving the million-dollar transfers. There was no evidence that the financier's business provided money-laundering services for other clients.

Both types of operations may be components of the market. Some customers in high-risk occupations (for example, cigarette smugglers) with continuing needs in a number of locations may seek out specialized launderers. Others who have a one-time need may be content to find an acquaintance capable and willing to provide the service to just one customer. There is also self-laundering, for example through acquisition of a small business that is on the "exempt" list at a bank (i.e., for which it is not necessary to file a currency transaction report for large cash transactions that are consistent with the regular pattern of the business). No one at the bank or any professional except perhaps a forgiving accountant needs to be involved, at least in the placement stage. The Egmont Group (2000), which provides accounts of investigations by financial intelligence units worldwide, tells of a Western European family of drug traffickers that ran a currency exchange bureau that served as both a cash-intensive front company and a means of laundering money.

As discussed in chapter 3, although professional money launderers certainly exist, they are surprisingly rare in reported cases. A great deal of the revenues from crimes is self-laundered. This is important for both policy and research purposes. The rationale behind the current AML regime is based in part on the implicit assumption that the regime provides tools to apprehend and punish a set of actors who provided a critical service for the commission of certain kinds of crime and who had previously been beyond the reach of the law—an assumption that makes the market model a useful heuristic device for analyzing the effects of laws and programs.

However, if money laundering is mostly done by predicate offenders or by nonspecialized confederates, then the regime accomplishes much less. There is no new set of offenders, just a new set of charges against the same offenders, and the potential gains from the additional tool represented by the AML regime, while valuable in increasing the efficiency of law enforcement, are likely to be substantially more modest than posited (Cuéllar 2003).

For research purposes, this implies that the market-model concept is a strained analogy. Price may not be well defined to most participants because the service is rarely purchased. Risk may also be hard to observe because it is derivative from participation in other elements of the crime. Assessing how interventions increase risks and prices for those transactions that do involve stand-alone launderers will have only modest value. Finally, stand-alone service providers may be scarce.

Thus, the market model may work well for some kinds of predicate offenses and offenders, but less well for others. How this element of heterogeneity in the money-laundering underworld affects the research agenda for improving AML regimes will be taken up in chapter 8.

Performance Measures

To what extent does the market framework help assess the effectiveness of an AML regime in reducing predicate crime? While useful for analyzing some of the basic questions, the available data do not permit application for assessing effectiveness. One source of difficulty is that the price of money-laundering services itself is not an adequate indicator. Enforcement, as noted above, aims at both the demand and supply sides. Demand-side efforts such as stings against customers have the effect of lowering observed prices. By raising the nonmoney cost of purchasing money laundering, which includes some risk of arrest, incarceration, and financial penalties, such stings reduce demand. Supply-side efforts directed at the launderers should raise the price. Both efforts should reduce the quantity of laundering and the net returns from crime, the ultimate goal, but price can then only be interpreted along with estimates of quantity.

Quantity estimates, however, are not available, as there are no systematic estimates of amounts laundered, either through US institutions or globally (chapter 2). The US Congress has pressed FinCEN to develop estimates with a documented analytical base, but no such estimates have been produced as yet. Nor is it likely that such estimates can be developed in the foreseeable future, given the lack of even the beginnings of a data collection apparatus to support this activity.

An alternative performance measure for assessing the effectiveness of the AML regime in controlling predicate crime is the volume of predicate offenses. Apart from the problem of developing a counterfactual—How much predicate crime would have occurred without the AML regime?—there is a fundamental problem of measuring predicate offense levels.

Consider again illegal drugs, the best studied of the activities generating a demand for money laundering. While there are a number of possible measures—total revenues, prices, or quantities consumed—none is precise enough to be useful for analytical purposes. For example, the error band around existing drug revenue estimates for the United States is very large, with an official estimate of $50 billion in 1998 (Office of National Drug Control Policy 2000) that should be viewed as the center point of a uniform distribution from $25 billion to $75 billion. A decline of 25 percent in a five-year period would be hard to detect with confidence.

Alternatively, one might use drug prices, since the mechanism by which money-laundering controls are expected to reduce drug use is by raising the cost of distribution rather than by reducing demand. A recent National Research Council report (Manski, Pepper, and Petrie 2001) expressed considerable skepticism that the current system of data collection for prices could detect any but the very largest changes in prices. Moreover, there have been large revisions in the estimated prices for cocaine and heroin for a given year in successive estimation efforts, reinforcing the sense of frailty in those estimates.

A third potential measure is the number of dependent drug users. The AML regime is intended to support drug policy efforts to reduce this number. Estimates of the number of dependent users are also imprecise, though less so than estimates of quantities or prices. The official estimates (which are subject to frequent and substantial revisions) do not provide error bands, but any realistic assessment of their precision would suggest that a change of 5 percent would be difficult to detect.

Moreover, it is unlikely that the AML regime itself could have very large effects on the extent of drug use. Low-level drug dealers earn too little to require money-laundering services, yet they account for the bulk of total earnings. Price markups along the distribution system (conservatively estimated at 50 percent at each level) show that more than 60 percent of revenues go to low-level wholesalers and retailers, who are predominantly independent agents rather than employees of larger organizations. At the peak of the crack cocaine market in 1988, average annual earnings of retail drug dealers in Washington, DC, were estimated at $28,000 (Reuter,

MacCoun, and Murphy 1990). More recent studies report much lower earnings (e.g., Bourgois 1995, Levitt and Venkatesh 2000).

High-level dealers, the only ones who need money-laundering services, account for no more than 25 percent of total drug revenues. Assume that in the current regime money launderers charge customers approximately 10 percent of the amount laundered. Now assume that an improved system raised the price for money-laundering services by half, to 15 percent. The result would be an increase in the price of drugs of only 1.25 percent, far too small to be picked up by existing monitoring systems. This is not an argument that money-laundering controls are neither effective nor cost effective, but only that their success cannot be empirically assessed this way.

The performance assessment situation is even less promising for criminal offenses other than drug distribution. Systematic estimates of the volume of these crimes or revenues are often not available or are effectively made up from thin air. It is implausible, for example, that one could reliably detect a reduction of 10 percent in the volume of (or revenues from) embezzlement or corporate fraud.

Performance measurement is an increasingly important component of responsive and responsible public policy, so the difficulty in finding credible measures of AML regime performance in reducing crime is a major problem. Perhaps more sophisticated versions of market models will help in this respect, but their utility has not been established.

Improving Criminal Justice System Performance

This chapter noted earlier that AML regimes might have two other benefits in addition to controlling crime: improving the efficiency of the system or catching offenders who otherwise would escape. Mariano-Florentino Cuéllar (2003) concedes that such regimes might have improved efficiency in drug control and in reducing a few related criminal activities, but argues that they have failed in the second area. The US AML regime principally has been used to increase the penalties with which prosecutors can threaten predicate offenders. The regime has had little success in apprehending professional money launderers or high-level criminals.

The paucity of cases against stand-alone launderers and investigations that have their origin in money-laundering information supports the criticism that the AML regime has brought in few new offenders. There are no systematic data on the origins of cases against major criminals such as principal drug dealers, so it is impossible to tell whether more of them are being captured through money-laundering laws and investigations.

How Risky Is Money Laundering?

However crude, an estimate of how risky money laundering in the United States has become as a result of the AML regime is helpful in assessing regime performance. About 2,000 people are convicted of money-laundering offenses (primary or otherwise) each year in the United States. For the moment, assume that all of those convicted are providers of, rather than customers for, the service. This assumption imparts an upward bias to our risk estimate, since we know that some of those convicted are not standalone providers of money-laundering services.

To estimate risk, a figure for the total number of persons who launder money is also needed. No such estimate is available, so an indicative calculation is all that can be offered. Assume total US money laundered annually is near the low end of conventional estimates, say $300 billion. Only 20 percent of those convicted are reportedly involved with laundering more than $1 million, but that is the amount involved in the specific transactions detected, not an annual flow. If an average money launderer handles $10 million per annum (which might generate a gross income of $500,000 to $1 million), then there would be 30,000 money launderers, and the probability of conviction would be about 6.7 percent (2,000/30,000). For comparison, there are estimates available that the probability of incarceration for selling cocaine in the late 1980s was approximately 25 to 30 percent (Reuter, MacCoun, and Murphy 1990). Though dated, these are the only such estimates for an illegal market.

This exercise is highly speculative; there are other assumptions that might generate a higher estimate of risk without overly straining plausibility. For example, in addition to those who were convicted of money laundering, there may be substantially more individuals for whom those charges were dropped in exchange for information about the predicate offense or for pleas to some other involvement in the predicate offense, even though the individual's principal role was money laundering. If half of those who were caught laundering money were convicted only on other charges, then the risk figure might rise to 13.3 percent. For money launderers with valuable legitimate labor market skills, that risk might generate a very high premium for their services. Compared with drug dealers with little education, such professionals require a higher incentive to risk the same amount of prison time.

These assumptions generously favor a finding that supports the effectiveness of the AML regime. Most of those convicted of money laundering are also convicted of other offenses, and many are probably customers rather than providers. The assumption that each money launderer handles an average of $10 million per annum imparts a similar upward bias; actual cases point to launderers with much lower volume. That is certainly the case if many of them work for only one client. It is quite plausible that even now, with an elaborate regime in place, money launderers face a less than one in twenty probability of incarceration in the United States. The financial penalties collected by the federal government represent the most modest of taxes, even assuming low-end estimates of money laundering.

However, it must be reemphasized that this is not a complete assessment of the effectiveness of the AML regime. The figures employed cover only those individuals who were themselves involved directly in the money-laundering transaction. It may well be that SARs and other elements of the regime generate useful evidence against larger numbers of drug dealers, but that the final indictments and convictions are for the predicate crime alone. The lack of information on this possibility is a major omission in the current system of data collection.

Conclusions

For both conceptual and empirical reasons, it is impossible to assess directly how much the current AML regime has reduced the volume of white-collar crime, drug dealing, and other illicit market activity. Little information is available about the prices charged by money launderers, and that price itself is a poor representation of the total client cost of money laundering. Even without having found enough data in the public domain to judge whether prices have risen for particular types of transactions, it would appear that money laundering is not a particularly risky business, given the record of federal convictions. Nor does it seem plausible that a more effective anti–money laundering regime would increase costs to criminal offenders, even drug dealers, enough to be observable with current data series.

The most useful assessment would be an index of the difficulty of laundering money, with difficulty measured as a combination of cost, risk, and inconvenience. Such an assessment would require the systematic collection of data on prices using everything from undercover operations to debriefing those arrested for purchasing or providing services. Such a data collection effort is part of the research agenda put forth in chapter 8.

6

Protecting Financial System Integrity

An oft-stated goal of anti–money laundering (AML) regimes is to protect the integrity of the financial system, particularly banks, which are at the core of that system. Other types of financial and nonfinancial institutions such as money service providers and real estate agents, which also are generally covered by the AML regime, are important to financial system development but less so for the day-to-day functioning of the economy. Banking services are central to the smooth functioning of a market economy.

The role of AML regimes in supporting efforts to protect and facilitate functional financial systems is well established. For example, the 2003–08 Strategic Plan of the US Treasury's Department's Financial Crime Enforcement Network (FinCEN 2003a, 8) links its AML activities directly to achieving one of Treasury's key objectives, which is to "preserve the integrity of financial systems." In Title III (the International Money Laundering Abatement and Anti–Terrorist Financing Act Sec. 302 (a) (3)) of the USA PATRIOT Act of 2001, the US Congress reported: "Money launderers subvert legitimate financial mechanisms and banking relationships by using them as protective covering for the movement of criminal proceeds and the financing of crime and terrorism, and, by so doing, can threaten the safety of United States citizens and undermine the integrity of United States financial institutions and of the global financial and trading system upon which prosperity and growth depend."

Nor are AML regimes important only to the US financial system. William Gilmore (1999, 83) quotes the Australian president of the Financial Action Task Force (FATF), Tom Sherman, as stating in 1992: "Combating money laundering is not just a matter of fighting crime but of preserving the integrity of financial institutions and ultimately the financial system as a whole."

This chapter examines the nature of the AML goal to protect financial system integrity and presents a framework for examining how well the regime is accomplishing that goal. Looking at the limited available evidence through the lens of that framework leads to the tentative conclusion that the AML regime appears to have made substantial progress in protecting the financial system, but we offer several qualifications regarding that progress.

Financial System Integrity as an AML Goal

Much of the initial focus of the global AML regime was on the core financial system and particularly banks, since the banking system plays a central role in the collection and movement of funds. While the principal objectives were to make it more difficult (expensive) for criminal offenders to launder the proceeds of their crimes, and to employ the financial system in the investigation and prosecution of those crimes, an important subsidiary objective has been to protect the integrity of the financial system itself. Thus, for example, in a report on customer due diligence for banks, the Basel Committee on Banking Supervision (2001, 2) noted that "know-your-customer" policies and procedures "are critical to protecting the safety and soundness of banks and the integrity of banking systems."

Society today disapproves of turning drug revenues into legitimate funds. Financial institutions that accept money from drug dealers, even if they do not face criminal charges, are perceived to be less than law-abiding. The role of mainstream financial institutions, particularly banks, is to provide public goods such as banking services and liquidity to the financial system and the economy, and they are expected to share and abide by generally accepted social and ethical codes of behavior. Further, since core financial institutions to varying degrees are regarded as quasi-public utilities with access to such government safety nets as deposit insurance, access to the discount window, and payment services, they have now been called upon to assist in supplying another public good, which is the prevention of money laundering. In the process, they help protect the integrity of the core financial system as a whole.

In this context, once the social objective to combat money laundering has become well established, a bank's reputation suffers if it becomes associated in the public mind with that crime, though the seriousness of that decline in reputation may vary from society to society. In Switzerland, for example, it can be very serious, since asset management accounts for as much as half of Swiss banks' output, and private clients generate as much as 85 percent of this business (Pieth and Aiolfi 2003, 20). The Swiss bankers' association contracts for polls on the subject, and a 2004 survey of public attitudes toward Swiss banks found that 80 percent of respondents believed that their banking institutions enjoy a positive reputation abroad (M.I.S. Trend 2004). At the same time, 57 percent felt that Switzerland is not doing enough to fight money laundering, but 76 percent want to maintain bank secrecy. This nicely illustrates the tensions and cross-currents around this subject. In other countries, moreover, reputation may not be as valuable an asset, so banks may be less sensitive to being perceived as committing a violation related to money laundering. It can be said, however, that if banks and other financial institutions at the center of the financial system are to play their assigned role in the economy, their customers should at the very least trust them. Such confidence helps to prevent runs on banks, which can undermine the stability not only of the financial system but also of the economy as a whole.

Finally, given the AML regime, a financial institution that fails to establish appropriate AML-compliance procedures incurs legal and financial liability that can impact its bottom line as well as its reputation. Money-laundering regulations can be viewed as a way to insulate banks and similar institutions from direct connections with illegal activities. To this end, supervisors of banks and other core financial institutions have over time implemented a structure to induce institutions to take their AML responsibilities seriously. Supervisors have linked compliance to sound risk management, which is central to minimizing the costs of financial intermediation to the institution and the system as a whole. They have embraced a proactive supervisory posture in support of compliance with the overall regime.

Senator John Kerry (D-Mass.), drawing on his experience as chairman and ranking member of the US Senate Subcommittee on Terrorism, Narcotics, and Operations, has described the interaction of organized crime, corruption, money laundering, and a weakened financial system in Russia (Kerry 1997, 164–65). Criminal groups intent on hiding the proceeds of their crimes gain control of banks, which allows them to corrupt the business and financial system more broadly, which in turn taints the government and other institutions of society. Ultimately the phenomenon spreads and mixes with money laundered from crimes in other countries.

At the extreme, as argued in a report by the UK Performance and Innovation Unit (2000, chapter 3, 7), "the accumulation of criminal assets in a country's financial system can influence decisions about national banking policies or about co-operation in international investigations, transparency and accountability rules." The case of the Bank of Credit and Commerce International (BCCI) illustrates this extreme. BCCI caused substantial disruption to the international financial system when its nefarious activities were finally uncovered in 1991. The institution was found guilty of numerous violations of the banking laws in a number of countries. BCCI was a thoroughly corrupt institution that operated outside the laws and regulations of a large number of countries, and its collapse resulted in losses for a range of creditors, mostly individuals but some governments as well. BCCI had been viewed by many of its customers as a sound institution, and its operations supposedly had been examined—incompletely as it turned out—by supervisory authorities in major nations. Thus, the AML regime has to be judged on the basis of the extent to which it protects the integrity of international as well as national financial systems.

Evaluating Progress

How can the effectiveness of the AML regime in protecting the integrity of national or international financial systems be measured? Indirect indicators, if available and carefully interpreted, should provide a reasonable picture. Examining actual money-laundering prosecutions can provide evidence on general use of the financial system for money-laundering purposes (particularly in the placement phase) and the nature of that use. It should be possible to distinguish among institutions that are corrupt and actively solicit money-laundering business, those that have willing or rogue employees who provide such services on an ad hoc and noninstitutionalized basis, and those that are unwitting accomplices in money-laundering operations. Within this third category of unwitting accomplices, it also is important to distinguish institutions that have deficient internal AML controls that may contribute to facilitating money laundering.

With respect to the integrity of major national financial systems and the global financial system, as a first approximation the test of success of the AML regime should be whether institutions have been linked to either of the first two money-laundering categories in terms of laundering the proceeds of crimes committed in their home countries. A distinction must be made between a bank's internal systems and business activities that aid and abet money laundering and therefore can reasonably be associated with weakening financial system integrity (a relatively low hurdle), and on those internal systems and business activities that fail to stop money laundering and deter the underlying crime (a much higher hurdle).

In addition, scrutiny of suspicious activity reports (SARs) submitted by and about institutions should aid in identifying each institution's potential vulnerability, though there are biases and defects in such measures that might warrant controls for other factors such as size, location, and clientele. If institutions that show up frequently in prosecutions file small numbers of SARs, that information might indicate that they are failing to meet their responsibilities. However, extreme threats to the integrity of a country's financial system, which might create financial instability on the scale of BCCI, are difficult to detect or measure systematically other than after the fact. BCCI was an example of a fraud and conspiracy conducted from within the institution itself. Had the crimes been detected at an earlier date, the implications of the BCCI collapse would have been essentially the same.

These types of data are not generally or systematically available to the public in the United States or any other country, which constrains the ability of researchers to conduct either type of analysis. For this study, we developed two databases of cases. We drew upon those databases to suggest how the analysis of money-laundering cases might be used to produce a fuller assessment of the progress of the AML regime in protecting core financial system integrity.

The first database included international cases reported in seven annual FATF reports on money-laundering typologies and in occasional reports by the Egmont Group, an international association of financial intelligence units (FIUs). Of 223 cases entered in the database, 185 involved core financial institutions, exclusively banks, and excluding such entities as casinos and insurance companies. Because these exercises were designed to identify and share information about new methods of laundering money, they are not necessarily a representative cross-section of money-laundering prosecutions that in principle would best serve this type of analysis. Given that qualification, 3 percent of the cases involved active solicitation by the bank, and 3 percent involved the activities of rogue employees. In the remaining 94 percent of cases, the banks were unwitting accomplices, although it was not possible to determine whether or the extent to which their internal AML controls (or lack of them) could be blamed.[1]

The second database included 60 cases of money laundering assembled from descriptions in various sources, such as books, newspaper articles, and the *National Money Laundering Strategies*.[2] Because cases reported by the media, in particular, are likely to be sensational, the bias probably is in the direction of direct involvement by banking institutions or their employees that were judged to be culpable. We were able to identify the role of banks in 55 of these cases.[3] Six involved active solicitation, four involved rogue employees, and six fell under the heading of negligence with respect to AML controls. However, in the remaining cases, which constituted 71 percent of the total, the banks were unwitting accomplices.[4]

Fourteen of the cases involved large banks, and of these, one case involved active solicitation, two involved rogue employees, four involved negligence on the part of the banks, and seven involved banks as unwitting accomplices to money laundering. With respect to the predicate crime, six of the 14 were drug cases, all in the first half of the 1990s, and three were

---

1. Interestingly, 59 percent of the cases involved more than one bank as part of the money-laundering operation.

2. This sample is neither exhaustive nor necessarily random. Had we deliberately set out to find cases in which large banks had been involved in money laundering, there certainly would have been a different distribution of the nature of bank involvement in cases and types of cases.

3. In 75 percent of the cases, the underlying (predicate) crime was committed at least in part in the United States, while in 62 percent of cases the initial placement of proceeds of the crime was in the United States.

4. Fairly consistent with the findings using the first database, 62 percent of the cases in this second database involved more than one bank as part of the money-laundering case.

corruption or kleptocracy cases, while real estate fraud and gambling accounted for one case each. The three remaining cases involved bank violations of money-laundering (Bank Secrecy Act) rules and regulations, one (Bank of New York) was associated with a rogue employee, and two were the result of negligence.

The anecdotal information provided through the second database of cases suggests that in recent years only a small number of US institutions have been involved in active solicitation of money-laundering business. Even in cases where a financial institution is found to have actively solicited money-laundering business, however, it is not necessarily closed down. Such was the case of the Broadway National Bank in New York City, as was described in box 5.1. In these situations, the interests of law enforcement authorities sometimes differ from those of the supervisory authorities, in that the former may value the deterrent effect of closing down an institution while the latter are concerned about financial stability and not provoking a costly run on the bank. A compromise is often found by removing or charging officers of the institution and imposing a large fine, while at the same time rehabilitating the institution with new owners and management under the watchful eyes of the supervisors.

In a case like that of Great Eastern Bank of Florida, also described in box 5.1, the bank received a substantial fine for what might be called gross negligence, but its offense was not quite in the category of active solicitation of money-laundering business.

Similarly, the number of large US institutions with willing employees who facilitate money laundering from within appears to have been small in recent years. The most prominent recent case involved the Bank of New York, through which $7 billion was laundered by way of an account belonging to Benex, a company linked with a purported Russian mobster. One of the bank's vice presidents pleaded guilty to money laundering, but the bank itself was not accused of wrongdoing (*New York Times*, September 5, 1999, 3-1). It was, however, subjected to extensive and expensive supervisory guidance to improve its compliance with AML laws and regulations. This type of case as well as some in the third category—unwittingly assisting money laundering in a context in which the institution's deficient AML compliance regime contributed to the problem—now routinely result in financial penalties and costly and ongoing supervisory scrutiny until the institution has demonstrated improvements in its compliance procedures. It appears possible that JP Morgan Chase will be subjected to similar formal sanctions in the wake of the criminal conviction of Beacon Hill Service Corporation as an unlicensed money transmitter that used JP Morgan Chase to make $6.5 billion in wire transfers over a six-year period (Morgenthau 2004). We assume the institution has already been subjected to informal sanctions as part of its annual supervisory examinations.

Supervisors also review SARs submitted by institutions in order to identify an institution's potential vulnerability to rogue employees or weak AML compliance systems. Along with regular reviews of an appropriate sample of money-laundering prosecutions, supervisors could support efforts to measure regime effectiveness, as well as make the regime more transparent, by issuing a periodic public scorecard of AML regime progress in protecting the integrity of the financial system.[5]

An illustration of some of these points came in the spring of 2004, when the attention of the local Washington, DC, community focused on various money-laundering allegations involving Riggs National Bank, a financial institution that dates back 165 years and has served a number of presidents.[6] What is known is that Riggs, a relatively small regional bank with about $4.2 billion in deposits, catered extensively to deposits from the diplomatic community, which reportedly accounted for almost 25 percent of its total. An estimated 95 percent of Washington embassies had Riggs accounts. Among other transgressions, the bank allegedly failed to submit required reports involving large cash transactions by Saudi Arabian accounts. A senior vice president was fired and is under criminal investigation for participation in a possible money-laundering operation involving corruption and the president of Equatorial Guinea. The bank is also suspected of collaborating with former Chilean President Augusto Pinochet to hide some of his wealth that may have had questionable origins. A $25 million fine was imposed on the bank, and it was put under close management scrutiny by the Office of the Comptroller of the Currency and the Federal Reserve System, the severest penalty short of closing the institution. In effect, the bank's reputation was ruined, and its owners were forced by a combination of market forces and supervisory encouragement to put it up for sale.[7]

The Riggs case illustrates three aspects of money laundering as it relates to efforts to protect the integrity of the core financial system. First, Riggs demonstrated "willful and systematic" lack of compliance with mandated internal controls involving money laundering, and it was this failure rather than an actual conviction for money laundering that triggered the regulators' stern responses. Second, a bank can so tarnish its reputation via such failure that it is no longer viable as a stand-alone institution even if it retains substantial institutional value. Third and related, some of the principal money laundering–related failures involved a special category of private banking—providing services to embassies and their governments. The

---

5. Although US bank supervisors routinely use this type of information in connection with their AML examinations of individual banks, we were not able to gain access to the data.

6. The Riggs case was not included in the anecdotal database because the full story was still coming out as our study was completed.

7. The offer by the PNC Financial Services Group valued at about $24 per share is higher than the Riggs stock, which reported is closely held, has traded since 1998; Riggs stock had traded as low as $10 a share since then and only slightly below $15 a share in the year before its announced sale.

clear lesson is that this type of private banking, along with government officials, should not receive special treatment under the AML regime.

Conclusions

Several qualified conclusions can be drawn from evaluating the progress of the AML regime in protecting the integrity of the core financial system. The regime, which has now been in place in major jurisdictions for more than 15 years, has altered how banks and other core financial institutions approach their responsibilities and conduct business. The AML regime has induced banks to take seriously their obligation to avoid direct contact with criminal money by putting in place reporting systems and developed monitoring techniques that make them less attractive for money laundering. The emerging global AML regime makes it more difficult to use banks and mainstream financial institutions to place funds, although there is little evidence that these efforts have made money laundering substantially more expensive. Nevertheless, the global regime appears to have largely achieved one of its primary goals, which is to eliminate the threat from money laundering to the integrity of banking systems, at least for large institutions in the major jurisdictions.

This is not to say that the threat has been permanently eliminated—witness the Beacon Hill case referred to earlier—or that more cannot or should not be done to promote further global progress. Financial institutions that have been unwitting accomplices to money laundering could have had tighter AML controls in place. Those controls might have been helpful in detecting the underlying crime or, more likely, might have prompted the criminals to take their business elsewhere.

The assessment in this chapter should be qualified in four important respects. First, the principal concern in connection with money laundering and the integrity of core national financial systems and the global system has to do with the placement stage of the three-stage laundering process. It is at that stage that the financial institution, and by extension its financial system, is most vulnerable to corruption and the loss of reputation. Preventing the involvement of core financial institutions in money laundering at the layering or integration stages is a different and more difficult matter.

The global AML regime has recently been extended to correspondent banking relationships, which often are an integral aspect of the layering and integration stages of money laundering. The USA PATRIOT Act contained some tough and groundbreaking provisions to address the correspondent banking aspect of the AML regime. In addition, recommendation 7 of the 2003 FATF Forty Recommendations incorporates new provisions with regard to cross-border correspondent banking and similar relationships. Detection of money laundering in the layering and integration stages of the anti–money laundering process requires close cooperation between the AML regime's prevention and enforcement pillars. Extensive use of a financial institution in a major jurisdiction in these later stages could undermine the institution's stability, integrity, and reputation, in turn undermining customer confidence in the financial system.

Second, financial institutions could be used more extensively and effectively in connection with the investigative element of the AML regime's enforcement pillar. One example is in sting operations, and another is in more effective use of SARs and similar reports. As noted in chapter 4, the US private sector has been quite critical of the government's tendency to operate as a one-way street on money laundering with respect to the provision of information. Similar complaints can be found in the KPMG (2003) report on the reporting regime for SARs in the United Kingdom. One sometimes hears complaints that banks and their supervisors resist cooperating with law enforcement authorities.[8]

Third, the jury is still out with respect to money laundering in connection with the "private banking" activities of major international banks. There have been major problems in the recent past, such as the difficulties that occurred in Mexico as a result of the United States' Operation Casablanca in 1998 (chapter 4). Such activities often involve the proceeds of crimes—such as corruption—committed outside the home countries of major financial institutions, and therefore only indirectly affect the integrity of those countries' financial systems. Nevertheless, in response to these and other concerns related to public confidence in banking systems, 12 major private international financial institutions adopted Global Anti–Money Laundering Guidelines for Private Banking in October 2000 (Wolfsberg Group 2002).[9] In addition, recommendation 6 of the 2003 FATF Forty Recommendations calls for enhanced due diligence with respect to "politically exposed persons" whose source of wealth may not be legitimate.

Finally, the tentative assessment that the global AML regime is generally effective in protecting the integrity of core financial systems of major countries leaves to one side the issue of institutions at least notionally headquartered outside major financial centers, as well as their capacity to abuse and undermine the integrity of the global financial system. Again, these

---

8. Martin Mayer wrote in the *New York Times* (January 14, 2004) that the Federal Reserve Board would not allow regional banks to reveal the identity of purchasers of large blocks of US currency. He did a disservice to the public and the AML regime by putting forward his unsupported accusation. The Federal Reserve routinely shares such information with law enforcement agencies.

9. The Wolfsberg Group revised its guidelines for private banking in 2002 and also adopted principles on the suppression of this financing of terrorism and AML principles for correspondent banking. In 2003, the group issued a statement on procedures for monitoring, screening, and searching, which carries CDD beyond initial customer contacts and establishment of an account relationship. The procedures can be used for investigative purposes and have the potential to help identify layering operations.

institutions and jurisdictions pose less of a direct threat to the financial systems of the major countries, but the risks are not negligible. This concern, as well as those regarding the proceeds of corruption often associated with private banking, is more relevant to the role of the AML regime in targeting the global "public bads" of terrorism, kleptocracy, and failed states, which will be discussed in chapter 7.

While the global AML regime appears to have successfully protected the integrity of banks via core financial institutions headquartered in the major financial centers, the regime may not have reduced the total volume of criminal proceeds laundered globally; the activity has perhaps been pushed into more peripheral institutions and jurisdictions. As a result, the AML regime has been expanded to pursue laundering taking place through those institutions and locations. The net effect may have been positive with respect to protecting the integrity of the core financial system but minimal with respect to achieving other AML goals.

7

Combating Global "Public Bads"

Three types of objectives for national and global anti–money laundering (AML) regimes have been identified: (1) the central goal of reducing a range of predicate crimes (chapter 5); (2) the more narrowly focused goal of protecting the integrity of the core financial system (chapter 6); and (3) a group of national security or systemic goals under the heading of global "public bads"—terrorism financing, corruption and kleptocracy, and failed states. In examining the progress of the AML regime in achieving this final group of goals, this chapter will consider each of the "bads." The global AML regime can and does play a constructive role in limiting each of these global problems, but the regime is just one tool, the development and use of which poses many challenges given the international context in which these goals must be pursued.

Terrorism

The first complication in assessing AML regime effectiveness in combating terrorism financing is that resources for such activities are laundered before, as opposed to after, the crime. The traditional AML focus is on the placement stage, when funds enter the financial system, but taking action when funds are already in the hands of terrorist organizations can be too late to stop the intended terrorist act.

Thus, the role of the AML regime with respect to terrorism financing is principally prevention in the full defensive sense of the word. Financial trails may be helpful after the terrorist act has occurred in terms of identifying and apprehending supporters of terrorism, but the goal is to stop those acts before they happen. The anti–money laundering enforcement pillar serves at best on the margin as a deterrent to terrorism, perhaps by making potential terrorists recognize the difficulty in acquiring funds. However, enforcement is more relevant to the actual blocking, seizure, and confiscation of resources financing terrorism. As detailed by the GAO (2003b), and R. E. Bell (2003) in the UK context, terrorist organizations use a range of alternative or nontraditional means to earn, move, and store their assets. Consequently, the full panoply of tools of the AML regime must be used to combat terrorism financing. Bell also emphasizes that privacy and human rights considerations are more complex than with respect to conventional anti–money laundering because some sources of financing are legitimate even if the uses are not.

The Eight Special Recommendations on Terrorist Financing adopted by the Financial Action Task Force (FATF) in October 2001 (FATF 2001a) draw a parallel between other forms of money laundering and the financing of terrorism. Hastily assembled following the September 11, 2001, terrorist attack on the United States and based on the model of the original FATF Forty Recommendations, the Eight Special Recommendations emphasize issues that are more relevant to combating the financing of terrorism—such as the role of nonprofit entities and informal funds transfer mechanisms—than conventional money laundering. In general, the Eight Special Recommendations reflect the fact that the AML regime as it applies to terrorism financing is analogous to its application to other money-laundering activities, but with some important differences in concept and application.

The Eight Special Recommendations call for (1) ratifying and implementing the 1999 UN International Convention for the Suppression of the Financing of Terrorism (parallel to recommendation 1 of the original FATF Forty Recommendations to ratify and implement the 1988 Vienna Convention against Illicit Traffic in Narcotic Drugs and Psychotropic Substances); (2) criminalizing the financing of terrorism (parallel to FATF recommendation 4 on criminalizing money laundering); (3) freezing and confiscating funds and assets of terrorists (parallel to FATF recommendation 7); (4) reporting suspicious transactions (parallel to FATF recommendations 15–18); (5) international cooperation (parallel to FATF recommendations 33–34 and 36–40); (6) measures against nontraditional channels of value transmission (analogous to FATF recommendations 8 and 9, extending the framework to nonbank financial and nonfinancial institutions); (7) special attention to wire transfers (analogous to FATF recommendation 9); and (8) reviewing laws and regulations that relate to nonprofit entities (analogous to FATF recommendation 25 with respect to the abuse of shell corporations).

Of course, combating the financing of terrorism predated the September 11 tragedy. In the wake of the bombing of Pan American flight 103 on December 21, 1988, over Lockerbie, Scotland, the 1989 G-7 Summit issued a declaration on terrorism that focused on deterring terrorist acts. President

Clinton invoked the International Emergency Economic Powers Act on January 23, 1995, to prohibit financial transactions with terrorists and groups financing terrorism. Following the bombing in Dhahran, Saudi Arabia, on June 26, 1996, the G-7 Summit issued another declaration on terrorism that included a reference to the financing of terrorism. The United Nations also reached agreement in 1999 on the International Convention for the Suppression of the Financing of Terrorism. In June 2000, the Bremer Commission report on Countering the Changing Threat of International Terrorism was submitted to the US Congress. A tug of war then ensued within the new Bush administration about implementing the report's recommendations, including US ratification of the UN International Convention on the Suppression of the Financing of Terrorism. The inter- and intra-agency infighting was resolved only in the wake of the September 11 attacks, which put combating terrorism financing at the top of the agenda of the US AML regime. September 11 also shifted some of the attention away from an exclusive focus on state sponsorship of terrorism.

The effort to enhance the AML regime to block and seize funds intended to finance terrorism was impressive even scaled by the enormity of the World Trade Center attack. Richard Spillenkothen, director of the division of supervision and regulation at the Federal Reserve Board, testified before the US Senate: "The US government's response to the terrorist attacks on September 11 has necessitated unprecedented cooperation among federal bank supervisors, the private sector, law enforcement agencies, and the international financial community" (Spillenkothen 2002, 1).

From the standpoint of effectiveness, if the AML regime were to prevent a single major terrorism incident each year on the scale of those in Bali, Indonesia on October 12, 2002, or Madrid, Spain on March 11, 2004, then it surely would be judged worthwhile. However, it is difficult if not impossible to establish connections between terrorism averted and any specific element of the AML regime; only where a specific terrorist plot is foiled, fairly late in its development, can a connection be made. In turn, inasmuch as the regime is justified on the basis of preventing international terrorism incidents, it is less likely to be examined on a cost-effectiveness basis as much as on its efficacy in measurably contributing to preventing an incident.[1]

It would be a stretch to consider statistics on the incidence of global terrorism as a useful indicator of the effectiveness of the AML regime per se in reducing terrorism, in part because prevention involves much more than interdicting financial flows, and in part because of the low-cost nature of most terrorist operations. Paul Pillar (2003) argues that financial instruments play a secondary role in counterterrorism because terrorism is cheap

---

1. Bell (2003, 120–21) in a thoughtful article on combating the financing of terrorism suggests only indirect measures of success: number of forfeiture orders, value of assets diverted, reduced revenues to terrorist organizations, and international cooperation indexed by active participation in blocking operations.

and the modest flows of funds are difficult to track. Unlike some other criminal activities that are financed from the accumulated stock of the proceeds of crime, financing of actual terrorist incidents primarily involves small flows of financial resources in the tens or hundreds of thousands, rather than millions, of dollars.

One should distinguish, however, between the marginal cost of a particular terrorist operation and the much larger total cost of creating and maintaining a sponsoring organization. In this sense, combating terrorism financing has a good deal in common with combating money laundering in the context of conventional organized criminal organizations such as the Mafia, drug cartels, and street gangs. In addition, some countries and organizations that sponsor terrorism are also involved in conventional criminal activities such as drugs and cigarette smuggling.

Similarly, one cannot conclude much about the effectiveness of the AML regime from the total amount of funds frozen or seized since September 11, 2001. The global total as of March 24, 2004, was estimated at $203 million as a result of 173 jurisdictions having issued freeze orders.[2]

A slightly better measure of AML regime effectiveness might be the amounts that are blocked, seized, or confiscated each time a new channel is added to the list of sources of terrorist financing, such as a new charity or a name of a new individual linked to such an activity. By this metric, results since September 11, 2001, are open to a variety of interpretations. As of the end of 2001, $112 million had been blocked or seized, which is a quite substantial amount relative to what is needed for individual terrorist operations. The amount 27 months later had risen to just over $200 million, but only $3.5 million had been added to the total in the final eight of those 27 months, indicating that the process had slowed considerably. Some of the previously blocked funds ($27.7 million) were used to help finance the new government in Afghanistan, and some went to pay legal fees, so the $200 million understates the total of all funds block or seized on a continuous basis.[3] Moreover, freezing often blocks a pipeline for fund transfer. Anecdotal reports suggest that such actions have a negative effect on fundraising, but they do not produce quantitative measures.

To illustrate the difficulty of going from these statistics to measures of effectiveness in preventing terrorism, assume that the unadjusted total of funds frozen, seized, or impeded was $300 million, or about $10 million a

---

2. This is the sum of blocked or frozen funds plus seized or confiscated funds. Funds are first blocked or frozen and later may be seized or confiscated via a separate legal proceeding. There may be some double counting in the data because they draw on a number of non-US sources. Some funds have been released to finance government activities. The total includes $64 million seized with the balance frozen. The data are from the US Treasury based on Zarate (2004).

3. Some funds may have been blocked and later released by the courts in the countries involved for lack of sufficient evidence to justify the initial blocking or subsequent seizure.

month over the 27 months from December 2001 through March 2004. If the AML regime had a 33 percent success rate, which would be remarkable, then about $20 million a month slipped through the net. On the one hand, if each major terrorist act costs on average $400,000—the FBI estimates the budget for the September 11 attacks at between $300,000 and $500,000 (US Treasury 2003, footnote 50)—as many as 1,350 such acts might have been financed over the 21¼-year period. On the other hand, US intelligence officials have been quoted as saying that al Qaeda operates on a budget in the tens of millions a year (*Washington Post*, December 20, 2003, A16), so an estimate of $300 million blocked, seized, or impeded over this period could be considered significant. This arithmetic is intended neither as an indictment of the AML regime as it has operated to combat terrorism financing since September 11, nor to suggest that the larger amounts frozen or seized imply that more has slipped through the net. Rather, the aim is simply to illustrate the challenge that the regime faces based on this metric, and to demonstrate why we prefer to measure effectiveness through a flow test (how much is blocked in each new antiterrorist financing action) rather than a stock test (total amounts frozen or seized).

Pillar (2003) offers a more positive interpretation of events, citing the interdiction of terrorist finances as "one of the biggest post-9/11 improvements of any of the counterterrorist instruments." In addition to the legal powers expanded as a result of 9/11, he argues that the higher priority attached to terrorism by the US government has stimulated more cooperation from foreign governments.

Prior to September 11, US and non-US official policy toward international terrorism focused to a substantial degree on state-sponsored terrorism and the use of economic sanctions to discourage the harboring of terrorist groups. Even now, the United States continues to designate state sponsors of terrorism, foreign terrorist organizations, and specially designated terrorists, as it has been doing since the early 1970s. This type of sanction has been used against Afghanistan, Cuba, Iran, Iraq, Libya, Sudan, and Syria, with limited impact. Sanctions or the threat of sanctions also can be lifted to provide positive incentives in certain situations, as was done in the wake of September 11. Gary Hufbauer, Jeffrey Schott, and Barbara Oegg (2001, 13) conclude "it would be illusory to expect that the arsenal of economic sanctions can play more than a modest role in the war against terrorism." They cite the limited success against state sponsors, terrorist groups, and major drug lords. Nevertheless, this is an area where modest contributions can be important.

As with other uses of the anti–money laundering regime, AML tools are only one important instrument in the fight against the financing of terrorism. Blocking or seizing funds intended to finance terrorism are only part of the overall effort to combat such activities and their financing. As stated by the US Treasury on August 29, 2003, in a press release about a UN report on sanctions to block the flow of funds to al Qaeda: "The point isn't grabbing dollars in bank accounts when freezing orders go into place, it is destroying the financial infrastructure of terrorism. That means seizing money, but it also involves dismantling the channels of funding, deterring those who would give aid and support to terrorists, and following the leads to terrorist cells." In a modest step along these lines, the US Treasury on May 12, 2004, for the first time invoked a provision of the 2001 USA PATRIOT Act (section 311) to declare the Commercial Bank of Syria—the principal government-owned bank—an institution of "primary money laundering concern" in connection with the bank having been used by terrorists. The action prohibited US financial institutions from having any direct or indirect dealings with the Syrian institution or any of its subsidiaries.

In stressing the complexities and challenges of counterterrorist policy, Pillar (2003, 217) describes terrorism as "a problem managed, never solved." Among his recommendations are to disrupt terrorist infrastructure worldwide, to use all available methods while not relying heavily on any one of them, to legislate sparingly, and to keep terrorist lists honest. Each of Pillar's points provides perspective on the role of the AML regime in combating terrorism financing. The complexities of the phenomena of terrorism, on the one hand, and money laundering, on the other, militate against simplistic, overarching solutions such as the creation of a new international organization dedicated solely to issues involving terrorist financing, as suggested by the Council on Foreign Relations (2002, 27) report on the subject, but dropped from its 2004 update.

The call for honesty in compiling lists of terrorists suggests the need for some care in blocking or seizing assets. Blocking assets in error, even well-intentioned error, only to have them later released via a judicial process, can undermine support for some of the more draconian (but perhaps necessary) methods applied to combating the financing of terrorism. Ron Suskind (2004, 191–93) describes the frantic US efforts to open a financial front in the war on terror on the basis of evidence that might not stand up in court. He concludes with a quotation he attributes to US Treasury General Council David Aufhauser, "It was almost comical. We listed out as many of the usual suspects as we could and said, 'Let's go freeze some of their assets.' "

In this context, any metric for judging the success of the AML regime in combating the financing of terrorism will not be entirely satisfactory.[4] However, the amount of assets frozen or blocked and seized or confiscated is relevant to an overall assessment of the AML regime's contribution. Consequently, after the initial success and more recent modest accomplishments in combating such financing, US and other authorities have stressed better compliance with international obligations in this area and

---

4. Metrics for judging the success of overall counterterrorism efforts such as arrests, convictions, and attacks prevented (more problematic to measure) often have little to do with the AML regime per se. Recall the discussion in chapter 5 of the temporary surge in terrorism-related SARs in the wake of the September 11 attack.

an increasing focus on informal money transfer mechanisms. The FATF has issued best-practice papers on the freezing of terrorist assets (FATF 2003d) and on combating the abuse of nonprofit organizations (FATF 2002a). The G-7, under US leadership, has also exhorted other countries to cooperate more effectively in combating terrorist financing. For example, the G-7 finance ministers and central bank governors issued a Joint Statement on Combating Terrorist Financing in April 2004 following a meeting with the finance ministers and central bank governors of 12 other countries, the FATF president, and the heads of the International Monetary Fund (IMF), World Bank, and the European Commission. They pledged closer cooperation and emphasized the importance of dealing collectively with the problem of terrorist financing.

As with other objectives of the AML regime, international cooperation is crucial to the success of the regime in combating the financing of terrorism. Notwithstanding various statements of strong support, however, cooperation in this complex area is only as effective as the political will to take costly or politically unpopular stands that might face domestic resistance. For example, the FATF's 2002–03 annual report said that the full compliance rate with its Eight Special Recommendations on Terrorist Financing was only 75 percent. The average full compliance rate by FATF members with the original FATF Forty Recommendations as of the same date was more than 90 percent.[5] Although there were shortfalls in compliance with each of the recommendations on terrorist financing, failures to comply fully were most frequent with those relating to wire transfers and to ratification and implementation of UN conventions and resolutions. For example, as of April 2004 only 112 countries had carried out the first of the FATF's special recommendations, which was to ratify the 1999 UN International Convention for the Suppression of the Financing of Terrorism. Another 41 countries, including six FATF countries, had signed the convention but not yet ratified it.[6] To cover the entire 191 members of the United Nations another 38 countries also would have to accede to the convention via ratification.

In general, efforts to rapidly implement measures to combat the financing of terrorism have met with considerable indifference and resistance. A UN monitoring group (United Nations 2003a) reported that 108 members had failed to submit reports on terrorism financing six months after the

---

5. Reporting on its pilot project with the World Bank to assess compliance with standards to combat money laundering and terrorism financing, the IMF (2004c) also found that compliance with the original FATF Forty Recommendations was much higher than with the Eight Special Recommendations on Terrorist Financing. The assessment noted that in many countries, the legislation necessary for the latter group of recommendations had not yet been adopted.

6. The FATF countries were Argentina, Belgium, Brazil, Germany, Greece, and Ireland. The United States, leading the war on terrorism, did not itself ratify the convention until June 26, 2002.

agreed submission date. The report said that 25 of those countries were of special interest because of other information suggesting that al Qaeda or its associates might be active within their borders. Among the most prominent were Egypt and Indonesia. Eight European countries also had not submitted reports, including Ireland and Luxembourg.[7] On the other hand, Saudi Arabian authorities touted their passage of the FATF review of Saudi compliance with the 40 + 8 recommendations on anti–money laundering and terrorism financing (*Financial Times*, March 8, 2004, 3), notwithstanding the fact that the actual review, while saying that Saudi Arabia was "compliant or largely compliant" with the recommendations, pointed to the country's lack of a clear definition of terrorist financing, failure to issue implementation rules for its 2003 AML legislation, and shortcomings in the area of customer due diligence (FATF 2004a, annex C, 9). A report by the Council on Foreign Relations (2004), while praising some Saudi actions over the previous two years, is also very critical of the implementation of its regime to combat money laundering and the financing of terrorism.

In addition, a large number of countries have not put in place legislation permitting them to freeze terrorist assets without delay, as called for under UN Security Council Resolution 1373. Following the March 11, 2004, attack in Madrid, the European Council of Heads of Government cited Resolution 1373 and called on all EU members to implement previous decisions on freezing property and evidence by December 2004 and on confiscation of proceeds by June 2004. The council did not list the countries that had thus far failed to comply, but it is reasonable to conclude that there was more than one.

With respect to tightening the US AML regime as it applies to the financing of terrorism, the American Civil Liberties Union has challenged some of the provisions of the USA PATRIOT Act on privacy grounds.[8] Opponents have criticized the elimination of the distinction between criminal and intelligence classifications, and have filed legal briefs opposing post–9/11 policies.[9] The effects of such resistance may well be taking their toll, for better or for worse. After the US government charged US Islamic leader Abdurahman

---

7. Another example of the limited urgency attached to international efforts to extend the AML regime to cover the financing of terrorism is the weak response of the 184 members of the IMF to a voluntary questionnaire on anti–money laundering and countering terrorism financing that was authorized in November 2001. By September 2002, only 49 countries had responded, and four G-7 countries (Canada, Germany, Japan, and the United Kingdom) were among those that had not.

8. Steinberg, Graham, and Eggers (2003) make a plea for public guidelines on how these important new powers should be implemented.

9. On the other hand, Richard Falkenrath, former deputy homeland security adviser to US President George W. Bush, wrote in the *Financial Times* (July 7, 2004, 13) that the failure of European governments to eliminate this same "wall" between law enforcement and intelligence has prevented them from "connecting the dots" with respect to terrorist attacks in Europe such as that which occurred in Madrid.

Almoudi with money laundering and engaging in prohibited financial transactions in October 2003, the *New York Times* (October 24, 2003, A19) noted that he had not been charged with terrorist financing, perhaps because prosecutors were gun-shy as a result of mixed results in earlier such cases.

Regarding the previously mentioned UN report on sanctions directed at blocking the flow of funds to al Qaeda, the *Washington Post* (August 29, 2003) reported that the Schengen Information System, used by 13 European Union and two other European countries to monitor border crossings, contained only 40 of the 219 names on the UN list of suspect individuals and institutions. Several members of the Schengen group reportedly are precluded by their national laws from placing the names of their own citizens on national watch lists without an appropriate judicial basis. Following the Madrid attack, the EU resolved once again to step up its efforts to implement a 2001 decision to create a Europe-wide arrest warrant.

As with other aspects of the AML regime, differences in legal as well as regulatory structure and philosophy sometimes get in the way of cooperation. For example, Germany has criticized US and UK authorities for resisting the extension of financial supervision regulations to "underground banks" such as the *hawala* system of international money transmission (*Financial Times*, June 18, 2003). But for the moment, US and UK authorities are satisfied with applying registration, customer due diligence, and suspicious activity report (SAR) requirements to these institutions, stopping short of a full supervisory regime. Similar differences in regulatory philosophy underlie opposing positions regarding the regulation of hedge funds in Germany and France as opposed to the United States and United Kingdom.

Such differences interfere with establishing a seamless global AML regime as it applies to the financing of terrorism. To cite another example, Jochen Sanio, a German then president of the Financial Action Task Force (FATF), said in 2003 that "no German bank had yet filed a spontaneous report saying that someone had transferred money or was suspected of being involved in the financing of terrorism" (*Reuters News Services*, January 14, 2003)—the apparent implication being that such reporting requirements were of limited utility. The United States has been pressing other countries to crack down on cash transfers, in part out of concern that they are increasingly used to channel funds to terrorist groups. On the other hand, a frequent complaint abroad about the US financial enforcement apparatus is that when the Treasury's Office of Foreign Assets Control (OFAC) requests that the assets of certain individuals be frozen, it fails to provide the necessary information that foreign authorities need to defend their actions in court.

The United States has also been urging other jurisdictions, starting with its G-7 colleagues, to introduce cash reporting requirements along the lines of its currency transaction reports (CTRs) and reports of international transportation of currency or monetary instruments (CMIRs). To date, however, the US effort has not been successful. In its report on conducting due diligence on current customers with whom a client relationship had been established prior to April 1994, Pricewaterhouse Coopers (2003, 64) notes: "Firms said that they would be in favor of the current customer review if they thought that it would stop even one terrorist act, but they thought that the likelihood of this was so low that any benefit was negligible."

Costs as well as benefits figure in to decisions regarding application of the AML regime to combating terrorist financing. For some poorer countries, the costs are large and the direct benefits are not valued highly. An appropriate response is stepped-up technical assistance, as was suggested for the United States in the report by the Council on Foreign Relations (2002, 25) on terrorist financing. The G-8 Counter Terrorism Action Group has responded by addressing capacity building, and the FATF uses its Technical Assistance Needs Assessment exercise for the same purpose.

In conclusion, the global AML regime has contributed to combating the particular global pubic "bad" of financing terrorism. However, the regime is just one part of what is a complex effort for which measures of success are imprecise and indirect. Just like the pursuit of other AML objectives, efforts to strengthen application of the global AML regime to terrorism financing face the usual range of challenges associated with aligning different national regimes and structures. In addition, combating terrorism financing involves unique difficulties because of the relatively small amounts of money involved, and because the resources that need to be tracked, rather than deriving from a crime, finance crimes that authorities desperately need to prevent.

Corruption and Kleptocracy

Corruption is a major public policy issue that has been called "the most important economic issue facing the world today" (Hills 2001, 1). "The extent of worldwide corruption is staggering," writes Daniel Kaufmann (2003, 1). "A conservative estimate of the value of corrupt worldwide income would not merely be measured in terms of billions of dollars, but instead in the low US$ trillion range . . . [and] the additional indirect and long-term costs would further enlarge such rough estimates."[10]

Corruption is a manifestation of the economic activity of rent seeking. While empirical studies clearly have demonstrated the substantial economic costs of corruption and the weak governance often associated with it, and while the phenomenon is widely recognized and extensively studied,

---

10. Kaufmann's estimate of the total annual amount of corruption, which he describes as "rough," is based on surveys. While the precision of his specific estimate is debatable, no one disputes that the amounts involved are large, certainly in the hundreds of billions of dollars annually.

actually designing policy approaches to reduce substantially the incidence and extent of corruption is a major challenge (see Kaufmann, Kraay, and Zoido-Lobatón 1999; Knack and Keefer 1995; and Mauro 1995).

Paolo Mauro (2002) offers a pair of theoretical models to explain the strategic complementarity between corruption and weak governance. In one model, corrupt behavior by a group of officials contributes to the corruption of all officials and helps to explain the resulting multiple equilibria in which rampant corruption mires a country in the "bad" equilibrium. In another model, corruption contributes to political instability because one government official's corruption induces his or her colleagues to follow the example, which shortens the effective time horizon of the government and reduces its chances of reelection. The policy conclusions from such models point toward comprehensive rather than gradual reforms to move decisively away from the bad equilibrium. The conclusions also support improved disclosure and transparency as devices to motivate public opinion and ultimately discipline office holders.

Corruption is a broad phenomenon often found in relationships between the public and private sectors, but some would argue that it occurs in purely private sector activities as well.[11] The World Bank (1997, 8) defines corruption as "the abuse of public office for private gain." Transparency International (1996, 7), the most prominent nongovernmental organization that has focused on this issue, employs a less concise definition: "Corruption involves behavior on the part of officials in the public sector, whether politicians or civil servants, in which they improperly and unlawfully enrich themselves, or those close to them, by the misuse of the public power entrusted to them."

Corruption of a public official is connected de facto with money laundering, regardless of whether corruption is a predicate crime for a money-laundering prosecution in the jurisdiction where the corruption occurs. The public official will place his or her proceeds where they are relatively safe. The safe location may be a business or piece of real estate in the official's own country, but often it is in a foreign country, which reinforces the cross-border link between money laundering and corruption.

Kleptocracy is corruption by high-level public officials who use their positions systematically to line their pockets directly or indirectly with funds from the public purse.[12] Kleptocracy is a subcategory of political

---

11. The new UN Convention Against Corruption (United Nations 2003b) does not cover private-to-private sector corruption, to the disappointment of some private sector observers.

12. Moody-Stuart (1997, 63) provides a nice classification of official corruption: "Five percent of $200,000 will be interesting to a senior official below the top rank; 5 percent of $2 million is in the top official's area; 5 percent of $20 million is real money for a minister or his key staff; 5 percent of $200 million justifies the serious attention of the head of state." The kleptocrats are the last and the next-to-last levels of officials in this classification.

corruption, which is more commonly found in societies with less well-developed systems of justice and limited transparency in the public and private sectors. Of course, the line between political corruption and political contributions is not an easy one to draw. The relativistic view of public corruption of Robert Neild (2002, 202) defines it as the "breaking by public persons, for the sake of private financial or political gain, of the rules of conduct in public affairs prevailing in a society in the period under consideration." Not surprisingly, he is not optimistic that the standards for public conduct in much of the world will soon evolve to a level close to those found today in northwestern Europe.

The prevention pillar of the AML regime can play an important role in reducing the incidence and scale of kleptocracy through rigorous application of customer due diligence (CDD) regarding "politically exposed persons," defined by the FATF (2003c) as "individuals who are or have been entrusted with prominent public functions in a foreign country, for example heads of state or of government, senior politicians, senior government, judicial or military officials, senior executives of state-owned corporations, important political party officials." Applying AML procedures such as CDD can help to limit the success of kleptocrats, since they generally have little interest in keeping their ill-gotten gains invested in their own jurisdictions, where any change in government might threaten control of those assets.

The enforcement pillar can play a role as well via both the punishment of kleptocrats and confiscation of the proceeds of their crimes. Both elements of the enforcement pillar are important not only because they punish the individuals but also because they send messages to junior officials who may be tempted into similar behavior.

Such condign punishment outside of the jurisdiction of the underlying offense is particularly relevant to bribery and corruption. Corrupt officials in poor nations who control the justice system there may be unreachable except through money-laundering investigations in other countries. For example, Pavel Nickolayevich Lazarenko, the former prime minister of the Ukraine, was indicted, placed under house arrest, and convicted in June 2004 in the United States for money laundering. This case was the first brought under US money-laundering law using as a legal foundation the proceeds of extortion that was committed entirely overseas. The underlying offenses of receiving bribes and extortion, which notionally occurred in the Ukraine even though the money did not change hands in Kiev, could not be prosecuted there. Prosecution of the prime minister in the United States, based on use of US banks and brokerage accounts, served to improve justice in a salient and important way.

Similarly, the prosecution of kleptocrats and confiscation of the proceeds of their crimes provide a positive example for limiting garden-variety corruption in the home countries. Thus the incidence of corruption is linked to the incidence of kleptocracy. Widespread corruption, in turn, can undermine the integrity of the financial system.[13]

Assessing the effectiveness of the AML regime in reducing kleptocracy more narrowly, and corruption more broadly, relies to some extent on indirect measures such as surveys and other indicators of the prevalence of these phenomena, for example those put out by Transparency International and the World Bank. In general, the AML regime is not the only or even the major element contributing to success in combating kleptocracy, but it has a role to play and can reasonably take some credit for any improvement, or blame for some deterioration, in the incidence of the phenomenon.

A reasonable proximate measure of the effectiveness of the AML regime in dealing with kleptocracy would be the flow of convictions of kleptocrats or the amount of funds frozen and returned to their countries of origin. Unfortunately, data to construct such a measure are not currently available, and anecdotal information is uneven. Various public and private international organizations have made ongoing efforts to raise the profile of work against kleptocracy and corruption, but none has yet developed a comprehensive database that would permit measuring progress in combating these crimes.

Transparency International's *Global Corruption Report 2004* illustrates both the progress to date and the need for systematic database construction. The publication includes a summary table of the activities of 10 major kleptocrat presidents and prime ministers who served from 1965 to 2002, starting with Joseph Mobutu in Zaire and ending with Arnoldo Alemán in Nicaragua (Transparency International 2004, 13).[14] They embezzled amounts believed to have ranged from $78 million to $35 billion while in office. A few of the individuals on the list, such as Alemán as well as Joseph Estrada in the Philippines, were convicted of corruption, and some of the stolen funds located in foreign banks were frozen and returned to their countries. Some of the funds stolen by former president Sani Abacha of Nigeria also were returned to that country.

Transparency International's list demonstrates that, even though a complete database is not yet available, information on kleptocracy and indirectly

---

13. Note that without the AML regime, criminal funds could be passed through the financial system without any payment of additional bribes. In this sense the regime itself creates a threat to the integrity of the financial system in the form of corrupt practices. The AML regime, in turn, seeks to cleanse banks and other financial institutions not by reducing the problem of bribes paid to violate regulations but by maintaining a distance between the underlying criminal acts and the financial sector.

14. The others in order of the estimated size of their embezzlements are Suharto of Indonesia, Marcos of the Philippines, Abacha of Nigeria, Milosevic of Serbia/Yugoslavia, Duvalier of Haiti, Fujimori of Peru, Lazarenko of Ukraine, and Estrada of the Philippines. Mobuto ranks third on the list and Alemán ninth. The list, of course, is not exhaustive. Any number of other names could have been added—e.g., Benazir Bhutto of Pakistan, Chiluba of Zambia, Moi of Kenya, and Taylor of Liberia.

on the AML regime's role in its prevention and prosecution is gradually being assembled. One reason for the slow progress is the general lack of attention in the policy community to developing systematic measures of the effectiveness of the AML regime. However, there are other reasons as well. The global AML regime has been slow to incorporate public corruption, and by extension kleptocracy, into its set of objectives. In the United States, foreign corruption became a predicate offense for a money-laundering prosecution only with the passage of the USA PATRIOT Act in 2001, despite earlier executive branch proposals and pressures from other countries to do so.

The Organization for Economic Cooperation and Development (OECD) ratified its Convention on Combating Bribery of Foreign Public Officials in International Business Transactions in 1997. But action followed these good intentions rather slowly. The convention did not enter into force until 1999, when 12 countries had deposited their instruments of acceptance, approval, or ratification.[15] Many countries were slow to pass legislation necessary to implement the convention, in particular criminalizing foreign bribery, which the United Kingdom did only as part of legislation passed in the wake of the September 11 tragedy. Prosecutions for foreign bribery, in fact, have been quite limited outside the United States,[16] and the OECD has been criticized for weak enforcement monitoring. Finally, the convention itself has come under fire for loopholes, such as noncoverage of foreign subsidiaries, bribery of officials of political parties, and private-sector bribery (Heimann 2004).

At the international multilateral level, negotiations began on the UN Convention Against Corruption in December 2000, and 95 countries signed the final text in December 2003.[17] The UN convention includes prevention measures such as establishment of anticorruption bodies, requires the criminalization of a range of acts of corruption, mandates increased international cooperation, and, importantly, has a chapter on asset recovery. Of course, the convention does not satisfy everyone—Transparency International, for example, has criticized it for failing to address monitoring mechanisms and for not mandating the criminalization of bribery.

With respect to kleptocrats, in particular, only recommendation 6 of the 2003 FATF Forty Recommendations explicitly addressed "politically exposed persons." One breakthrough in this area was the passage in May

---

15. As of March 2004, 34 countries, including five nonmembers of the OECD (Argentina, Brazil, Bulgaria, Chile, and Slovenia) had adhered to the convention.

16. Bribery of a foreign official has been a crime under the US Foreign Corrupt Practices Act (FCPA) since the 1970s, but prosecutions are infrequent. In May 2003, James Giffen and ExxonMobil were charged under the FCPA in connection with payment of a $51 million "service fee" in Kazakhstan related to an oil contract. Giffen allegedly received more than $78 million from Mobil and other companies, passing some of the funds on to senior Kazakh officials.

17. At the end of March 2004, Nigeria announced that it would also sign.

2003 of UN Security Council Resolution 1483, which called for freezing the funds, assets, and economic resources of Saddam Hussein and other senior officials of the former Iraqi regime and their immediate family members. However, to date there is little evidence that this requirement has produced financial results.

Pursuing known or suspected kleptocrats before they have been driven from power is politically sensitive for governments that often need the cooperation of other governments on other issues, even if they are corrupt. In this connection, a noteworthy development was the establishment in 2003 of a US government task force to systematically target high-level present and former Latin American officials involved in corruption (*New York Times*, August 23, 2003, A9). Such proactive concern with the issue of kleptocrats appears to have produced some results. When Alemán of Nicaragua was convicted of corruption in December 2003, a US judge approved forfeiture of a multimillion-dollar Florida condominium and seizure of $150,000 from the former revenue director in Alemán's finance ministry. Another important case that emerged in early 2004 was the investigation of a senior official with the Riggs National Bank in Washington, DC (see chapter 6) for alleged involvement with the kleptocratic activities of the president of Equatorial Guinea, Teodoro Obiang, and his son.

It is no easy matter to deal with kleptocrats after they have been driven from office. In part, this is because allegations of corruption may involve the settling of political scores,[18] or because new leaders may not be entirely serious about taking action, as evidenced, for example, by neglecting to provide information that might form the basis for legal action by another country. One reason for such bait-and-switch tactics is that the requesting authorities sometimes are in the process of following the example of their kleptocratic predecessors rather than practicing what they preach. Even when home country authorities are serious, they need authorities in other jurisdictions to share their concern, devote resources to the matter, and cope with due process requirements in their jurisdictions. Such complications often impede the type of quick cooperation necessary to identify, block, and confiscate the proceeds of high-level official corruption. As usual, political and legal standards differ across jurisdictions.

---

18. Suspected political motivations for prosecutions in the home countries of alleged kleptocrats may sometimes underlie findings that the evidence presented by those authorities is too weak to justify extradition or the freezing and seizure of assets. In a case that comes close to allegations of kleptocracy, a Greek court, following the example of courts in Spain and the United Kingdom, declined in 2003 to extradite oligarch Vladimir Gusinsky to Russia on money-laundering charges possibly associated with capital flight, which is covered by money-laundering statutes in some countries but is not compatible with FATF recommendations. The reason cited for denying extradition was that Russian authorities had failed to substantiate the charges, and the independent Greek legal system turned them down. The European Court of Human Rights subsequently rebuked the Russian government for its pursuit of Gusinsky (*Financial Times*, October 15, 2003, 4; May 20, 2004, 2).

The Swiss authorities scored a public relations coup with their early pursuit of the assets of Nigeria's Abacha, but that case involved the Swiss legal regime, which has fewer or less cumbersome due process protections than those in many other developed countries. Authorities also benefited from the Abacha family's apparent misperception that their ill-gotten gains were safe in Swiss institutions.[19] Other jurisdictions, however, have been less successful in pursuing the Abachas' assets. The UK's Financial Services Authority announced in 2001 that it had the power to investigate allegations against the Abachas and sanction institutions involved for failing to comply with AML controls but not to freeze assets that may be the proceeds of crime. UK authorities eventually did return about $8 million to Nigeria's Economic and Financial Crimes Commission on the basis that cash previously seized at Heathrow belonged to the Nigerian central bank. By the second half of 2003, however, UK authorities had largely abandoned efforts to track the Abacha family's assets, despite evidence assembled by the Financial Services Authority that as much as $1.3 billion may have been processed through London between 1996 and 2000. No reason was given for the decision, but one can speculate either that Nigerian authorities had not provided the United Kingdom with sufficient information to pursue the matter, that the assets could not be reached, or that UK authorities reached the conclusion that it was not worth the effort to seize assets and return them to Nigeria, where there is no assurance that they might not be stolen again.

In the United States, the White House or the State, Treasury, Justice, or Homeland Security Departments may receive requests for assistance with respect to corruption by former officials in other countries. The US government bureaucracy generally is not structured to respond quickly to such requests, resulting in delays that at the least can be politically embarrassing. For example, the US government in late 1999 received a publicized request from Indonesia for assistance in finding the assets of former president Mohamed Suharto. The request went unanswered for 10 months, and the eventual response was that the Indonesian government would have to provide more detailed information if the US government was to be of any assistance.

Such instances were the principal motivation behind an action item in the US Treasury's 2000 National Money Laundering Strategy that established an interagency working group to streamline and improve coordination in handling such requests and inquiries. The group succeeded in establishing new procedures, but under US law the government is still constrained from responding proactively to assertions by foreign governments that various former officials were corrupt and that their assets in the United States should be turned over to the new government. Requests for assis-

---

19. It was reported in January 2004 that Swiss authorities are cooperating with Argentine authorities investigating money laundering by 200 former officials of President Menem's administration.

tance must contain a factual or legal basis to allow the US government to act, such as evidence that the funds were the proceeds of a US crime (including corruption). Despite such constraints, the US government has sometimes taken actions, as seen in the previously mentioned Lazarenko and Alemán cases.

Kleptocracy and international bribery cases are complex and expensive, as acknowledged even by those writing on behalf of proactive organizations such as Transparency International. Fritz Heimann (2004, 129) notes: "Prosecutors may be reluctant to bring foreign bribery cases because they lack the professional resources to pursue complex international cases. Procedures for obtaining evidence from abroad are often cumbersome and often unproductive." He prescribes technical assistance in connection with cases in developing countries.

The inquiry by Kenyan President Mwai Kibaki into corruption by the government of his predecessor, Daniel arap Moi, offers a glimpse into both the financial and political constraints to such initiatives. The inquiry has required bringing in a costly team of business investigation consultants working with forensic investigators. Moreover, since many of the alleged recipients of earlier corruption payments are in the new government, the political pressures to scale back the inquiry have been substantial.

Nigeria established the Economic and Financial Crimes Commission primarily to deal with private-sector corruption such as money laundering, fraud, and tax evasion. Given Nigeria's history of public-sector corruption and interference in legal proceedings, however, public- and private-sector corruption are difficult to separate, and resistance is entrenched. The commission faces an uphill battle in getting Nigeria to conform to the global AML standards established by the FATF. Executive Chairman Nuhu Ribadu was granted only 6.25 percent of his budget request for fiscal year 2004—$2.2 million out of a request for $35.5 million (*Financial Times*, February 24, 2004, 3).

In recent years, G-8 summit meetings have addressed corruption issues. Building on an initiative at the Evian Summit in 2003, the Sea Island Summit produced agreements the following year with four countries—Georgia, Nicaragua, Nigeria, and Peru—to combat corruption and promote transparency, with the latter focused on the process for granting licenses in the extractive sectors. Complementary actions by the G-8 are limited to technical assistance, denial of safe havens to convicted kleptocrats, and dealing more effectively with recovering the proceeds of corruption. The last action restated a commitment made the Okinawa Summit in 2000.

In conclusion, the hope is that in the future the AML regime and associated political structures will be more effective in dealing with kleptocrats before and after they have left power. Doing so would improve the anticorruption climate, but substantive progress in the future is likely to be slow, as it has been in the past. As part of this progress, better measures of success than surveys of corruption perceptions should also be developed.

Failed States

Kleptocracy and corruption generally are associated with failed states in which the entire political structure has imploded or been perverted in the pursuit of personal economic or political gain. Examples include Nigeria during the rule of Sani Abacha and Myanmar/Burma under the current military junta. In failed states, governments and public institutions normally expected to enforce laws are actively engaged in undermining or ignoring them, which in turn contributes to economic, financial, and political instability. A high degree of internal or cross-border violence is often associated with such states.

Kleptocracy and corruption, as well as other predicate crimes (such as theft, extortion, and drugs) normally associated with money laundering, contribute to the failure of states. Once a state begins to fail, the process feeds on itself, and those in nominal control of the instruments of the governmental process have an interest in systematically employing those instruments for personal rather than public gain. The systemic concern associated with the global public "bad" of failed states is not just the breakdown of law and order, but the fact that such states become a breeding ground for other public "bads" such as terrorism and other forms of violence, which may then be exported to other countries. Examples in recent years include Afghanistan and the Democratic Republic of the Congo.

The prevention and enforcement pillars of the AML regime have a role to play in identifying, isolating, and ultimately rehabilitating failed states. However, the AML regime is ancillary to broader efforts directed at bringing about profound structural changes in the government and society. Successful implementation of AML regimes requires resources that are generally lacking in failed states because most of their financial resources have been stolen, or because the revenue-raising apparatus of the public sector has broken down. In addition, an effective AML regime requires the political and institutional capacity lacking in failed states.

Money Laundering and Failed States

A number of indicators can be used to assess the relationship between failed states and money laundering, as well as the effectiveness of the AML regime in helping to reduce the number of such states. The focus here will be on the linkages between failed states (based on two political indices and one economic index), money laundering (based on two indicators in particular countries and territories), and corruption (based on the Transparency International index). The information used dates primarily from 2002 or 2003, with the exception of data from the FATF's Non-Cooperative Countries and Territories initiative, which since 1999 has assessed the extent to which countries cooperate with global anti–money laundering efforts. A time series for these various indicators would help measure the progress of the global AML regime in this area, but consistent time series are not available for most indicators.

Table 7.1, which summarizes information on failed states for 2002, draws on what is known as the Polity IV study (Gurr, Harft, and Marshall 2003) and on a study by Robert Rotberg (2003) on indicators of political failure. The latter study describes failed states as "tense, deeply conflicted, dangerous and contested bitterly by warring factions . . . [with] the following features: they have internal violence, they can no longer deliver positive political goods to their inhabitants, they cannot control borders, they have flawed institutions, they have deteriorated or destroyed infrastructures" (Rotberg 2003, 5). Polity IV concentrates on four indicators of violence or political instability: revolutions, ethnic wars, adverse regime changes, and genocides or "politicides."[20]

Polity IV and Rotberg identify the same seven countries as "failed states": Afghanistan, Angola, Burundi, the Democratic Republic of the Congo, Sierra Leone, Somalia, and Sudan. Rotberg also includes Liberia and Polity IV includes Myanmar/Burma in the "failed" category. There is much less concordance between Rotberg's category of 21 "weak states"—defined as countries with a shorter list of dimensions of failure—and Polity IV's category of 20 "complex states," defined as countries with two or more linked wars or crises (box 7.1). Six countries are common to the two lists of "weak" or "complex" states, which will be characterized together here as "failing" states.[21]

With respect to states that have failed or are failing economically, we draw on the most recent Country Policy and Institutional Assessment (CPIA) by the World Bank Group's International Development Association (IDA 2003). A World Bank (2002) task force used this type of analysis in a report on what it called "low-income countries under stress," characterized by weak policies, institutions, and governance. We identified as economically "failed" or "failing" those states that had CPIA ratings or "public-sector management and institutions" ratings in the fourth and fifth quintiles in 2002.[22] The 11 countries in the fifth quintile on both criteria were classified as

---

20. Adverse regime changes include abrupt shifts in patterns of governance, periods of severe elite or regime instability, and shifts away from democracy and toward authoritarian rule. "Politicides" are defined as civil disturbances that result in the deaths of a substantial portion of a political group.

21. The countries in common are Colombia, Georgia, Indonesia, Lebanon, Sri Lanka, and Tajikistan.

22. Elements of the rating for public-sector management and institutions are property rights and rule-based governance, quality of budgetary and financial management, efficiency of revenue mobilization, quality of public administration, and transparency, accountability, and corruption in the public sector (World Bank 2003b, 11). This is one of four rating categories that make up the overall CPIA rating, which also includes economic management, structural policies, and policies for social inclusion and equity. It should be noted that the CPIA exercise covers only countries that are eligible to borrow from the IDA.

Table 7.1   Failed and failing states in 2002

Country	Failed states Rotberg[a]	Polity IV[b]	CPIA[c]	Failing states Rotberg[d]	Polity IV[e]	CPIA[f]	Not included on CPIA list[g]
Afghanistan	X	X					X
Algeria					X		X
Angola	X	X	X				
Azerbaijan						X	
Bolivia				X			
Burkina Faso				X			
Burundi	X	X				X	
Cambodia				X		X	
Cameroon						X	
Chad				X	X		
Central African Republic			X				
Colombia				X	X		X
Comoros						X	
Congo, Democratic Republic of	X	X				X	
Congo, Republic of					X		
Djibouti					X		
East Timor				X			X
Ecuador				X			X
Egypt					X		X
Fiji				X		X	
Gambia, The					X		
Georgia				X	X	X	
Ghana				X			
Guinea				X		X	
Guinea-Bissau				X	X		
Guyana					X		
Haiti			X	X			
Indonesia				X	X		
Iran					X		X
Iraq				X		X	
Israel				X		X	
Kyrgyz Republic						X	
Kiribati						X	
Laos			X	X			
Lebanon				X X		X	
Liberia	X					X	
Moldova				X			
Myanmar/Burma		X					X
Niger				X		X	
Nigeria			X				
Pakistan				X			
Papua New Guinea						X	
Paraguay				X			X
Philippines					X		X
Rwanda					X		

(*table continues next page*)

Table 7.1   (continued)

Country	Failed states Rotberg[a]	Polity IV[b]	CPIA[c]	Failing states Rotberg[d]	Polity IV[e]	CPIA[f]	Not included on CPIA list[g]
São Tomé and Príncipe						X	
Senegal					X		
Sierra Leone	X	X				X	
Solomon Islands			X	X			
Somalia	X	X				X	
Sri Lanka				X X			
Sudan	X	X	X				
Tajikistan		X		X	X		
Thailand					X		X
Togo			X				
Tonga					X		
Turkey					X		X
Uganda					X		
Uzbekistan			X				
Vanuatu						X	
Yemen						X	
Zimbabwe			X		X		
Total	**8**	**8**	**11**	**21**	**20**	**23**	**18**

CPIA = Country Policy and Institutional Assessment rating

a. Rotberg defines "failed" states as "tense, deeply conflicted, dangerous and contested bitterly by warring factions."
b. State failure includes four types of events according to Polity IV: revolutions, ethnic wars, adverse regime changes, and genocides or politicides.
c. In the fifth quintile in both the "overall" category and the "public-sector management and institutions" category of the CPIA rating.
d. States with one or more failed state features.
e. Two or more temporarily linked wars or crises.
f. In the fifth or fourth quintile of the "overall" category or the "public-sector management and institutions" category of the CPIA rating and defined as having not failed.
g. Countries rated as politically failed or failing states that are not included in CPIA ratings.

Sources: CPIA ratings in IDA (2003); Rotberg (2003); Gurr, Harft, and Marshall (Polity IV study) (2003).

economically "failed" states; the other 23 countries in either the fourth or fifth quintiles on either criterion were classified as economically "failing."

Table 7.1 shows that only two countries (Angola and Sudan) of the 11 cited as failed economically are listed as failed politically by Rotberg or Polity IV. Five others are listed as failing politically (Haiti, Laos, Solomon Islands, Tajikistan, and Zimbabwe).[23] Three of the nine countries that are listed as failed politically are classified as failing economically (Burundi,

---

23. Zimbabwe today would probably be classified as "failed" as opposed to "failing" politically. The remaining four countries characterized as failed economically, but which are neither failed nor failing politically, are the Central African Republic, Nigeria, Togo, and Uzbekistan.

Box 7.1 "Failed" or "failing" states

The Polity IV study (Gurr, Harft, and Marshall 2003) provides a time series of "failed states"—states so ridden by conflict as to be essentially ungoverned—and what it calls "complex" or failing states, which are sufficiently conflicted as to be in danger of becoming failed states. Although continuity is considerable, a state may be classified as failed or failing in one year but not similarly classified the next or the previous year. Of the eight states scored by Polity IV as failed in 2002, five were scored as failed or failing a decade earlier in 1992: Afghanistan, Angola, Burundi, the Democratic Republic of the Congo, and Somalia. Liberia also was scored as failed in 1992 by Polity IV, but not in 2002, when it was scored as failed by Rotberg (2003), the other index used in this examination. In addition, three states were scored by Polity IV as failed or failing in 1992 that were scored as failing in 2002: Algeria, Lebanon (scored as failed in 1992), and Tajikistan. The only country that was scored as failed or failing in 1992 and was not in either category in 2002 was Peru.

Polity IV classified 87 countries as failed or failing one or more years between 1992 and 2001. More than 75 percent of those classifications were on the combined list for 2002 shown in table 7.1. The exceptions were two failed states (Bosnia over nine years and Lesotho for two years) and six failing states: Albania (one year), Armenia (two), Belarus (two), Nepal (one), Peru (one), and Zambia (one). More than 80 percent of the countries that Polity IV lists as failed in at least one year between 1992 and 2001 are on the list in table 7.1 as failed or failing in 2002. Again, Bosnia and Lesotho are the exceptions. Those countries most frequently listed as failed (five years or more) are Afghanistan, the Democratic Republic of the Congo, Lebanon, Sierra Leone, and Somalia.

the Democratic Republic of the Congo, and Sierra Leone).[24] Most of the remaining countries classified as failing politically had estimated incomes per capita in 2002 too high to be included as IDA borrowers, for which the threshold in fiscal year 2004 was $865.

For assessments of the seriousness of money laundering in various national jurisdictions, we used information from the money-laundering and financial crimes section of the *International Narcotics Control Strategy Report* (INCSR) of the US State Department (2003), as well as the results of the Financial Action Task Force's Non-Cooperative Countries and Territories (NCCT) initiative.

The INCSR classified 190 national jurisdictions as to whether they are of "primary concern" or "concern" with respect to money laundering, with a final category sued for jurisdictions that are just "monitored." Jurisdictions of primary concern are major money-laundering countries defined by statute as those "whose financial institutions engage in currency transactions

---

24. The other four countries classified as politically but not economically failed were explicitly not rated by the CPIA process, even though in principle their per capita incomes are low enough that they could borrow from the IDA. Myanmar/Burma, Liberia, and Somalia are inactive IDA borrowers, and Afghanistan lacked the information necessary to receive a CPIA rating as of 2002. East Timor, a new IDA borrower, was not included in the 2002 CPIA exercise because of a lack of information.

Table 7.2 Inclusion of countries in INCSR ratings and FATF reviews (number of countries)

FATF treatment	INCSR rating			Total
	Primary concern[a]	Concern[b]	Monitored[c]	
Not reviewed	12	24	78	114
Reviewed	41	26	9	76
Failed[d]	*5*	*1*	*0*	*6*
Failed/passed[e]	*10*	*7*	*0*	*17*
Passed[f]	*7*	*13*	*3*	*23*
FATF member[g]	*19*	*5*	*6*	*30*
Total	53	50	87	190

INCSR = *International Narcotics Control Strategy Report*
FATF = Financial Action Task Force

a. Jurisdictions whose financial institutions engage in currency transactions involving significant amounts of proceeds of narcotics trafficking.
b. Jurisdictions where money laundering takes place but is not considered a critical problem.
c. Jurisdictions reviewed that do not pose an immediate concern.
d. Countries that have failed to satisfy the FATF Non-Cooperative Countries and Territories (NCCT) criteria.
e. Countries that initially failed to satisfy the NCCT criteria, but subsequently satisfied them.
f. Countries that initially satisfied the NCCT criteria.
g. Countries and territories that are members of the FATF and have not been subject to NCCT reviews, but that have been subject to FATF mutual evaluations.

involving significant amounts of proceeds of narcotics trafficking." However, the INCSR recognizes the difficulty of distinguishing between the proceeds of narcotics trafficking and the proceeds of other serious crime and, therefore, explicitly applies a broad definition of the scope of money laundering.

The FATF's NCCT initiative—dubbed the "name and shame" process because it calls countries to task for failing to cooperate with global anti–money laundering efforts—is somewhat different in that it focuses on a jurisdiction's compliance with criteria regarding its legal and regulatory framework, international cooperation on money laundering, and resources allocated to anti–money laundering activities (see box 4.3 in chapter 4).

Table 7.2 summarizes the overlap between the INCSR and FATF rating and review processes. While there are important differences in coverage, the FATF review process includes a substantial number of countries and territories identified in the INCSR as jurisdictions of "concern" with respect to money laundering (about 50 percent) and a higher number of jurisdictions of "primary concern" (about 80 percent). In all, 80 percent of FATF members subjected to multilateral review, including the United States, are rated by the INCSR as jurisdictions of "primary concern" or "concern" because of the substantial amount of money laundering that occurs there despite having adequate AML regimes in place. The six FATF members rated as needing only to be "monitored" by the INCSR are Denmark, Finland, Iceland, New Zealand, Norway, and Sweden.

Table 7.3 Failed and failing states and INCSR ratings
(number of countries)

States and territories	INCSR rating					
	Primary concern[a]	Concern[b]	Monitored[c]	Total rated	Not rated	Total
Political						
Failed[d]	1	0	5	6	3	9
Failing[e]	10	4	17	31	4	35
Economic (additional)						
Failed[f]	1	0	2	3	1	4
Failing[g]	0	2	9	11	3	14
Total failed or failing	12	6	33	51	11	62
Not failed or failing	35	37	52	124	4	128
Total states	47	43	85	175	15	190
Dependent or autonomous territories	6	7	2	15	0	15
Total	53	50	87	190	15	205

INCSR = *International Narcotics Control Strategy Report*

a. Jurisdictions whose financial institutions engage in currency transactions involving significant amounts of proceeds of narcotics trafficking.
b. Jurisdictions where money laundering takes place but is not considered a critical problem.
c. Jurisdictions reviewed that do not pose an immediate concern.
d. Rotberg (2003) combined with Polity IV study (Gurr, Harft, and Marshall 2003); see notes *a* and *b* in table 7.1.
e. Rotberg combined with Polity IV study (Gurr, Harft, and Marshall 2003); see notes *d* and *e* in table 7.1.
f. In the fifth quintile in both the "overall" category and the "public-sector management and institutions" category of the Country Policy and Institutional Assessment (CPIA) rating.
g. In the fifth or fourth quintile of the "overall" category or the "public-sector management and institutions" category of the CPIA rating, and rated as not failed.

Sources: Country Policy and Institutional Assessment (CPIA) ratings in IDA (2003); Rotberg (2003); Gurr, Harft, and Marshall (Polity IV study) (2003); US Department of State (2003).

Because of the broader coverage of the INCSR, its rating system is used here to assess the link between money laundering and "failed" or "failing" states. Table 7.3 shows that only 18 (35 percent) of the 51 politically or economically failed or failing states that the INCSR rated are classified as jurisdictions of "primary concern" or "concern."[25] This percentage is less than the 52 percent of the 175 countries covered by both classifications that are of "primary concern" or "concern." Those 18 "failed" or "failing" states account for 20 percent of the 90 countries of "primary concern" or of "con-

---

25. Of the limited number of relevant FATF reviews—nine of the 62 failed or failing states—seven states did not pass their initial reviews. The two that passed were Turkey, which is a FATF member and is classified by Polity IV as politically failing, and Vanuatu, classified as economically failing on the basis of the CPIA review. However, the seven failed or failing states account for only about 30 percent of the 23 jurisdictions that initially failed their FATF reviews.

cern" in the INCSR, less than the 29 percent of the 175 countries covered by both classifications that are "failed" or "failing."[26]

This lack of a close association between money laundering and failed states should not be particularly surprising. As argued by Donato Masciandaro and Allesandro Portolano (2002), money launderers or their clients attach high importance to keeping their money safe and like to exploit legal protections to do so, which is no easy task in politically or economically failed or failing states. The only politically failed state that is rated by the INCSR as of primary concern is Myanmar/Burma, and the only economically failed state is Nigeria. Both failed their NCCT reviews. Myanmar/Burma might be considered in a different category of rogue states where there is order accompanied by violence inflicted by the authorities. Such states— North Korea could be considered to be in the same category—might be content to flout international norms by dealing with criminal gangs that operate globally.[27]

Money Laundering and Corruption

Table 7.4 presents a cross-tabulation of the assessment of the seriousness of money laundering on the basis of the INCSR, and the assessment of the extent of corruption on the basis of the Corruption Perceptions Index (CPI) published by Transparency International (2003). A total of 23 (43 percent) of the 53 countries that are in the fourth or fifth quintiles on the CPI and are rated in the INCSR are classified as jurisdictions of "primary concern" or "concern" as part of that rating process, less than the 56 percent of the 130 countries covered by both classifications that are classified as countries of "primary concern" or "concern." Those states account for 32 percent of the 73 jurisdictions that are classified as a "primary concern" or "concern" by the INCSR and also are ranked by the CPI, less than 40 percent of the 130 countries covered by both classifications that are in the fourth or fifth CPI quintiles.[28] The association between money laundering and corruption is not quite as weak as that between money laundering and failed states, but it is still less than would be expected statistically if there were a positive association.

---

26. The calculation excludes dependent or autonomous territories covered by the INCSR that presumptively cannot be full-fledged failed or failing states, such as the Cayman Islands and the Isle of Man.

27. North Korea, however, did not make any of our lists of failed or failing states in 2002, and along with South Korea is rated by the INCSR only as a country of "concern" with respect to money laundering.

28. The association is essentially neutral using the FATF reviews for cross-tabulation with the CPI, but these cover a much smaller sample of countries. Of the 20 countries with CPI ratings that did not pass their first reviews under the FATF's NCCT Initiative, eight (40 percent) were rated in the fourth or fifth CPI quintile.

Table 7.4 Money laundering and corruption (number of countries)

CPI[a] quintile	Primary concern[b]	Concern[c]	Monitored[d]	Total rated	Not rated	Total
Fifth	6	4	15	25	3	28
Fourth	6	7	15	28	0	28
Fourth and fifth	12	11	30	53	3	56
First to third	31	19	27	77	0	77
Total CPI rated	43	30	57	130	3	133
Not rated[e]	10	20	30	60	12	72
Total	53	50	87	190	15	205

INCSR = *International Narcotics Control Strategy Report*

a. Corruption Perceptions Index (CPI), Transparency International (2003).
b. Jurisdictions whose financial institutions engage in currency transactions involving significant amounts of proceeds of narcotics trafficking.
c. Jurisdictions where money laundering takes place but is not considered a critical problem.
d. Jurisdictions reviewed that do not pose an immediate concern.
e. Rated by the INCSR but not by Transparency International. Includes 14 dependent and autonomous territories that are rated by the INCSR.

Sources: INCSR, US Department of State (2003); CPI, Transparency International (2003).

As with the link between money laundering and failed states, many countries for which the perception of corruption is high do not show up as jurisdictions regarding which there is great concern about money laundering. The explanation may be similar: where there is a lot of corruption, with the possible exception of corruption principally by senior government officials, the proceeds of other crimes, over and above "living expenses," may not be safe. However, the data reviewed here do identify 11 countries that are of "primary concern" or "concern" with respect to global money laundering, are politically and/or economically "failed" or "failing" states, and also score poorly when it comes to corruption: Bolivia, Myanmar/Burma, Ecuador, Haiti, Indonesia, Lebanon, Nigeria, Pakistan, Paraguay, the Philippines, and Yemen.

The lack of evidence of linkages between failed states, money laundering, and corruption does not imply that there is no role for the global AML regime's prevention and enforcement efforts in dealing with failed states. The role, however, may be ancillary to broader efforts directed at bringing about profound structural changes in these countries' governments and societies. A credible AML regime requires the political and institutional capacity necessary to put it in place. Implementation of an effective AML regime also requires resources that failed states generally lack, either because they have been stolen or because the government has limited or no revenue-raising capacity.

Consider the case of Afghanistan, which is still classified as a failing state, though one would hope a postconflict, recovering one. The 2003 INCSR rated it only as a country to be "monitored," and Transparency International does not yet cover it in its ratings of corruption, presumably because there is insufficient international business activity to carry out the necessary surveys for the ranking process. Its apparent progress notwithstanding, Afghanistan remains a potential venue for money laundering because of its location and the fact that the opium sector may account for about half of overall GDP (IMF 2003a, 2). A summary report in 2003 of the views of IMF executive directors reflects these concerns. While commending the creation of a supervision department in the central bank, the executive directors "emphasized the importance of further developing regulatory and supervisory capacities and restructuring and privatizing state banks; urged tighter control of informal mechanisms of financing, the introduction of anti–money laundering, and controlling the financing of terrorism legislation; . . . [and] were concerned about the serious risks posed by the rise in poppy cultivation and the production of opium in Afghanistan to the levels of the late 1990s." In encouraging Afghan authorities to prepare the groundwork for privatization of state-owned companies, the executive directors "saw several key areas of reform as preconditions, including putting in place a functioning financial system, a market-oriented regulatory framework, and a functioning and fair legal system to firmly establish the rule of law and the security of property rights" (IMF 2003a, 3–4).

In this context, it is not difficult to understand why it may be a number of years before Afghanistan graduates from the status as failed or failing state and scores well on anti–money laundering and corruption indices.

The NCCT Process and Global AML Standards

Besides strengthening compliance with the global AML regime, the FATF's Non-Cooperative Countries and Territories initiative has played an important role in distinguishing between jurisdictions that reject making any effort to comply with international norms and standards, and those jurisdictions that accept or can be persuaded to accept such a responsibility. A country that can be persuaded to conform to global norms may be less likely to become a failed or failing state.[29] Two critical questions are: How effective has the NCCT approach been in terms of using the threat of adverse publicity and application of countermeasures to motivate reform? How much improvement has there been as a result of the NCCT process and what can be expected going forward?

---

29. The NCCT "name and shame" process is a soft type of targeted sanction. The NCCT process has been reasonably successful because the sanctions focus primarily and narrowly on the financial sector, using market forces as incentive devices, and have substantial multilateral support. See Hufbauer, Schott, and Elliott (2004) for a full analysis of economic sanctions and the reasons for their successes and failures.

For the first question, it is instructive to look at the case of Nauru, a Pacific island nation with a population of about 12,500 and an income per capita estimated at $5,000. Nauru is so small that it is not a member of either the IMF or the World Bank, and therefore is not included in the CPIA rating. The INCSR, however, listed Nauru as a country of "primary concern" regarding money laundering, and the country failed its first NCCT review in June 2000. Nauru passed AML legislation in August 2001 at least partly in response to the FATF review, but the provisions in that legislation with respect to supervision and regulation did not cover the offshore banking sector. As a result, the FATF in December 2001 recommended the application of countermeasures to Nauru, which prompted the government to amend its AML legislation to cover offshore banks, but did not lead to their actual licensing and supervision. The legislation was further amended in March 2003, but the FATF still would like Nauru "to take additional steps to ensure that previously licensed offshore banks are no longer conducting banking activity and no longer are in existence" as a condition for considering the removal of countermeasures (FATF 2003b, 12).

What has all this activity accomplished with respect to Nauru? After all, no money actually flows to or through the island in any physical sense in connection with its offshore banking sector; the flows are virtual, electronic, and controlled from elsewhere.[30] Reportedly, there has been a decline in the number of shell banking organizations, or at least in the rate of increase—as many as 400 such banks along with numerous other shell-type entities were said to have been registered in Nauru at one point (FATF 2003b, 11). If they so choose, countries can forbid their banks or nonbanks from dealing with those organizations to the extent that they know their names or whether they are entities known to be incorporated or registered in Nauru. In effect, Nauru and its offshore banking entities can be largely, if not completely, quarantined.

There is some hope that Nauru may further amend its legislation and implementation of it in order to cooperate more fully with the FATF and international law enforcement authorities. While it appears that Nauru has to some extent been made an example for purposes of a "demonstration effect," it has a way to go.[31] On the other hand, it seems unlikely that a large amount of proceeds from crimes in industrial countries has been laundered there—but it is impossible to prepare even a rough estimate without more cooperation from the Nauruan authorities. What is clear is that Nauru has made some progress, and that its money-laundering role has been at least somewhat reduced as a result of the application of countermeasures.

---

30. Wechsler (2001, 48) notes that Nauru banks were involved in some of the money flows from Russia through the Bank of New York in the late 1990s.

31. We met with the director of Nauru's police force (Bernard Junior Dowiyogo) in January 2003. He informed us that when requests came to him from abroad seeking cooperation in international investigations, he passed them on to the responsible government agency and had nothing further to do with them!

Masciandaro and Portolano (2002) worry that the NCCT process is not uniformly applied and that countries may not effectively implement their AML regimes once they have passed the NCCT review. They argue for complementary measures better to integrate jurisdictions into the global financial system, as well as for the development of stronger sanctions for noncompliance. Guy Stessens (2000) notes two types of "noncooperation" with global AML standards. The first may be an unwillingness to cooperate, in which case the appropriate response is to quarantine the country's financial system to encourage it to modify its behavior. The second may be insufficient capacity due to governance problems or a lack of financial or nonfinancial resources. If the world is serious about establishing a comprehensive and global AML regime, this latter type of noncooperation would seem best addressed with technical assistance.

Regarding the broader issue of moving ahead with promoting compliance with global AML standards, it should be noted that 17 jurisdictions that initially failed FATF reviews subsequently passed.[32] Most were offshore financial centers such as the Cayman Islands, Lebanon, Liechtenstein, and Panama, but the list includes a number of countries of larger significance such as Egypt, Hungary, Israel, Russia, and Ukraine.[33] As of early 2004, three sizable countries remained on the FATF's noncooperation list: Indonesia, Nigeria, and the Philippines. These countries, whose combined population tops 350 million, have made sufficient progress since their FATF reviews so as not to be subject to countermeasures, with which the Philippines was threatened in 2001. It remains to be seen, however, how these countries will perform or be dealt with in the future. If they fail to meet international standards, it will be much more challenging politically and technically to apply a Nauru-type quarantine to them.

In addition, the monitoring of observance of global AML standards was largely turned over to the IMF and the World Bank following development of a common methodology with the FATF (chapter 4). This transfer of responsibility has the benefit that reviews are now conducted by organizations with near-universal membership, rather than by a self-selected group of countries. Because of the broader coverage, the reviews are conducted at arm's length rather than as a peer-review process that sometimes limits frank criticism. The growing number of FATF and FATF-style regional groups also participate in and sometimes conduct the reviews. At the conclusion of the 12-month IMF/World Bank pilot project, a joint report concluded that the wealthier the country, the more developed its

---

32. The FATF has not excluded the possibility, however, of listing a country or territory as uncooperative if there is backsliding.

33. Russia made it all the way from FATF's "name and shame" list to full membership in the FATF within a very short period principally because it had met the "minimum requirements" for membership with respect to its AML regime and because of its classification as a "strategically important country" (FATF 2003a, 10–18).

AML regime, though jurisdictions regardless of financial resources had shortfalls with respect to frameworks for combating terrorism financing (IMF 2004b, 2). The most frequent implementation weaknesses included intragovernmental coordination problems, ineffective law enforcement, weak supervision, inadequate controls in financial firms, and shortfalls in the area of international cooperation.

Countries must "volunteer" for the IMF/World Bank reviews, and while countries can choose not to have the results published, the reviews are available to other member governments. Still, while the peer pressure, transparency, and accountability of the process are enhanced by the involvement of international institutions such as the IMF and the World Bank, there is today less capacity to apply meaningful pressure than when the reviews were carried out exclusively by the FATF.

For example, China, Colombia, India, Pakistan, Thailand, and Venezuela are six large and politically important countries that are rated as a "primary concern" regarding money laundering by the INCSR but were not reviewed by the FATF.[34] Will they volunteer or be induced to volunteer for an IMF/World Bank review of their compliance with international standards on anti–money laundering and combating terrorism financing, and will they volunteer or can they be shamed into allowing those reports to be published?[35] In fact, a number of IMF executive directors (IMF 2004a, 4) commented critically on the fact that the FATF has reserved the right to conduct further rounds of its NCCT process on its own. Their view was that if the FATF were to take the initiative to place new countries on its NCCT list, the IMF should reconsider its collaborative work in this area. They argued that the IMF's work on compliance with global standards and codes is based on the uniform, voluntary, and cooperative nature of its activities. Moreover, countries may be reluctant to volunteer for reviews if they risk being subjected to sanctions as a consequence. On the other side, a report by the Council on Foreign Relations (2004) has called for reinvesting the FATF with the authority to "name and shame" jurisdictions for falling short in implementing their regimes for combating money laundering and the financing of terrorism.

In India, an anti–money laundering law passed in early 2003 has yet to be fully implemented, and questions have been raised about several ele-

---

34. China and India have been targeted for membership by the FATF and will be subject to FATF-style mutual evaluations if they become members. China has stated (Zhou 2004, 5) that the FATF should be more representative.

35. The United Kingdom set a good example by volunteering to be reviewed under the IMF/World Bank program and allowing publication of the report. The United States also volunteered for a review of its compliance with standards and codes on money laundering and the financing of terrorism, but not for the broader financial-sector assessment program. The review was not carried out, and the United States has since "volunteered" for a FATF mutual assessment, which is much less rigorous.

ments of the Indian AML regime as it is being put in place, among them whether suspicious activity reports will be required or voluntary. Interviews in India for this study suggest that money laundering is not perceived as a major problem there, which may be why motivation is lacking to adopt and implement full-scale global AML standards. For example, drugs are said not to be a problem.[36] The informal money transfer system, though technically illegal for international transactions, is widely used in India because of the country's tight exchange regime and other types of financial controls. But as these controls are in the process of being relaxed, the perception seems to be that whatever problems there might be with money laundering will likely fade away.

Apart from the question of whether countries will willingly subject themselves to AML regime compliance reviews is the question of whether the IMF—known for its tough stands on countries' monetary and fiscal policies—can be equally tough on money laundering. The IMF has leverage only when a country comes to it to request financial assistance, but it is unlikely that improving implementation of an AML regime can be justified as a condition for restoring macroeconomic stability—much less gain the support from IMF member countries necessary for adoption.[37]

Take the example of the Philippines, whose AML regime was cited by the FATF as inadequate, and which was subsequently threatened with countermeasures. Compliance with FATF standards, however, could not realistically have been required of the Philippines for access to IMF resources during 2000–03, when that country had an IMF-supported macroeconomic adjustment program.[38] The link between money laundering and macroeconomic stability is simply not sufficiently well developed to sell such a linkage.

Another example is Vietnam, rated by the INCSR as a country warranting "concern" but not "primary concern" regarding money laundering. An IMF review of the Vietnamese economy in 2003, when the country was operating under an IMF-supported adjustment program, urged passage of "an effective anti–money laundering decree by year-end, followed by rigorous implementation," and also emphasized "the importance of an

---

36. The actual level of drug trafficking in India is extremely difficult to estimate. The UN figures suggest that India has more heroin addicts than any other nation, the combination of a moderate prevalence rate and a huge population, but the estimates are highly conjectural because of the lack of a national survey of drug use.

37. One possible exception might be assistance to failed states, where a case can be made that a substantially improved AML regime could be key to the rehabilitation process, as in the case of Afghanistan outlined earlier in this chapter.

38. Wechsler (2001, 52) does point out, however, that when the United States abstained on a vote on an IMF program for the Philippines in 2000 because of concerns that the country had not fulfilled its previous fiscal, monetary, and financial-sector commitments, the vote was interpreted as a sign of concern about the weak Philippine AML regime.

independent external audit of the central bank in accordance with internationally accepted standards" (IMF 2003b, 4). Vietnam's reluctance to agree to such an audit was holding up an IMF disbursement at the time, and the Fund's support for Vietnam's adjustment program eventually was terminated in April 2004 because of this issue, which had been judged to be central to the IMF's macroeconomic policy concerns.

In sum, the answer to the two questions posed earlier about the effectiveness and improvement associated with the NCCT process is that there has been progress. The global AML regime is now well established, and FATF standards are broadly accepted and have been endorsed by the IMF and World Bank. However, the success rate is far from 100 percent, and effective implementation is difficult both to achieve and to assess.

Conclusion

While the surveys and databases cited in this section have shown some broad connections between global anti–money laundering initiatives and failed states, the major instruments for dealing with such states lie outside the AML regime. At the same time, unless the global AML regime is used proactively as a prevention tool, failing or failed states may become huge gaps in the global AML regime, particularly in the case of large countries such as Nigeria. Moreover, the links between large-scale kleptocracy, money laundering, and the failure of states appear to be stronger than those between garden-variety corruption, money laundering, and state failure. That finding confirms a role for the AML regime in efforts to aid failing and failed states, but it also suggests that the deeper connections between the various global "bads" need to be studied further.

Improving the Global AML Regime

While the initial focus of the US anti–money laundering (AML) regime was the intersection of organized crime and drugs, the focus subsequently widened to include the proceeds from many crimes. Today the AML regime has multiple goals, including those identified throughout this study: reducing the incidence of crime, which includes but is far from limited to drug-related crimes; protecting the integrity of the core financial system; and controlling a number of global "public bads," particularly terrorism, corruption and kleptocracy, and failed states.

From its earliest days, money laundering has frequently involved cross-border transactions, since moving dirty money across borders is an effective way to disguise its trail. With the increased globalization of the financial system, money laundering has evolved into an activity affecting societies and financial systems everywhere in the world. Money laundering is a principal area of abuse of the global financial system—what has been called a dark side of globalization.

Based on our analysis of money laundering and assessment of the global AML regime, this chapter presents conclusions and recommendations for improving the global regime in seven areas: the appropriate scope of the AML regime, the regime as a means to various ends, challenges to US implementation of the AML regime, challenges to global implementation of the regime, opportunities for international cooperation, implications for domestic law enforcement, and a research agenda for an ongoing and comprehensive assessment of the regime as it adjusts to changing conditions.

Scope of the AML Regime

The scope and detail of the US and global AML regimes built up over a period of less than two decades is impressive. If diligently implemented on a global basis, the 2003 Forty Recommendations issued by the Financial Action Task Force will expand the global regime even further, particularly the prevention pillar.

The evolution of the enforcement pillar, with the exception of expanding the number of predicate offenses covered by the AML regime, has been less dramatic. In many jurisdictions enforcement still is minimal. Moreover, as is often true of structures resting on two pillars, there is tension between them including which should receive greater emphasis in implementation.

It is unlikely, and may well be undesirable, that the global AML regime will continue to expand at its recent pace. Even in high-profile areas such as terrorism, there are practical limits to extending the prevention pillar and resource constraints to aggressive use of the enforcement pillar.

Money launderers can be expected to change their tactics in response to enhancements in the global AML regime, so the task of combating money laundering is not likely to get any easier in the years ahead. However, it is reasonable to ask just how much can be expected of governments and the private sector. Constructing a zero-tolerance regime that was consistent with the smooth flow of finance would be costly and politically unacceptable. At the margin, the broadly defined costs of extending the regime are not likely to be worth the modest reduction in money laundering and small contributions to ultimate goals to which such an extension would contribute. The challenge, especially with respect to prevention, is to identify the margin where costs are roughly equal to expected benefits.

The 2003 FATF Forty Recommendations will provide additional challenges in terms of compliance with, and implementation of, the global AML regime. The standard for national regimes has been raised substantially through the explicit extension of the global regime to nonfinancial businesses and certain professions. Applying the basic elements of the prevention pillar (customer due diligence and reporting) to certain professionals such as lawyers and accountants will be resisted, and monitoring and enforcing compliance (supervision and sanctions) will be even more difficult. Almost all jurisdictions will fall short of perfection with respect to design and certainly with respect to implementation.

The issue will be the impact of such shortfalls on overall acceptance of the global regime. For example, if the United States is unwilling to apply the prevention pillar of the AML regime to lawyers and accountants, will this adversely affect US capacity to stiffen controls on terrorist financing? The answer surely is yes, but a sufficient case has not yet been made to overcome US political resistance to applying the prevention pillar more fully to these professions. The examples cited in FATF (2004b, 24–27) of lawyers and accountants acting as "gatekeepers" relate almost exclusively to their direct involvement in facilitating money laundering. As they are already liable for such activities under criminal statutes, little would be gained by subjecting them to due diligence and reporting requirements.

Moreover, the costs that would be imposed by comprehensively extending the AML regime to lawyers, in particular, could be substantial. Law offices would be required to have a compliance officer and to develop mechanisms to implement a customer due diligence (CDD) program, which would involve training and internal and external audits. In addition, many lawyers are solo practitioners or work in small firms with limited financial and technical resources for tracking and linking dispersed information on clients and their activities. Finally, lawyers' insurance requirements no doubt would increase. Since there is no study on the role of lawyers in money laundering in the United States, it is impossible to assess whether the cost of extending the US AML regime to the legal or other professions is worth the benefits. At the very least, however, professional organizations should enhance their educational activities and standards in this area.

Money laundering is likely to evolve over the years in response to technological, economic, and social developments. The AML regime will correspondingly have to be adapted, and that task will be made difficult by the lack of hard information on either the costs or the effectiveness of the regime. Although the financial and nonfinancial costs of the current regime are most likely bearable for advanced economies and large institutions, they loom far larger for less developed economies and smaller institutions. The financial costs for institutions are to a considerable extent fixed, as in the case of having to adapt existing data management systems to meet new reporting requirements. These fixed costs are more difficult for smaller institutions to absorb. The nonfinancial costs are often associated with deadweight losses that are more burdensome for poor countries. In effect, combating money laundering is a luxury good, a reality that argues for increased technical assistance financed by the countries that particularly value the benefits of the AML regime. It also argues for direct financial assistance to countries to increase the probability of effective implementation.

The designers of the AML regime are aware of these circumstances and constraints, at least as they affect decisions involving financial institutions in the major centers. Consistent with the 2003 FATF Forty Recommendations, US authorities have embraced a risk-based approach in several areas. US financial institutions are expected to apply one level of CDD scrutiny to normal customers—having presorted them using a risk-based approach to their actual and potential use of the institution—and a higher level for "politically exposed persons," based essentially on the judgment of the institution. The level of scrutiny applied to potential sources of terrorist financing is higher still, as the authorities require institutions to do name checks for individuals and organizations against lists supplied by the government.

Thus, it is possible to adjust the calibration of the risk-based system. However, the nature and magnitude of the challenge is such that errors will occur. On the one hand, money laundering or terrorist financing will slip into and through the financial system. On the other, individuals will be wrongfully denied access to the financial system or subject to harassing investigations, undermining the self-policing of compliance on which the regime primarily relies. If the AML regime erects excessive barriers for legitimate customers, transaction costs rise, the reputations of businesses are unnecessarily tarnished because of false links to money laundering, and the regime itself comes under stress.

Mariano-Florentino Cuéllar (2003, 453) offers a completely different take on the scope of the US regime and, implicitly, the global one. He argues that the regime's scope—particularly the long list of predicate crimes on which money-laundering charges can be based—is too broad. As a result, law enforcement officials use the AML regime to prosecute those who committed the underlying crime, but are distracted from focusing on the disruption of criminal finance, which he argues was the original intent of US money-laundering legislation. He proposes revising the US money-laundering statutes to provide a much narrower focus.[1]

The Cuéllar position is implicitly predicated on an unsophisticated application of the market model of money-laundering activity and an associated view that there are large numbers of stand-alone money launderers offering their services to criminal networks. The evidence reviewed in chapters 3 and 5 of this study suggests that stand-alone money launderers are the exception rather than the rule. In general, money laundering is an integral part of the underlying offense, or the money launderer is integrated in an overall criminal operation.

Cuéllar (2003, 456) advocates the use of information technology and artificial intelligence to review patterns of wire transfers to create "money profiles" and uncover the operations of criminal finance. But it is questionable whether developing such unique profiles in the transactions of money launderers is even possible. The US Congress Office of Technology Assessment (OTA 1995), whose report Cuéllar cites as supporting his view, is also skeptical. Robert Litan (2004) makes a similar proposal that is more promising as a research project: the US Financial Crime Enforcement Network (FinCEN) could examine a broad range of financial transactions by various types of criminals to look for patterns that could be shared with private-sector institutions and might enhance the detection of money laundering.

If other information were brought to bear in the examination of wire transfers, for example, origins and destinations, then Cuéllar's approach might be more fruitful. But the OTA report notes that this would likely lead

---

1. The National Association of Criminal Defense Lawyers (2001, 1) made a similar proposal to rewrite the US money-laundering statutes. The association is critical of the "alarming expansion" of the scope of those statutes that, as interpreted and applied, subject unwary individuals and businesses to "overreaching investigations and prosecutions unrelated to drug trafficking or organized crime."

to a large number of false positives and raise a host of privacy concerns both domestically and internationally. Even if the technology were available at low cost to provide a passport and vaccination certificate for each dollar that moves through the global economy and the financial system, the suppliers and purchasers of goods and services and the financial system would balk at participating in such a regime. A "Big Brother" approach to money laundering, much less other issues, generally is not acceptable in democratic societies. The US political debate about renewing the USA PATRIOT Act in 2005 illustrates that such an approach is not universally accepted even in the special case of terrorism.

Moreover, if the AML regime becomes overloaded with requirements, pressures will mount to roll it back in all dimensions. In the mid-1990s, the US AML regime was scaled back by Congress with respect to the submission of suspicious activity reports (SARs) in response to criticism that some requirements were excessively burdensome. Cuéllar (2003), among others, advocates trimming the AML regime, and that view has considerable support in the US Congress.

Means to What Ends?

The global AML regime is a means to an end and a tool to be used to help achieve certain goals, but not an end in itself. In the United States as well as many other jurisdictions, the principal initial motivation in criminalizing money laundering was to support the war against illegal drugs and associated criminal gangs.

This rationale was based implicitly on the market model for money-laundering services and the hypothesis that there were large numbers of money launderers, associated with financial institutions, offering their third-party services. The policy implication of this view was that closing down the money launderers would sharply curtail the underlying crime. As economists, we embarked on this study from the same starting point. However, the evidence presented in chapters 3 and 5 suggests that the applicability of an unsophisticated market model to money laundering is limited, and that the hypothesis that there are a substantial number of stand-alone money launderers is not supported.

Nevertheless, the AML regime as it has evolved is employed to pursue a wide range of law enforcement and other social objectives, which has two consequences: first, the regime should be recognized as a policy tool, though only one of many, to achieve those objectives; and second, the AML regime is no longer all about drugs. Recognizing that the AML regime is a means to multiple ends, and not just directed at combating illegal drugs or organized crime, means that assessing its effectiveness depends in part on the particular objective being considered. This study has examined the contribution of the AML regime to three broad objectives: reducing crime, maintaining the integrity of the core financial system, and controlling the global "public bads" of terrorism, corruption and kleptocracy, and failed states. But any assessment is limited at this point because it has to rely on indirect indicators of regime effectiveness. Better indicators can and should be developed, and we discuss some possibilities in the research agenda presented in this chapter. Data constraints aside, however, it should also be pointed out that multiple objectives require multiple indicators. In particular, even if it were possible to measure accurately the aggregate annual volume of money laundering globally, the findings would not adequately represent the precise contribution of the AML regime to combating terrorism, inhibiting the drug trade, discouraging white-collar crime, or protecting the integrity of the core financial system.

Following the money was an important law enforcement tactic long before money laundering was criminalized. However, criminalizing money laundering expands that tactic by enlisting the private sector in the process, and by allowing for targeting stand-alone professional launderers, to the extent that they exist. Criminalization also provides the basis for developing the prevention pillar, which is essential to protecting the integrity of the core financial system.

The prevention pillar has some deterrent effect on certain methods of money laundering, although it also creates incentives for the mutation of the phenomenon. The prevention pillar (most notably the reporting element) provides information for use in investigation, which is part of enforcement. The investigative element operates through several channels: as a primary tool to bring criminals to justice, leading to stand-alone prosecutions; as a secondary tool to expand cases and develop leads with respect to matters and persons already under investigation; and as a tertiary tool where money laundering merely turns up in the course of an investigation and adds to possible charges.

Two policy implications can be drawn from these observations. First, the AML regime can be proactively used to pursue certain objectives, as in sting operations that attract those seeking money-laundering services.[2] And second, to be effective as a law enforcement tool, the AML regime must be a two-way street in which the private sector not only supplies information but also is enlisted to participate in achieving regime objectives.

Both of these policy implications are controversial, particularly the latter. The private sector does not always welcome being coopted by government, yet cooperation by private-sector institutions is often essential to success. For its part, law enforcement often is reluctant to take private businesses into its confidence out of fear of damaging its case either prior to or during the prosecutorial stage. Given the extent to which the AML regime already relies on the quasi-voluntary cooperation of various private-sector institu-

---

2. Cuéllar (2003) implicitly endorses a proactive AML strategy, and James (2002, 6) takes a similar position.

tions, US law enforcement authorities would likely best serve anti–money laundering efforts by cooperating more closely with the private sector, particularly when it comes to providing more information about what they are looking for and why.

Implementation Challenges for the United States

The United States has taken the lead in developing and establishing the global AML regime, recognizing that money laundering is inherently not only an issue without borders but, more importantly, one for which borders can impede progress. US authorities reached this conclusion in part as a result of efforts to level the international playing field for US financial institutions whose assistance is critical to effectively combat money laundering.

The United States faces several challenges going forward, including implementing the 2003 FATF Forty Recommendations, determining the future of the National Money Laundering Strategy (NMLS), and maintaining its global leadership role.

FATF Forty Recommendations

The 2003 FATF Forty Recommendations appear at first not to require a great deal from the United States, but issues lurk below the surface in at least two areas: application of the prevention regime to certain professionals (particularly lawyers and accountants), and the treatment of special purpose vehicles.

Many nations and territories face challenges from certain professions that have banded together globally to resist participation in the AML regime at the level recommended by the FATF. Resistance in the United States is likely to be particularly acute because of the interplay of privacy issues and the regulatory structure of the US federal system. Regulation and (limited) supervision of professionals occurs largely at the state level, which in part explains why the accounting profession has until recently been lightly controlled.[3] Regardless of current US arrangements, the fact that these professions will be included at least on a pro forma basis in regimes in other jurisdictions poses a problem for the United States.

The second issue for the United States with respect to the FATF Forty Recommendations involves the establishment and role of shell corpora-

---

3. Lawyers also have generally been regulated by the states, but federalism is not an absolute barrier to federal regulation in the financial area. Much federal financial law explicitly preempts state law, and even where it does not, the federal banking supervisors and, to a lesser extent, the Securities and Exchange Commission have effectively preempted the states. In addition, the recent Sarbanes-Oxley legislation imposed a regulatory regime on lawyers representing corporations as a matter of federal securities law.

tions and special purpose vehicles at home (i.e., Nevada or Delaware) or abroad (i.e., the Cayman Islands or Bermuda) as part of a US business or financial structure, as well as ongoing pressure from some other jurisdictions for greater transparency as regards such arrangements. Authorities in many European jurisdictions favor the imposition of CDD and reporting requirements on such entities.[4] This issue involves the philosophy and the structure of regulation. In the United States, the structure, again, is one where the presumption is that matters are left to the states, and increased federal involvement requires jumping political and constitutional hurdles. The philosophy of regulation in the United States is one of limited regulation at every level—an activity is legal unless it has been decided it is illegal. In contrast, in many other nations with fully developed financial sectors, such as those in continental Europe, the philosophy is more along the lines that nothing is legal unless government has approved it.

The global AML regime associated with the 2003 FATF Forty Recommendations has relatively weak supervision and sanction elements in its prevention pillar, but they are there. The International Monetary Fund (IMF) and World Bank will evaluate performance under the new standards. The FATF has reserved the possibility of resuming its "name and shame" role. If the United States is found to have a low level of compliance, its capacity to exert leadership in this area will be adversely affected. Mark Pieth and Gemma Aiolfi (2003) have criticized both the United States and the United Kingdom for uneven application of the previous FATF Forty Recommendations.

National Money Laundering Strategy

The US Congress in 1998 mandated the annual development and publication of a *National Money Laundering Strategy* (NMLS) by the executive branch via an interagency process for five years, ending in 2003. Should the mandate be renewed?

On balance, the NMLS was a constructive instrument to focus executive branch attention and, more importantly, promote better interagency cooperation on money-laundering issues. On the other hand, it was far from successful in molding an integrated and coherent approach to money laundering, which must ultimately be based on a firm foundation of research and analysis. The preparation of annual national strategies on money laundering should be reauthorized, but with several important modifications

---

4. Some US observers express similar views. Wechsler (2001) flagged the issue of Delaware corporations, and Jack Blum, a prominent voice on such matters, has called for national registration of corporations that identifies where they can be served with civil and criminal process. In addition, a Financial Stability Forum (FSF 2000) report on offshore financial centers focused attention on the need to better identify the beneficial owners of corporate vehicles established in those jurisdictions as part of the effort to enhance financial stability and fight financial fraud.

to encourage more analytical content, less wheel spinning, and greater continuity.[5] We offer the following four recommendations with respect to a revised NMLS mandate:

- A strategy document should be developed and publicly presented every third year, with annual updates on progress. Annual strategies tend to be wheel-spinning exercises. No sooner is the production cycle for the last document completed than the cycle for the next one must begin. The achievements of the previous strategy will not yet be manifest, however, so the next strategy will likely have a defensive air to it. Furthermore, money laundering is not such a rapidly evolving activity as to require annual adjustments in the AML regime. The annual progress updates can include amendments as needed in connection with any changes in emphasis, as in the case of the shift to focusing on terrorist financing in the wake of the September 11 attack.

- A review of progress during the period in achieving previously identified goals, which appeared only once in the previous five NMLS, should be institutionalized. The constructive precedent in 2002 was not followed in the 2003 NMLS, except for an appendix on online terrorist financing that had been identified as an objective in 2002.

- The NMLS should include and report analytical work on money laundering, which is essential to developing a transparent and defensible policy. The 2001 and 2002 NMLS contained more analytical material than the previous two strategies or the one that followed. Rigorous analysis enhances communication, and an important role of the NMLS is as a communication device not just between the executive and legislative branches but also with the general public and the world at large.

- Oversight hearings should be employed systematically in connection with the NMLS and its annual updates on progress. Hearings enhance communication among the branches of government and promote interagency cooperation, which is a chronic problem in dealing with issues as complex as the AML regime.

Global Leadership

Although the United States has been a driving force in shaping the global AML regime, continuing in that leadership role will require addressing a number of challenges in the years ahead. The first concerns the issues raised above with respect to leading by example in complying with the 2003 FATF Forty Recommendations. The power of persuasion depends in

---

5. This position is similar to that found in General Accounting Office (2003a), although we reached our conclusions via a somewhat different route.

part on a demonstrated commitment to global norms, even those that may not be at the top of the US list of priorities. To the extent that the US authorities are unable or unwilling to implement FATF recommendations regarding the legal and accounting professions, shell corporations, and special purpose vehicles, the United States will have to explain and justify its position. One useful step in this regard would be for US authorities to articulate that they are open to expanding the US AML regime in these areas once it is demonstrated that there are substantial net benefits.

A related aspect of this challenge is whether the United States is willing to follow the United Kingdom and submit to a full assessment of its financial-sector regulation by the IMF and World Bank, including its compliance with international standards in the area of money laundering. The United States did volunteer for a review of its compliance with the old FATF Forty Recommendations and the Eight Special Recommendations on terrorist financing as part of the IMF/World Bank pilot program. The United States has since volunteered for the FATF assessment of its regime, a review that would employ the revised methodology endorsed by the FATF, IMF, and World Bank.[6] However, this type of review would not result in a formal assessment or rating of the US regime, but rather only a report on US compliance with the FATF 40 + 8 recommendations.

The United States has argued, with some merit, that scarce IMF/World Bank resources to conduct such full assessments should be devoted to other countries where risks to the global AML regime are greater. On the other hand, the United States is in a position to set an example for the rest of the world by submitting to the review, yet has elected not to do so. Moreover, a case can be made that money laundering is substantial in the United States and should receive special attention as part of the global AML regime. Because of the central role of the US financial system, as well as the role of the US dollar as a medium of exchange and a standard of value in the global financial system, many if not most criminals want the proceeds of their crimes ultimately to be in dollars and potentially integrated into the US economy, even if the crimes were committed in other jurisdictions. The United States should reconsider its position and volunteer for a full IMF/ World Bank assessment of its financial sector.

A second challenge to US global AML leadership is the choice of priorities. Over the past three years, the United States, understandably, has emphasized combating terrorism financing but has not garnered as much global support as it might have hoped (chapter 7). Terrorism financing is not the top priority of most countries' AML regimes, and many of these regimes are supported by very limited resources. Some countries may prefer to concentrate on extending the global regime to cover accountants, smuggling, or tax evasion. Those efforts, even if they do not match US pri-

---

6. In the meantime, the US Treasury Web site has posted previous self-assessments of US compliance with FATF standards on combating money laundering and terrorism financing.

orities, warrant increased bilateral and multilateral technical assistance. The United States, along with other major countries, should consider stepping up such assistance to jurisdictions that are struggling to establish or implement their regimes.

A related third challenge to US global AML leadership involves the frequent criticism that the US regime is overly selective in the list of foreign predicate crimes that qualify as money-laundering offenses under US law. For example, the 2003 FATF Forty Recommendations designates 20 categories of high-priority offenses that should be covered by national money-laundering statutes. However, seven of those offenses related to money laundering—including sexual exploitation, trafficking in human beings, and counterfeiting—cannot be prosecuted in the United States if the underlying crime was committed abroad.

Foreign or domestic tax evasion—other than failure to pay US taxes on the proceeds of a crime—also does not qualify as an underlying crime for US prosecution as a money-laundering offense. While US prosecutors can work around this lacuna and do not regard it as an impediment to an effective US AML regime, the absence of foreign tax evasion as a predicate offense under US law is often cited as impeding international cooperation.[7] Latin American leaders, for example, often complain privately that while the US insists on cooperation on issues it considers important, the US itself often fails to cooperate on issues of importance to other countries, such as evasion of taxes on income from assets held abroad. In this context, the US policy becomes a barrier to leadership. Thus, US law should be changed to make tax evasion, whether in the United States or elsewhere, a predicate offense for money-laundering prosecution.

The United States also needs to be more forthcoming in helping to enforce the tax laws of other countries. The interaction of capital flight and tax evasion is a particular problem where governments have difficulty raising adequate revenues to finance their expenditures, resulting in a run-up of unsustainable stocks of sovereign debt to foreign as well as domestic holders. Though macroeconomic policy failures in Latin American countries and elsewhere often provide substantial inducement for capital flight, the United States also is regarded as one of the world's leading tax havens, which contributes to fiscal problems in other countries. US critics counter that many countries' tax laws are flawed, but what country's are not, to one extent or another? A compromise approach might be to condition increased US cooperation in the tax area on criteria that apply to the structure and efficiency of the other country's tax system. For example, the criteria might address the balance between direct and indirect taxes, or the maximum tax rate applied to earned income. One should not be too sanguine about the

---

7. Such criticism is not directed only at the United States. An IMF (2001, 24) review of Cyprus as an offshore financial center observed that international cooperation would be strengthened if Cyprus were to clarify that tax evasion is an offense under its money-laundering laws and regulations.

chances of agreement on mutually acceptable criteria, but the effort might produce some positive results over time and reinforce the willingness of other countries to cooperate with the United States on money laundering in general, and the financing of terrorism in particular.

Chapters 4 and 7 explained how the legal framework of the AML regime aimed at kleptocrats is in its infancy, especially with regard to enforcement. The United States should ratify the new UN Convention Against Corruption (United Nations 2003b) to accelerate the development process, and implement streamlined procedures (which might require changes in US laws) to facilitate cooperation with other countries in freezing, confiscating, and returning the assets of kleptocrats to the home countries from which they stole them.

Global Implementation Challenges

Even if one accepts the premise that expansion of the global AML regime will slow in the years ahead, the regime still will have to be regularly adjusted, in part to address the continually changing mechanisms of money laundering and the tactics of those needing to launder the proceeds of their crimes. The FATF's mandate was renewed in May 2004 for another eight years. While it is premature to speculate about when the Forty Recommendations should again be revised, it is reasonable to expect that adjustments and a new set of recommendations will be required at some point in the future. What is significant and disturbing about the announcement of the renewal of the FATF's mandate is that it made no mention either of the importance of research on, or ongoing assessments of the costs and benefits of, an effective anti–money laundering regime.

In the meantime, the principal global issue is implementation of the AML regime on the basis of the 2003 FATF Forty Recommendations. Monitoring compliance with global AML standards has been largely turned over to the IMF and World Bank following a common methodology worked out with the FATF (chapters 4 and 7). This transfer of responsibility has the benefit that reviews are now conducted by organizations with near-universal membership, rather than by a self-selected group of countries that may be reluctant to render frank criticism of fellow members.

On the other hand, while peer pressure, transparency, and accountability are enhanced by the involvement of the IMF and World Bank, the fact that their mandates are far more diffuse has substantially reduced the capacity to apply meaningful leverage, as compared with a process that was exclusively run by the FATF. It is unrealistic to presume that money laundering will rise to the level of importance of fiscal, monetary, exchange rate, and banking policies in connection with IMF support for member countries' economic programs (chapter 7).

A clear challenge ahead to the global AML regime will be to balance the role of the FATF, as the standard-setting body, with the involvement of the international financial institutions. Countries that some members of the IMF and World Bank might see as candidates for peer pressure in terms of improving their AML regime compliance with international standards may not be seen as candidates by other member nations or by the managements of those institutions.

A related international challenge lies in the scope and utility of sanctions invoked against countries that do not comply with the global regime. As noted in chapter 7, experience with the FATF's Non-Cooperative Countries and Territories (NCCT) initiative has generally been positive, but not completely successful or without controversy. In response to the initiative's "name and shame" approach, about 70 percent of jurisdictions with initial shortcomings have brought their AML regimes into better alignment with international norms. Only Nauru and Myanmar/Burma have been quarantined. Although the process has not yet been fully effective in convincing Nauru to mend its ways or in shutting down Nauru as a host to money launderers, some improvements have been made. Nauru's role in money laundering appears to have been reduced if not eliminated, but it never was large! Myanmar/Burma has made even less progress.

An issue for the global system going forward is to develop criteria upon which similar sanctions can be imposed on other jurisdictions. Is it realistic to expect that such sanctions can in fact be imposed on jurisdictions that are more relevant to the international financial system than the two countries sanctioned to date? How will such countries as Indonesia, Nigeria, and the Philippines respond to pressures from the FATF, and what will the FATF do if their response is inadequate? Will the FATF try to add other countries to its list of uncooperative jurisdictions and incur the displeasure of at least some members of the IMF and World Bank? The standard for noncooperation will have to be raised substantially for this to happen.

This is an issue regarding which one must consider carrots as well as sticks. The concept of mutual recognition of the AML regimes of other countries—or at least institutions from other countries that have passed their FATF examinations or IMF/World Bank reviews—deserves more consideration than it received in the 2003 FATF Forty Recommendations or under the USA PATRIOT Act. As noted repeatedly in this chapter already, serious consideration should be given to increased technical and financial assistance to countries trying to establish and implement national AML regimes on the basis of international standards.

International Cooperation

The AML regime serves multiple though generally concordant goals, despite different emphases in different jurisdictions. Conflicts do sometimes arise as a result of different regulatory philosophies and issues regarding the allocation of limited resources.

International cooperation is often a challenge not only because of differences in AML regimes but because of differences across countries with respect to the structure and development of their financial systems. For example, the limited role of retail banking for both households and small businesses in Switzerland leads to less emphasis on the formal ex ante CDD aspects of the prevention pillar for Swiss banks and greater emphasis on identifying actual money-laundering operations through a cooperative relationship among financial institutions and the authorities.

The issue of limited resources is relevant both to choosing objectives for the global AML regime and determining to which of those selected objectives to allocate scarce governmental or private resources. Limiting money laundering was a high-profile public good in the United States even before September 11, 2001, but today it is still regarded as an unaffordable luxury good in some other jurisdictions.

Developing countries, in particular, are sometimes ambivalent about creating or giving priority to AML efforts. Brent Bartlett (2002) points out three common reasons why: (1) money laundering brings funds from developed economies to developing economies; (2) the crimes that generate the funds occur in developed rather than developing countries; and (3) money laundering adds to the demand for banking services in developing countries. Bartlett argues that that the data do not support any of these statements, that money laundering undermines confidence in the financial system, and that developing countries in general share a broad interest in an effective AML regime. Nevertheless, it is safe to say that reducing global "public bads" is not a high priority for many of these countries, which often are unattractive to begin with as locations for financial transactions because of a lack of integrity of domestic financial institutions. For countries with weak financial systems—as evidenced by extensive use of informal value transfer mechanisms—money laundering may seem a minor problem compared to inadequate supervision of lending practices or tracking of nonperforming loans. The sophisticated human and organizational resources required to create an effective AML regime are particularly scarce in such countries, which is one reason why the IMF and World Bank have been encouraged to develop technical assistance programs to help them develop those resources.[8]

It is an article of faith to the authorities in industrial countries that all nations need to have effective AML regimes, but resources are scarce. The global threat posed by weaknesses in poor countries may be quite minor, and complete convergence of national AML regimes is not necessary to achieve an effective global regime. The trick is to identify weaknesses that need to be addressed and regimes that need to be upgraded before they become major problems for the system as a whole.

---

8. The World Bank (2003a) and IMF have developed a reference guide for that purpose.

Having effective AML regimes in poor or small jurisdictions identified as offshore financial centers (OFCs) is particularly important to the global system. The IMF has identified 44 such countries and territories, most of which are classified as developing. These jurisdictions need unimpeded links to mainstream financial centers—even if it reduces their attractiveness to some investors. Thus, an AML regime that is certified by the FATF and international financial institutions is a critical asset. The rapid response of the Cayman Islands and most other OFC jurisdictions to the FATF's designation of them as uncooperative suggests that they understand the importance of cooperation.

Achieving a better alignment of national regimes with the global regime is complex. Russia struggled to align its AML legislation with global standards because of a desire to include broad and vaguely defined economic crimes within the ambit of its law, in part out of concern about capital flight. Chinese authorities have articulated a similar position in the context of the release of money-laundering rules by the People's Bank of China (*Financial Times*, January 14, 2003). India sees money laundering principally as an activity induced by capital and exchange controls, which it is slowly dismantling.

Continued progress in developing the global AML regime also will require better alignment of predicate offenses internationally. The 2003 FATF Forty Recommendations include a roadmap for cooperation with a list of core offenses, but there are important omissions.

Greater and ongoing international cooperation also is needed to forge consensus on global strategies that can adequately serve the disparate needs of the global community. Intensified efforts since September 2001 to combat the financing of terrorism illustrate both the potential for focusing the tools of the AML regime on particular objectives and the pitfalls associated with a failure to recognize that some countries consider other objectives to be of equal or greater importance.

One relatively weak test of international cooperation on money laundering will be the UN Convention Against Corruption (United Nations 2003b). To be effective, the convention must be ratified by the major nations, many of which will have to change their domestic legislation and then actually implement the convention's provisions, in particular its asset recovery provisions.

The enforcement pillar of the global AML regime, often constrained by tensions and differences between national criminal justice systems, will also have to evolve in the years ahead. For example, more fully streamlined modalities of information sharing in money-laundering cases should be established between law enforcement authorities to replace the cumbersome multistep processes of existing multilateral assistance arrangements that require the use of diplomatic channels. Global standards with respect to asset freezes and forfeitures are also needed so that such actions are not only internationally coordinated but also comprehensive in their effect. A third area where progress is needed is extradition. International agreement is needed to streamline procedures in connection with certain money-laundering offenses, perhaps those 20 designated by the FATF to be particularly important. Members of the European Union are considering implementing such procedures in connection with a specified list of crimes.

Consideration should also be given to producing a global equivalent of the US State Department's *International Narcotics Control Strategy Report* (INCSR) on money laundering. Although the INCSR identifies nations that the US believes have major money-laundering problems, the principal concern is with money laundering that facilitates drug trafficking. The report correctly states that this cannot be separated from money laundering problems more generally. Nonetheless, the INCSR presents a US perspective, whereas a periodic report from an international agency—such as the United Nations Office on Drugs and Crime, which has itself no actual regulatory responsibility—that rated nations in terms of the extent and nature of their money-laundering problems might serve a useful global educative function and support better analysis of money laundering and its control.[9] The ratings could draw on but be separate from IMF/World Bank reviews and FATF mutual assessments.

Domestic Law Enforcement

Regulation and supervision alone can do much to keep financial institutions clean of money laundering. Chapter 6 showed that the global AML regime has been quite effective in meeting this goal with respect to the core financial systems of the major financial centers. However, this success will tend to push money laundering to other less regulated and supervised channels, which in turn points to the importance of effective law enforcement cooperation across the global AML regime.

Unfortunately, it is difficult to judge the effectiveness of current money-laundering investigations because assessment of the enforcement pillar lags that of the prevention pillar, perhaps inevitably, since the former requires much more detailed knowledge of the underlying reality. Still, enforcement assessments have not even been attempted, so definitively determining their feasibility is difficult. Even the greater focus on law enforcement envis-

---

9. Winer (2002) proposes that the United Nations establish a "white list" of financial institutions committed to the global AML regime that have passed rigorous reviews of their compliance with and implementation of AML standards. Once on the white list, they would become exclusively eligible to receive and manage funds from the United Nations and other international organizations. This proposal apparently has received little attention since it was put forward two years ago. The cost of the administrative apparatus it proposes might exceed the benefits to the AML regime as a whole, but such a proposal nevertheless represents the type of imaginative thinking on international cooperation that warrants consideration.

aged in the 2003 FATF Forty Recommendations centers around organization and resources, which are important but do not emphasize results.

Money-laundering convictions in the United States average no more than 2,000 annually, even on a generous measure. Given the suspected scope of the activity, this suggests that money laundering is not a very risky activity, particularly when one considers that most convicted launderers are associated with sums of less than $1 million. A very speculative estimate of the risk of conviction faced by money launderers is about 5 percent annually. However, some who provide money-laundering services may only be convicted on other charges, probably related to the predicate offenses that can generate longer sentences.[10] This may be the result of plea bargaining or of a decision to bring only the charges with the longest sentences. Thus, there is no way to measure the actual risk a money launderer faces of going to prison. US seizures and forfeitures of $700 million annually suggest that either a trivial fraction of laundered money is seized, or that much less is laundered than is indicated by official statements about the scale of the activity.

Interviews with both former and current law enforcement officials suggest that the existing regulatory system and the information it generates is not well used in prosecutions. The US Customs and Internal Revenue Services use suspicious activity reports skillfully for specialized purposes, but the reports are rarely used to initiate investigations; instead they are used as additional information for making a case that has originated with another type of lead. Indeed, apart from sting operations, money laundering is rarely the initial offense for an investigation. Some knowledgeable observers have described the sting operations of the early 1990s, when a number of drug traffickers were brought down employing such techniques, as the heyday of money-laundering investigations. But they add that the culture of the major federal law enforcement organizations has since become less hospitable to making money laundering a central investigative focus. The deemphasis of drug investigations has apparently led to less commitment to money-laundering expertise in some key law enforcement organizations. The shift in focus by federal enforcement to countering terrorism financing also has likely been at the expense of more general money-laundering investigations.

However, the reduced emphasis on large-volume money-laundering operations also may reflect the training and orientation of the federal law enforcement community. Money laundering is complex and often difficult to follow for anyone without highly specialized knowledge of finance, and relatively few agents and prosecutors are in a position to acquire the skills necessary to pursue such cases. This is not a problem that can be solved

---

10. Cuéllar (2003) provides some evidence that prosecutors tend to pursue the easier money-laundering charges for low-level perpetrators rather than the more-difficult-to-establish charges for the underlying crime or major financing networks.

with a simple recommendation, but we do believe that finding a way to give more priority to money laundering as the initiating offense, and making better use of the existing SAR database, could improve the effectiveness of the AML regime in fighting crime.

The federal government, of course, has often run undercover money-laundering operations, sometimes to considerable investigative effect. However, these operations pose two interesting problems that have received little attention. First, in order to generate business, agents offer low-priced money-laundering services, which may drive down prices and thus actually facilitate laundering. This is a theoretical possibility and a difficult one to investigate, since it depends on how well the market actually operates. The market effect may well be insignificant, but it is a concern that should nevertheless be explicitly addressed when setting up these operations. Second, the operations do facilitate, temporarily at least, the workings of criminal enterprises. To catch senior drug dealers in Operation Polar Cap, a sting operation in the mid-1980s, federal agents allowed large amounts of money to be laundered successfully back to Panama. The trade-offs in terms of the targets apprehended may well be reasonable, but again these are issues that warrant explicit consideration and assessment.

Research Agenda

One clear finding of this study is that there has been little research on either money laundering or the anti–money laundering regime. The law enforcement community simply does not use the types of systematic measurements of inputs and outputs necessary to allocate scarce enforcement resources effectively.

The multiple goals and complex cost considerations of the AML regime point to the potential of using the cost-effectiveness of AML enforcement as a framework to assess the regime. The implied outcome measure is the cost of law enforcement with an AML regime in place as compared to the cost of enforcement without it. While it would be difficult to assemble the information necessary to estimate this difference in any formal sense—"experimenting" per se is impossible, and the effects of the regime on costs are too subtle to be measured—such an approach suggests at least at the conceptual level the value of obtaining data on the number of cases in which money-laundering controls generated valuable information, or provided the legal basis for conviction and incarceration, and on the costs of those controls.

Empirical research on money laundering is even more challenging than for most other criminal activities. There are no victimization surveys of the kind that allow measurement of the volume of other white-collar crimes. Population surveys that provide so much insight into drug distribution and other consensual crimes are unlikely to provide much information about the narrow set of participants involved in money laundering, most of whom are often closely linked to, if not part of, the crimes.

Nevertheless, the AML regime ought to be susceptible to research. Formidable bureaucratic obstacles arise from the complex structure of law enforcement, which involves multiple agencies that are parts of different cabinet departments, each with its own mission, expertise, and data systems. Data do not travel easily across such bureaucratic landscapes.

An active AML research program will not resolve every issue at hand, but six broad recommendations for a research agenda are offered below.

1. Create a Database of Detected Money-Laundering Transactions

A great deal of information can be gathered about money laundering through compilation of investigations in various countries. However, this information has yet to be systematically assembled into a searchable and researchable database. A starting point for money-laundering studies should be the creation of just such a database that contains all the investigative information, as has been done over the past 30 years in the study of terrorism by organizations such as the RAND Corporation (e.g., Fowler 1981). For each transaction, data would be available inter alia on the predicate offense, the price paid to the launderer and the total cost of laundering to the customer, the stages of money laundering covered by the transaction, and the characteristics of the customer and the provider.

The database would not constitute a representative sample of money-laundering operations, but rather the results of investigative decisions. Having such data available, however, would facilitate analyses of how prices vary across transactions, how they have changed over time for particular kinds of transactions, and how the patterns of utilization of different institutions vary across countries, offenses, and time. The results would only be suggestive, but nevertheless would provide insights that are currently not available.

2. Track Usage of Suspicious Activity Reports

The suspicious activity reporting system in the United States has expanded over time, particularly since the mid-1990s, and now represents a substantial effort by both the government and the private sector. The SARs database contains a vast amount of information assembled at considerable expense. The risk of information overload is real and substantial, and some argue that the system is essentially dysfunctional—valuable warnings and leads are lost, mislaid, or overlooked. No US agency has yet assessed how effective SARs are in contributing to the arrest and conviction of money launderers, or to achieving the specific goals of the AML regime such as combating terrorism financing. The GAO has tried to arrive at an assessment but has been unable to do so.

To be useful, the SARs database needs to be made available to many agencies that have neither the incentive nor the means to provide FinCEN with feedback about the outcome of their use of the information. For example, a particular SAR may be just one of many pieces of evidence that lead to a conviction many months if not years after the initial SARs database query. The inquiry may be initiated by one agency, but the information is passed on to another that then uses it to obtain a conviction.

Creating a system to report all successful uses of SARs is a daunting and expensive task. Universal reporting on outcomes may not be necessary, however; periodic targeted studies might be sufficient. A sample of queries could be followed up and traced to the end of the initial investigation, or a sample of cases involving crimes likely to be related to money laundering could be examined to determine whether and how SARs played a role in the convictions.[11]

Given the continued pressure to expand the range of institutions required to report suspicious activities, an effort must be made to assess whether the system does in fact produce enforcement information of sufficient value to justify that expansion. Without getting into specific details of the appropriate investigative approach for such a study, it might lead to improving the design of the SAR system in terms of the identification, selection, and coverage of information that is worth gathering.

3. Sponsor Research

More sponsored research on money laundering and how to improve the AML regime is needed at the national and international levels. In the United States, research funds should be earmarked in the budgets of the principal agencies responsible for the AML regime (the Homeland Security, Justice, and Treasury Departments). Research program design and results should be subject to outside evaluation, with a strong presumption that the results will be published. Other agencies responsible for supervision of the financial system, such as the Federal Reserve and the Securities and Exchange Commission, should be encouraged to have parallel programs.

At the international level, the FATF, IMF, and World Bank should support cooperative research programs.

4. Maintain a Scorecard on Core Financial System Integrity

Short of developing a more complete database of money-laundering cases, supervisory authorities should at least regularly assess (perhaps every two years) the extent to which money laundering threatens the integrity of the core financial system. If necessary, law enforcement authorities in the United States and other countries could assist in carrying out such reviews.

---

11. Gold and Levi (1994) conducted such analyses using data from the United Kingdom, which has made more progress with assessing SARs than has the United States.

Chapter 6 provided a prototype for this type of research project. Cases that involve core financial institutions should be classified into categories based on whether there was institutional solicitation, solicitation by a rogue officer, or unwitting participation or negligence. Cases should then be cross-classified by the size of the financial institutions involved. This exercise would provide an initial baseline against which subsequent reviews could assess progress of the AML regime in protecting the integrity of the core financial system. The results of these assessments should be published.

5. Measure AML Regime Costs

A major shortcoming of the AML regime is the lack of hard data on what it costs. Chapter 4 drew on the limited literature available and attempted to come up with a rough estimate of the gross financial costs of the US regime, including costs to taxpayers incurred by government, costs imposed on financial and nonfinancial businesses and institutions, and costs for customers. Former US Treasury Secretary Paul O'Neill was right to push for work on this topic, and it is unfortunate that he was not more successful. Developing more and better data on AML regime costs should be part of an overall research program.

6. Use Economic Modeling

While the first five suggestions for the research agenda have emphasized empirical research, establishing a firm empirical basis for decisions about the AML regime also requires developing models of money laundering. Theoretical economists have begun to work in this area, but at a very aggregate level that reflects only the most schematic knowledge of money laundering (Masciandaro 1999; Masciandaro and Portolano 2002; and Mauro 2002).

Also needed is a microeconomic research agenda that examines such elements of money-laundering analysis as the market model for laundering services, as well as how the activity might respond to different kinds of regulations and other interventions. The theoretical research could be strengthened by the empirical analyses recommended above.

Final Comments

The global regime that has been constructed to combat money laundering is as complex as the phenomenon itself, in part because of the regime's multiple goals, but also because of institutional and attitudinal differences across countries. These circumstances will continue to shape the international regime and strategies to control money laundering.

With the 2003 revision of the FATF Forty Recommendations on money laundering and the relatively recent promulgation of the Eight Special

Recommendations on Terrorist Financing, the global AML system confronts new challenges with respect to compliance, implementation, and sanctions. Even the United States, one of the principal architects of the AML regime, is unlikely to comply fully with the letter of the new FATF framework. To ensure an effective strategy going forward, the United States should submit to a full IMF review of its financial sector, including review of its anti–money laundering and terrorism financing policies. In addition, the United States should expand the list of foreign offenses that can lead to US money-laundering prosecutions to include tax evasion as well as other serious crimes not now covered and step up cooperation with other jurisdictions on actions against corruption and kleptocracy.

Different countries have different AML priorities, but cooperation is essential to achieve an effective overall global strategy. Ratification and effective implementation of the UN Convention Against Corruption will be a test for the AML system as a whole. The global AML regime clearly needs further development and promulgation of anti–money laundering strategies at the international as well as national levels. Cooperation with the private sector also should be enhanced, and more technical and financial assistance should be made available to poorer jurisdictions.

At present, there is no empirical base to assess the effectiveness of the current AML regime in terms of suppressing money laundering and the predicate crimes that generate it. Sifting of the limited available information suggests that the global AML regime has made progress in the general area of prevention, but without much effect on the incidence of underlying crimes. Critics argue that the regime has done little more than force money launderers to change their methods. Felons' lives are a bit more difficult and a few more are caught, but there is little change in the extent and character of either laundering or crime. Critics may well be right. To rebut such charges and continue to expand, the AML regime needs to demonstrate progress toward its announced goals. The research agenda set out in this study, if implemented conscientiously along with the other recommendations made here, could contribute substantially to further progress in combating money laundering for many years to come.

References

ABA (American Bar Association) Task Force on Gatekeeper Regulation and the Profession. 2003a. *Report to the House of Delegates*. Photocopy (February).

ABA (American Bar Association) Task Force on Gatekeeper Regulation and the Profession. 2003b. *Response to the Advance Notice of Proposed Rulemaking and Request for Comments*. Photocopy (June 9).

Abt, Vicki, James F. Smith, and Eugene Martin Christiansen. 1985. *The Business of Risk: Commercial Gambling in Mainstream America*. Lawrence, KS: University of Kansas Press.

Association of Certified Fraud Examiners. 2002. *2002 Report to the Nation on Occupational Fraud and Abuse*. Austin, TX. Photocopy.

Bartlett, Brent. 2002. The Negative Effects of Money Laundering on Economic Development. *Platypus Magazine* 77: 18–23.

Basel Committee on Banking Supervision. 1988. Prevention of Criminal Use of the Banking System for the Purpose of Money-Laundering. Basel: Basel Committee on Banking Supervision.

Basel Committee on Banking Supervision. 2001. Customer Due Diligence for Banks. Basel Committee Publications 85. Basel: Basel Committee on Banking Supervision.

Bell, R. E. 2001. Discretion and Decision Making in Money Laundering Prosecutions. *Journal of Money Laundering Control* 5, no. 1: 42–51.

Bell, R.E. 2003. The Confiscation, Forfeiture, and Disruption of Terrorist Finances. *Journal of Money Laundering Control* 7, no. 2: 105–25.

BIS (Bank for International Settlements). 2004. International Banking and Financial Market Developments. *Quarterly Review* (March).

Blades, Derek, and David Roberts. 2002. *Measuring the Non-observed Economy Statistics*. OECD Brief 5. Paris: Organization for Economic Cooperation and Development.

Board of Governors of the Federal Reserve System. 2002. *Report to Congress in Accordance with Section 356(c) of the USA PATRIOT Act*. Washington: Board of Governors of the Federal Reserve System.

Bourgois, Philippe. 1995. *In Search of Respect: Selling Crack in El Barrio*. New York: Cambridge University Press.

Buencamino, Leonides, and Sergei Gorbunov. 2002. *Informal Money Transfer Systems: Opportunities and Challenges for Development Finance*. United Nations Department of Economic and Social Affairs (DESA) Discussion Paper 26. November.

Bureau of Justice Statistics. 2003. *Money Laundering Offenders, 1994–2001*. Washington: Bureau of Justice Statistics.

Byrne, John J. 2004. Improving Financial Oversight: A Private Sector View of Anti–Money Laundering Efforts. Testimony on behalf of the American Bankers Association before the House Financial Services Subcommittee on Oversight and Investigations. Photocopy (May 18).

Calzaroni, Manlio. 2001. The Exhaustiveness of Production Estimates: New Concepts and Methodologies. Organization for Economic Cooperation and Development, Paris. Photocopy.

Camdessus, Michel. 1998. Speech to the Financial Action Task Force. Paris.

Caprio, Gerald, and Patrick Honohan. 2001. *Finance for Growth: Policy Choices in a Volatile World*. New York: Oxford University Press for the World Bank.

Carlson, Kenneth, Herbert Weisberg, and Naomi Goldstein. 1984. *Unreported Taxable Income from Selected Illegal Activities*. Cambridge. MA: Abt Associates, Inc.

CCBE (Council of the Bars and Law Societies of the European Union). 2003. Joint Statement by the International Legal Profession on the Fight Against Money Laundering. www. ccbe.org/doc/En/signed_statement_030403_en.pdf.

Center for Global Development. *On the Brink: Weak States and US National Security*. A Report of the Commission on Weak States and US National Security. Washington: Center for Global Development.

Council on Foreign Relations. 2002. *Terrorist Financing*. New York: Council on Foreign Relations.

Council on Foreign Relations. 2004. *Update on the Global Campaign Against Terrorist Financing*. New York: Council on Foreign Relations.

Cuéllar, Mariano-Florentino. 2003. The Tenuous Relationship Between the Fight against Money Laundering and the Disruption of Criminal Finance. *The Journal of Criminal Law and Criminology* 93: 312–466.

Da Vanzo, J., J. Hawes-Dawson, R. B. Valdez, and G. Vernez. 1994. *Surveying Immigrant Communities: Policy Imperatives and Technical Challenges*. Santa Monica, CA: RAND Corporation.

Dixon, H. 1999. Controversy: On the Use of the "Hidden Economy" Estimates. *Economic Journal* 109: F335–F337.

Egmont Group. 2000. *FIU's in Action: 100 Cases from the Egmont Group*. London: Egmont Group of Financial Intelligence Units.

Eizenstat, Stuart. 2000. Efforts to Combat Money Laundering. Congressional Testimony before the Committee on Banking and Financial Services. Federal News Service (March 9).

Eldridge, James E. 1986. The Bank Secrecy Act: Privacy, Comity, and the Politics of Contraband. *North Carolina Journal of International Law and Commercial Regulation* (summer): 677–96.

Elliehausen, Gregory. 1998. *The Cost of Bank Regulation: A Review of the Evidence*. Federal Reserve Staff Study 171. Washington: Board of Governors of the Federal Reserve System.

El Qorchi, Mohammed, Samuel Munzele Maimbo, and John F. Wilson. 2003. *Informal Funds Transfer Systems: An Analysis of the Informal Hawala System*. International Monetary Fund Occasional Paper 222. Washington: International Monetary Fund.

European Commission. 2003. *Eurobarometer: Public Opinion in the European Union*. Brussels: European Commission.

Eurostat. 1995. *European System of Accounts*. Brussels: Eurostat.

FATF (Financial Action Task Force). 1998. *1997–1998 Report on Money Laundering Typologies*. Paris: Financial Action Task Force.

FATF (Financial Action Task Force). 1999. *1998–1999 Report on Money Laundering Typologies*. Paris: Financial Action Task Force.

FATF (Financial Action Task Force). 2000. *Report on Money Laundering Typologies 1999–2000*. Paris: Financial Action Task Force.

FATF (Financial Action Task Force). 2001a. *Special Recommendations on Terrorist Financing*. Paris: Financial Action Task Force.

FATF (Financial Action Task Force). 2001b. *Report on Money Laundering Typologies 2000–2001*. Paris: Financial Action Task Force.

FATF (Financial Action Task Force). 2002a. *Combating the Abuse of Non-Profit Organizations: International Best Practices*. Paris: Financial Action Task Force.

FATF (Financial Action Task Force). 2002b. *Report on Money Laundering Typologies 2001–2002*. Paris: Financial Action Task Force.

FATF (Financial Action Task Force). 2003a. *Annual Report 2002–2003*. Paris: Financial Action Task Force.

FATF (Financial Action Task Force). 2003b. *Annual Review of Non-Cooperative Countries and Territories*. Paris: Financial Action Task Force.

FATF (Financial Action Task Force). 2003c. *The Forty Recommendations*. Paris: Financial Action Task Force.

FATF (Financial Action Task Force). 2003d. *Freezing of Terrorist Assets: International Best Practices*. Paris: Financial Action Task Force.

FATF (Financial Action Task Force). 2003e. *Report on Money Laundering Typologies 2002–2003*. Paris: Financial Action Task Force.

FATF (Financial Action Task Force). 2004a. *Annual Report 2003–2004*. Paris: Financial Action Task Force.

FATF (Financial Action Task Force). 2004b. *Report on Money Laundering and Terrorist Financing Typologies 2003–2004*. Paris: Financial Action Task Force.

FEE (Fédération des Experts Comptables Européens). 1999. Charter of the European Professional Associations in Support of the Fight against Organized Crime. www.fee.be/european/PDFs/Charter%20organisedCrime.pdf.

FEE (Fédération des Experts Comptables Européens). 2003. Fact Sheet FST 004. www.fee.be/secretariat/PDFs/Fact%20Sheet/FST004.Money.Laundering.pdf.

Feige, Edgar L. 1979. How Big is the Irregular Economy? *Challenge* 22(1): 5–13.

Feige, Edgar L. 1997. Revised Estimates of the Underground Economy: Implications of the US Currency Held Abroad. In *The Underground Economy: Global Evidence of its Size and Impact*, eds. Owen Lippert and Michael Walker. Vancouver: Fraser Institute.

Fields, Greg, and Mimi Whitfield. 2001. Prosecutions Helping Lift the Veil of Secrecy from Offshore Banks. www.clevelandtour.com/reyesboard/messages/7.html.

FinCEN (Financial Crimes Enforcement Network). 2002. *Use of Currency Transaction Reports. Report to Congress*. Washington: US Department of the Treasury.

FinCEN (Financial Crimes Enforcement Network). 2003a. *2003–2008 Strategic Plan*. Washington: US Department of the Treasury.

FinCEN (Financial Crimes Enforcement Network). 2003b. *The SAR Activity Review Report: Tips and Issues*. US Department of the Treasury Bulletin 5. Washington: US Department of the Treasury.

FinCEN (Financial Crimes Enforcement Network). 2004. *The SAR Activity Review: By the Numbers*. Washington: US Department of the Treasury.

Fowler, William Warner. 1981. *Terrorism Data Bases: A Comparison of Methods, Missions and Systems*. Santa Monica, CA: RAND Corporation.

Freiberg, Arie, and Richard Fox. 2000. Evaluating the Effectiveness of Australia's Confiscation Laws. *Australian and New Zealand Journal of Criminology* 33, no. 3: 239–65.

FSF (Financial Stability Forum). 2000. Report of Working Group on Offshore Financial Centres. Financial Stability Forum, Basel, Switzerland (April).

FSF (Financial Stability Forum). 2004. Review of Offshore Financing Centres Initiative. Financial Stability Forum press release. Basel, Switzerland (April 5).

GAO (General Accounting Office). 1996. *Money Laundering: A Framework for Understanding US Efforts Overseas*. GAO/GGD 96–105. Washington: General Accounting Office.

GAO (General Accounting Office). 1998. *FinCEN's Law Enforcement Support Role is Evolving*. GAO/GGD 98–117. Washington: General Accounting Office.

GAO (General Accounting Office). 2002. *Money Laundering: Extent of Money Laundering through Credit Cards is Unknown*. GAO/GGD 02–670. Washington: General Accounting Office.

GAO (General Accounting Office). 2003a. *Combating Money Laundering: Opportunities Exist to Improve the National Strategy*. GAO/GGD 03–813. Washington: General Accounting Office.

GAO (General Accounting Office). 2003b. *Terrorist Financing: US Agencies Should Systematically Assess Terrorists' Use of Alternative Financing Mechanisms*. GAO 04–163. Washington: General Accounting Office.

Gilmore, William C. 1999. *Dirty Money: The Evolution of Money Laundering Countermeasures*. Strasbourg, France: Council of Europe Publishing.

Godshaw, G. P., R. Koppel, and R. Pancoast. 1987. *Anti-Drug Law Enforcement Efforts and Their Impact*. Bala Cynwyd, PA: Wharton Econometric Forecasting Associates.

Gold, Michael, and Michael Levi. 1994. *Money-Laundering in the UK: An Appraisal of Suspicion-Based Reporting*. London: Police Foundation.

Grant Thornton. 1992. Regulatory Burden Phase II – National Opinion Survey of Community Banks. Study prepared for the Independent Bankers Association of America. Photocopy (June).

Grant Thornton. 1993. Regulatory Burden: The Cost to Community Banks. Study prepared for the Independent Bankers Association of America. Photocopy (January).

Gurr, Ted, Barbara Harft, and Monty G. Marshall. 2003. *State Failure Task Force Report: Phase III (Polity IV)*. McLean, VA: Science Applications International Corporation (SAIC).

Gutmann, P. M. 1977. The Subterranean Economy. *Financial Analysts Journal* 26, no. 34.

Heimann, Fritz. 2004. Will the OECD Convention Stop Foreign Bribery? In *Global Corruption Report 2004*, Transparency International. London: Pluto Press.

Hills, Roderick M. 2001. The Economics of Corruption. *Looking Ahead* 23, no. 2: 3–6.

HM Treasury (United Kingdom). 2002. Consultation Document on Proposed Revision of the Money Laundering Regulations 1993 and 2001. Photocopy (November).

Hufbauer, Gary Clyde, Jeffrey J. Schott, and Barbara Oegg. 2001. *Using Sanctions to Fight Terrorism*. Policy Brief 01–11. Washington: Institute for International Economics.

Hufbauer, Gary Clyde, Jeffrey J. Schott, and Kimberly Ann Elliott. 2004. *Economic Sanctions Reconsidered*. 3rd edition (forthcoming). Washington: Institute for International Economics.

IDA (International Development Association). 2003. *Allocating IDA Funds Based on Performance*. Washington: World Bank.

IFAC (International Federation of Accountants). 2002. Anti–Money Laundering. Photocopy. www.ifac.org.

IMF (International Monetary Fund). 2001. *Cyprus: Assessment of the Offshore Financial Sector*. Washington: International Monetary Fund.

IMF (International Monetary Fund). 2003a. IMF Concludes 2003 Article IV Consultation with the Islamic State of Afghanistan. IMF Public Information Notice 03/147, Washington.

IMF (International Monetary Fund). 2003b. IMF Concludes 2003 Article IV Consultation with Vietnam. IMF Public Information Notice 03/140, Washington.

IMF (International Monetary Fund). 2003c. Offshore Financial Centers—The Assessment Program—A Progress Report and the Future of the Program. Washington: International Monetary Fund.

IMF (International Monetary Fund). 2003d. *United Kingdom: Financial System Stability Assessment*. Washington: International Monetary Fund.

IMF (International Monetary Fund). 2004a. IMF Executive Board Establishes Standard for Anti–Money Laundering and Combating the Financing of Terrorism Assessments. IMF Public Information Notice 04/33, Washington: International Monetary Fund.

IMF (International Monetary Fund). 2004b. Japan: Report on the Observance of Standards and Codes—FATF Recommendations for Anti–Money Laundering and Combating the Financing of Terrorism. Washington: International Monetary Fund.

IMF (International Monetary Fund). 2004c. Twelve-Month Pilot Program of Anti–Money Laundering and Combating the Financing of Terrorism Assessments: Joint Report Prepared by IMF and World Bank. International Monetary Fund, Washington.

Inter-American Dialogue. 2004. *All in the Family: Latin America's Most Important International Financial Flow*. Washington: Inter-American Dialogue.

Interpol. 2003. Funds Derived from Criminal Activities (FOPAC). www.interpol.int/Public/FinancialCrime/FOPAC/default.asp.

Inter-University Consortium for Political and Social Research. 2003. National Archive of Criminal Justice Data 1995 and 2000. www.icpsr.umich.edu/NACJD/index.html.

Isachsen, Arne J., and Steinar Strom. 1980. The Hidden Economy, the Labor Market and Tax Evasion. *Scandinavian Journal of Economics* 82, no. 2: 304–11.

Isachsen, Arne J., and Steinar Strom. 1985. The Size and Growth of the Hidden Economy in Norway. *Review of Income and Wealth* 31, no. 1: 21–38.

Jackson, Dudley. 2000. *The New National Accounts: An Introduction to the System of National Accounts 1993 and the European System of Accounts 1995*. Cheltenham: Edward Elgar.

James, Alvin, Jr. 2002. Statement before the US Senate Committee on Banking Housing and Urban Affairs. Photocopy (October 3).

Joseph, Lester M. 2001. Money Laundering Enforcement: Following the Money. *Economic Perspectives*: An Electronic Journal of the U.S. Department of State. http://usinfo.state.gov/journals/ites/0501/ijee/justice.htm.

Kaplan, Lawrence J., and Salvatore Matteis. 1967. The Economics of Loansharking. *American Journal of Law and Sociology* 27:244

Kaufmann, Daniel. 2003. Anti-Corruption within a Broader Developmental and Governance Perspective: Some Lessons from Empirics and Experience. Statement by the Head of the World Bank Delegation to the High Level Political Signing Conference for the UN Convention Against Corruption, Merida, Mexico. Photocopy (December 9–10).

Kaufmann, Daniel, Aart Kraay, and Pablo Zoido-Lobatón. 1999. *Governance Matters*. World Bank Policy Research Working Paper 2196. Washington: World Bank.

Kerry, John. 1997. *The New War: The Web of Crime that Threatens America's Security*. New York: Simon and Schuster.

Key, Jack. 1979. Testimony before the Senate Permanent Subcommittee on Investigations of the Committee on Governmental Affairs, 96th Congress, 1st Session, December 7, 11, 12, 13, and 14, 1979 (Illegal Narcotics Profits). Washington: US Government Printing Office.

Knack, Stephen, and Philip Keefer. 1995. Institutions and Economic Performance: Cross-Country Tests Using Alternative Institutional Measures. *Economics and Politics* 7, no. 3: 207–27.

KPMG. 2003. *Money Laundering: Review of the Regime for Handling Suspicious Activity Reports*. London: National Criminal Intelligence Service.

Levi, Michael. 2002. Money Laundering and Its Regulation. *Annals of the American Academy of Political and Social Sciences*, no. 582: 181–94.

Levitt, Steven, and S. Venkatesh. 2000. An Economic Analysis of a Drug-Selling Gang's Finances. *Quarterly Journal of Economics* 115, no. 3: 755–89.

Litan, Robert. 2004. Drafting Finance in the War on Drugs. Council on Foreign Relations, New York. Photocopy (January).

Manski, Charles, John Pepper, and Carol Petrie, eds. 2001. *Informing America's Policy on Illegal Drugs: What We Don't Know Keeps Hurting Us*. Washington: National Academies Press.

Masciandaro, Donato. 1999. Money Laundering: The Economics of Regulation. *European Journal of Law and Economics* 7, no. 3: 225–40.

Masciandaro, Donato, and Allesandro Portolano. 2002. Inside the Black (List) Box: Money Laundering, Lax Financial Regulation, Non-Cooperative Countries. A Law and Economics Approach. Paulo Baffi Center, Bocconi University and Bank of Italy. Photocopy (May).

Mauro, Paolo. 1995. Corruption and Growth. *Quarterly Journal of Economics* 110, no. 3: 291–303.

Mauro, Paolo. 2002. *The Persistence of Corruption and Slow Economic Growth*. IMF Working Paper WP/02/213. Washington: International Monetary Fund.

Mirus, Rolf, and Roger S. Smith. 1997. Canada's Underground Economy: Measurement and Implications. In *The Underground Economy: Global Evidence of its Size and Impact*, eds. Owen Lippert and Michael Walker. Vancouver: Fraser Institute.

M.I.S. Trend. 2004. Les Questions Bancaires Actuelles 2004: Opinions et Représentations des Citoyens Suisses. Institut pour l'Etude des Marchés et les Sondages d'Opinion, Lausanne, Switzerland. Photocopy.

Moody-Stuart, George. 1997. *The Grand Corruption: How Business Bribes Damage Developing Countries*. Oxford: World View Publishing.

Morgenthau, Robert M. 2004. Testimony before the US Senate Finance Committee. July 21, 2004.

Muscato, Frank. 2003. Testimony before Field Hearing on Organized Retail Theft: Conduit of Money Laundering, House Committee on Government Reform, Subcommittee on Criminal Justice, Drug Policy, and Human Resources, Washington. *Congressional Record* (November 10).

National Association of Criminal Defense Lawyers (NACDL). 2001. Proposals to Reform Federal Money Laundering Statutes. NACDL Money Laundering Task Force. Photocopy.

National Crime Authority. 1991. *Taken to the Cleaners: Money Laundering in Australia,* vol. 1. Canberra, Australia: National Crime Authority.

National Criminal Intelligence Service (NCIS). 2003. *United Kingdom Threat Assessment of Serious and Organized Crime*. London: National Criminal Intelligence Service.

Neild, Robert. 2002. *Public Corruption: The Dark Side of Social Evolution*. London: Anthem Press.

OECD (Organization for Economic Cooperation and Development). 1998. *Harmful Tax Competition: An Emerging Global Issue*. Paris: OECD.

OECD (Organization for Economic Cooperation and Development). 2000. *Towards Global Tax Cooperation: Progress in Identifying and Eliminating Harmful Tax Practices*. Paris: OECD.

OECD (Organization for Economic Cooperation and Development). 2002. *Measuring the Non-Observed Economy—A Handbook*. Paris: OECD.

Office of National Drug Control Policy. 2000. *What America's Users Spend on Illicit Drugs, 1988–1998*. Washington: US Government Printing Office.

Office of National Drug Control Policy. 2001. *What America's Users Spend on Illicit Drugs, 1988-2000*. Washington: US Government Printing Office.

OTA (Office of Technology Assessment). 1995. *Information Technologies for the Control of Money Laundering*. Washington: US Government Printing Office.

Oxfam. 2000. Tax Havens: Releasing the Hidden Billions for Poverty Eradication. Policy Research Department of Oxfam (Great Britain). Photocopy.

Passas, Nikos. 2000. Informal Value Transfer Systems and Criminal Organizations: A Study into So-called Underground Banking Networks. Ministry of Justice, The Hague, Netherlands. Photocopy.

Performance and Innovation Unit of the UK Cabinet Office. 2000. Recovering the Proceeds of Crime. www.number-0.gov.uk/su/criminal/recovering/contents.htm.

Pieth, Mark, and Gemma Aiolfi. 2003. Anti–Money Laundering: Leveling the Playing Field. Basel Institute of Governance, Basel, Switzerland. Photocopy (June).

Pillar, Paul R. 2003. *Terrorism and US Foreign Policy*. Washington: Brookings Institution.

President's Commission on Organized Crime. 1987. *The Impact: Organized Crime Today*. Washington: US Government Printing Office.

Pricewaterhouse Coopers. 2003. *Anti–Money Laundering Current Customer Review Cost Benefit Analysis*. London: Financial Services Authority.

Public Broadcasting Service (PBS). 2000. Frontline: Drug Wars Interview with "David." www.pbs.org/wgbh/pages/frontline/shows/drugs/interviews/david.html.

Rahn, Richard, and Veronique de Rugy. 2003. *Threats to Financial Privacy and Tax Competition*. Cato Institute Policy Analysis 491. Washington: Cato Institute.

Reinicke, Wolfgang H. 1998. *Global Public Policy: Governing without Governments?* Washington: Brookings Institution.

Reuter, Peter. 1986. The Social Costs of the Demand for Quantification. *Journal of Policy Analysis and Management* 5(4): 807–12.

Reuter, Peter, Robert MacCoun, and Patrick Murphy. 1990. *Money From Crime*. Santa Monica, CA: RAND Corporation.

Robinson, Jeffrey. 1996. *The Laundrymen: Inside Money Laundering*. New York: Arcade Publishing.

Rotberg, Robert I. 2003. *State Failure and State Weakness in a Time of Terror*. Washington: World Peace Foundation.

Schneider, Friedrich. 2002. The Size and Development of the Shadow Economies and Shadow Economy Labor Force of 21 OECD Countries: What Do We Really Know? Photocopy.

Schneider, Friedrich, and Dominik Enste. 2000. Shadow Economies: Size, Causes, and Consequences. *The Journal of Economic Literature* 38, no. 1: 77–114.

Simon, Carl, and Ann Witte. 1982. *Beating the System: The Underground Economy*. Boston: Auburn House.

Spillenkothen, Richard. 2002. Testimony before the Committee on Banking, Housing, and Urban Affairs, US Senate. Board of Governors of the Federal Reserve System, Washington. Photocopy (January 29).

Stessens, Guy. 2000. *Money Laundering: A New International Law Enforcement Model*. Cambridge, UK: Cambridge University Press.

Steinberg, James B., Mary Graham, and Andrew Eggers. 2003. *Building Intelligence to Fight Terrorism.* Brookings Institution Policy Brief 125 (September). Washington: Brookings Institution.

Suskind, Ron. 2004. *The Price of Loyalty: George W. Bush, the White House, and the Education of Paul O'Neill.* New York: Simon and Schuster.

Suss, Esther C., Oral H. Williams, and Chandima Mendis. 2002. *Caribbean Offshore Financial Centers: Past, Present and Possibilities for the Future.* IMF Working Paper WP/02/88. Washington: International Monetary Fund.

System of National Accounts. 1993. Brussels, New York, Paris, Luxembourg: Eurostat, IMF, OECD, UN, World Bank.

Tanzi, Vito. 1980. The Underground Economy and Tax Evasion in the United States: Estimates and Implications. *Banca Nazionale del Lavoro Quarterly Review* 135.

Tanzi, Vito. 1999. Uses and Abuses of the Estimates of the Underground Economy. *Economic Journal* 109: 338–47.

Transparency International. 1996. *The TI Sourcebook*. Berlin: Transparency International.

Transparency International. 2003. *Transparency International Corruption Perceptions Index*. Berlin: Transparency International.

Transparency International. 2004. *Global Corruption Report 2004*. London: Pluto Press.

Truman, David R. 1995. The Jets and the Sharks are Dead: State Statutory Responses to Criminal Street Gangs. *Washington University Law Quarterly* 73(2): 683–735.

UNECE (UN Economic Commission for Europe). 2002. Inventory of National Practices in Estimating Hidden and Informal Economic Activities for National Accounts. Geneva: UN Economic Commission for Europe.

United Nations. 2003a. Second Report of the Monitoring Group Established Pursuant to Security Council Resolution 1363 (2001). United Nations Security Council S/2003/1070, New York.

United Nations. 2003b. UN Convention Against Corruption. United Nations, New York.

US Department of State. 2003. *International Narcotics Control Strategy Report*. Washington: United States Department of State.

US Department of the Treasury. 1999. *The National Money Laundering Strategy for 1999*. Washington: US Department of the Treasury.

US Department of the Treasury. 2000. *The National Money Laundering Strategy for 2000*. Washington: US Department of the Treasury.

US Department of the Treasury. 2001. *The National Money Laundering Strategy for 2001*. Washington: US Department of the Treasury.

US Department of the Treasury. 2002. *The National Money Laundering Strategy for 2002*. Washington: US Department of the Treasury.

US Department of the Treasury. 2003. *The National Money Laundering Strategy for 2003*. Washington: US Department of the Treasury.

US Senate Minority Staff of the Permanent Subcommittee on Investigations. 2001a. Correspondent Banking: A Gateway for Money Laundering (February 5). http://freedom.orlingrabbe.com/money_laundering/correspondent_banking.pdf.

US Senate Minority Staff of the Permanent Subcommittee on Investigations. 2001b. *Your Banker Is a Snitch.* http://freedom.orlingrabbe.com/lftimes/banker_snitch.htm.

US Sentencing Commission. 2002. *2001 Sourcebook of Federal Sentencing Statistics.* Washington: United States Sentencing Commission.

US Sentencing Commission. 2003. Monitoring of Federal Criminal Sentences, 1995 and 2000. Dataset. www.ICPSR.umich.edu/NACJD/archive.html.

van Duyne, Petrus C. 2003. Money Laundering Policy: Fears and Facts. In *Criminal Finances and Organising Crime in Europe.* eds. Petrus C. van Duyne, Klaus von Lampe, and James L. Newell. Nijmgen, Netherlands: Wolf Legal Publishers.

Wechsler, William F. 2001. Follow the Money. *Foreign Affairs* 80(4) (July/August): 40–57.

Winer, Jonathan M. 2002. Illicit Finance and Global Conflict. Paper prepared for the Fafo Program for International Cooperation and Conflict Resolution. Photocopy (March 25).

Wolfsberg Group. 2002. Global Anti–Money Laundering Guidelines for Private Banking. www.wolfsberg-principles.com/wolfsberg_principles_1st_revision.html.

Woolner, Ann. 1994. *Washed in Gold: The Story behind the Biggest Money Laundering Investigation in US History.* New York: Simon and Schuster.

World Bank. 1997. *The World Development Report 1997.* Washington: World Bank.

World Bank. 2002. *World Bank Group Work in Low-Income Countries under Stress: A Task Force Report.* Washington: World Bank.

World Bank. 2003a. *Reference Guide to Anti–Money Laundering and Combating the Financing of Terrorism.* Washington: World Bank.

World Bank 2003b. *World Development Indicators.* Washington: World Bank.

World Bank. 2004. *Doing Business in 2004: Understanding Regulation.* Washington: World Bank.

Zarate, Juan C. 2004. Testimony before the House International Relations Subcommittee on the Middle East and Central Asia. Photocopy (March 24).

Zhou, Xiaochuan. 2004. Statement to the International Monetary and Financial Committee. International Monetary Fund, Washington. Photocopy (April 24).

Glossary and Acronyms

AML. Anti–money laundering.

Annunzio-Wylie Money Laundering Act (1992). US statute that inter alia introduced suspicious activity reporting by financial institutions and made it a crime to operate an illegal money transmitting business.

Anti–Drug Abuse Act (1988). US statute that inter alia gave the IRS the power to seize property involved in the breach of money laundering laws.

AOC. US Administrative Office of the Courts.

APG. Asia-Pacific Group on Money Laundering. Established in 1998. The group's 26 current members are Australia, Bangladesh, Brunei Darussalam, Chinese Taipei, Cook Islands, Fiji, Hong Kong, India, Indonesia, Japan, Macau, Malaysia, Marshall Islands, Nepal, New Zealand, Niue, Pakistan, Republic of Korea, Palau, the Philippines, Samoa, Singapore, Sri Lanka, Thailand, the United States, and Vanuatu.

AUSTRAC. Australian Transaction Report and Analysis Center. Australia's anti–money laundering regulator and financial intelligence unit.

Basel Committee. Basel Committee on Banking Supervision, sponsored by the G-10 central banks; normally meets at the BIS.

BCCI. Bank of Credit and Commerce International.

BIS. Bank for International Settlements.

BSA. Bank Secrecy Act (1970). First US legislation on reporting and monitoring of currency transactions.

Caricom. Caribbean Community. Established in 1990. The community's 26 current members are Anguilla, Antigua and Barbuda, Aruba, Bahamas, Barbados, Belize, Bermuda, British Virgin Islands, Cayman Islands, Costa Rica, Dominica, Dominican Republic, Grenada, Haiti, Jamaica, Montserrat, Netherland Antilles, Nicaragua, Panama, St. Kitts and Nevis, St. Lucia, St. Vincent and the Grenadines, Suriname, Trinidad and Tobago, Turks and Caicos Islands, and Venezuela.

CCE. Continuing Criminal Enterprise Act. US legislation directed at combating organized crime, passed in 1970 along with the Racketeer Influenced and Corrupt Organizations (RICO) Act.

CDD. Customer due diligence. Procedure mandated in some countries for banks, financial institutions, some nonfinancial businesses, and certain professions to obtain information on customers before doing business with or for them.

CFATF. Caribbean Financial Action Task Force. Established in 1990. Its 26 current members are Anguilla, Antigua and Barbuda, Aruba, Bahamas, Barbados, Belize, Bermuda, British Virgin Islands, Cayman Islands, Costa Rica, Dominica, Dominican Republic, Grenada, Haiti, Jamaica, Montserrat, Netherlands Antilles, Nicaragua, Panama, St. Kitts and Nevis, Saint Lucia, Saint Vincent and Grenadine, Suriname, Trinidad and Tobago, Turks and Caicos Islands, and Venezuela.

CFT. Combating the Financing of Terrorism.

CICAD. Inter-American Drug Abuse Control Commission. An agency of the Organization of American States (OAS) established in 1986, with 34 current members.

CIP. Customer identification program. Term used in US regulations for CDD.

CIS. Commonwealth of Independent States. A group of countries that were part of the former Soviet Union with the exception of the Baltic countries.

CMIR. Report of International Transportation of Currency or Other Monetary Instruments. Report that must be filed to export more than $10,000 in currency from the United States.

CoE. Council of Europe. Established in 1949, with 45 current members.

CPI. Corruption Perceptions Index. An index published since 1995 by Transparency International that ranks nations according to their perceived level of corruption.

CPIA. Country Policy and Institutional Assessment. Annual report by the World Bank Group's International Development Association (IDA) to rate the performance of borrowers.

Crime Control Act (1990). US statute that inter alia established the US financial intelligence unit, the Financial Crime Enforcement Network (FinCEN).

CTAG. Counter Terrorism Action Group of the G-8.

CTIF-CFI. Belgian Financial Intelligence Processing Unit.

CTR. Currency transaction report. Form that US financial institutions are required to use to report currency transactions, generally exceeding $10,000, to the Internal Revenue Service.

DEA. US Drug Enforcement Administration.

Drug Trafficking Offenses Act (1986). UK statute categorizing money laundering as criminal offense.

EDU. Europol Drugs Unit.

Egmont Group of Financial Intelligence Group. International group of FIUs established in 1995 to share experiences, promote the creation of FIUs in nonmember states, and exchange data. The group has 84 current members.

Eight Special Recommendations on Terrorist Financing. Recommendations issued in October 2001 by the FATF to combat the funding of terrorist acts and terrorist organizations.

ESAAMLG. Eastern and Southern Africa Anti–Money Laundering Group. Established in 1999. The group's 11 current members are Botswana, Kenya, Malawi, Mozambique, Mauritius, Namibia, South Africa, Seychelles, Swaziland, Uganda, and Tanzania.

EU. European Union.

European System of Accounts. National accounting standards and definitions established in 1995 for countries in the European Union. Known as ESA95, the system is compatible with but somewhat more specific than the System of National Accounts (SNA93) used by most countries in the world.

Europol. European Law Enforcement Organization.

FATF. Financial Action Task Force. Established by the G-7 Summit in Paris in 1989 to examine measures to combat money laundering. Its 33 current members are Argentina, Australia, Austria, Belgium, Brazil, Canada, Denmark, the European Commission, Finland, France, Germany, Greece, the Gulf Cooperation Council, Hong Kong, Iceland, Ireland, Italy, Japan, Luxembourg, Mexico, the Netherlands, New Zealand, Norway, Portugal, the Russian Federation, Singapore, South Africa, Spain, Sweden, Switzerland, Turkey, the United Kingdom, and the United States.

FCPA. Foreign Corrupt Practices Act (1977). US statute that inter alia prohibited the bribery of foreign government officials by US persons and prescribes accounting and record-keeping practices.

FDIC.   Federal Deposit Insurance Corporation.

FEE.   European Federation of Accountants.

FHT.   Interpol Financial and High Tech Crimes Sub-Directorate.

FinCEN.   Financial Crimes Enforcement Network. US financial intelligence unit established in 1990 in the US Treasury Department.

FIU.   Financial intelligence unit. National center for the reception, analysis, and dissemination of suspicious transaction reports and other information regarding potential money laundering or terrorism financing.

FOPAC.   Fonds Provenant d'Activités Criminelles. Criminal Funds Investigation Group (Interpol).

Forty Recommendations.   Recommendations issued by the FATF to set international anti–money laundering standards. The recommendations were first issued in 1990, slightly revised in 1996, and thoroughly revised in 2003.

FSA.   UK Financial Services Authority.

FSAP.   Financial Sector Assessment Program. Joint reviews of financial systems in member countries by the International Monetary Fund and the World Bank.

FSF.   Financial Stability Forum. A multinational group established in 1999 by the G-7 to promote cooperation among financial authorities, supervisory groups, and international institutions.

FSSA.   Financial System Stability Assessment by the International Monetary Fund.

GAFISUD.   Regional Financial Action Task Force on Money Laundering in Latin America. Established in 2000. Its nine current members are Argentina, Bolivia, Brazil, Chile, Colombia, Ecuador, Paraguay, Peru, and Uruguay.

GAO.   US General Accounting Office (renamed the US Government Accountability office in June 2004).

G-7.   Group of Seven, established in 1975. Members are Canada, France, Germany, Italy, Japan, the United Kingdom, and the United States.

G-8.   Group of Eight: G-7 plus Russia.

G-10.   Group of Ten, established in 1962. Its 11 current members are Belgium, Canada, France, Germany, Italy, Japan, the Netherlands, Sweden, Switzerland, the United Kingdom, and the United States.

Hawala.   Arabic word for bill of exchange or promissory note. An informal money transfer system alternative or parallel to traditional banking or financial channels.

Hawaladar. Hawala operator.

IAIS. International Association of Insurance Supervisors.

IFAC. International Federation of Accountants.

IFIs. International financial institutions, primarily the International Monetary Fund and the World Bank.

IFT. Informal funds transfer system.

ILO. International Labor Organization.

IMF. International Monetary Fund.

IMFC. International Monetary and Financial Committee of the International Monetary Fund.

IMoLIN. International Money Laundering Information Network, established in 1996.

INCSR. US State Department's International Narcotics Control Strategy Report.

International Money Laundering Abatement and Anti–Terrorist Financing Act (2001). Title III of the USA PATRIOT Act, incorporating proposals to strengthen and expand the US AML regime.

IOSCO. International Organization of Securities Commissions. 105 current members.

IRS. US Internal Revenue Service.

JAFIO. Japan Financial Intelligence Office.

KYC. Know Your Customer. Another name for customer due diligence (CDD).

MLCA. Money Laundering Control Act (1986). US statute that inter alia made money laundering a crime.

MLSA. Money Laundering Suppression Act (1994). US statute that inter alia created the BSA Advisory Group, merged FinCEN and the Office of Financial Enforcement, and authorized the AML regulation of casinos.

Money Laundering and Financial Crimes Strategy Act (1998). US statute that inter alia mandated the National Money Laundering Strategy (NMLS) reports for five years (1999–2003).

Money Laundering Prosecution Improvements Act (1988). US statute that inter alia introduced liabilities and fines for facilitators of money-laundering activities, expanded the definition of financial institutions, and provided the legal basis for sting operations.

MONEYVAL. European Regional Financial Action Task Force, which consists of the Council of Europe Selected Committee of Experts on the Evaluation of Anti–Money Laundering Measures (2002). Formerly the PC-R-EV.

MOT. Meldpunt Ongebruikelijke Transacties (Office for the Disclosure of Unusual Transactions). Dutch financial intelligence unit.

MROS. Swiss Money Laundering Reporting Office.

MSB. Money service businesses involved in issuing money orders and traveler's checks, money transmission services, check cashing, currency exchange, etc.

NCCT. Non-Cooperative Countries and Territories identified by the FATF as not meeting global AML standards.

NCIS. UK National Criminal Intelligence Service.

NMLS. National Money Laundering Strategy. Annual US report to the US Congress from 1999–2003 on anti–money laundering efforts.

OAS. Organization of American States. Established in 1948. With 35 current members.

OECD. Organization for Economic Cooperation and Development. Established in 1961. With 30 current members.

OFAC. US Treasury Department's Office of Foreign Assets Control.

OFC. Offshore financial center.

OGBS. Offshore Group of Banking Supervision. Its 19 current members are Aruba, Bahamas, Bahrain, Barbados, Bermuda, Cayman Islands, Cyprus, Gibraltar, Guernsey, Hong Kong, Isle of Man, Jersey, Labuan, Macau, Mauritius, Netherlands Antilles, Panama, Singapore, and Vanuatu.

ONDCP. US Office of National Drug Control Policy.

PC-R-EV. Council of Europe Selected Committee of Experts on the Evaluation of Anti–Money Laundering Measures (1997). The committee conducted self-assessment and mutual assessment exercises of anti–money laundering measures in Council of Europe countries. Replaced by MONEYVAL in 2002.

PEP. Politically exposed person. Individuals in prominent public positions in their countries.

Polity IV. A 2003 study by Gurr, Harft, and Marshall of political regime characteristics and transitions.

RICO. Racketeer Influenced and Corrupt Organizations Act (1986). US statute that inter alia targeted the profits of criminal activities committed by organized crime.

ROSC. Report on Observance of Standards and Codes. Report by the International Monetary Fund on the extent to which members observe certain international standards and codes.

SAR. Suspicious activity report. Form that US financial institutions are required to use to report suspicious transactions, generally exceeding $5,000.

Smurf. (1) To divide large illicit bank deposits into several deposits, each less than $10,000, so they will not be subject to a CRT; also known as "structuring" of deposits. (2) Slang for a courier who makes such structured deposits.

STR. Suspicious transaction report. Report that financial institutions must file to a country's financial intelligence unit if a transaction is suspected to be linked to criminal activity or to terrorism. Used in certain countries other than the United States.

Strasbourg Convention (1990). Convention that required each Council of Europe member to adopt legislation that criminalizes money laundering.

System of National Accounts. National accounting standards and definitions established in 1993 and used by most countries in the world today. Often referred to as SNA93.

Technical Assistance Needs Assessment. A FATF exercise.

TEOAF. US Treasury Executive Office for Asset Forfeiture.

TI. Transparency International (see CPI).

TRACFin. French Unit for Processing Information and Action against Illegal Financial Flows.

UNECE. UN Economic Commission for Europe.

UNDCCP. United Nations Office for Drug Control and Crime Prevention.

UNODC. United Nations Office on Drugs and Crime.

USA PATRIOT Act. Uniting and Strengthening of America by Providing Appropriate Tools Required to Intercept and Obstruct Terrorism Act (2001). US statute on money laundering and terrorism financing enacted after the September 11, 2001, terrorist attack.

Vienna Convention (1988). UN convention against illicit traffic in narcotics drugs and psychotropic substances.

Wolfsberg Principles. Joint anti–money laundering initiative by 12 international banks setting common standards on private banking and other areas. The 12 banks are ABN AMRO, Santander Central Hispano, Bank of Tokyo Mitsubishi, Barclays, Citigroup, Credit Suisse Group, Deutsche Bank, Goldman Sachs, HSBC, JP Morgan Chase, Société Générale, and UBS.

Index

Kibaki, Mwai, 155
Klein, Adam, 66n
kleptocracy, 43, 71, 134, 149–55, 151n. *See also*
    bribery; corruption
    embezzlement cases, 151, 151n
    monetary classification of, 149n
    and money laundering, 156
    prosecution of, 150, 152n, 153n
    US pursuit of foreign offenders, 153–55
"know your customer" (KYC), 130, 197
KPMG, AML cost estimates, 99, 100, 100n

Lansky, Meyer, 121
Laos, 159
lawyers. *See also* professionals
    as an agent for money laundering, 34
    Canadian regulation of, 82
    and CDD, reporting requirements, 59n, 60–61
    expansion of AML responsibilities, 172–73
    and FATF Recommendations, 60–61
Lazarenko, Pavel Nickolayevich, 150, 151n
Lebanon, 167
Lesotho, 160b
Liberia, 67, 151n
Libya, 143
licensing, 57
Liechtenstein, 67, 85, 86, 167
lotteries, 29
Luxembourg, 88, 90, 146

macroeconomic estimates
    currency-demand approach, 11–12
    of money laundering, 10, 11–18
    and national income accounts, 16
mafia, 118
March 11, 2004, EU responses to, 146, 147
Marcos, Ferdinand, 151n
Marshall Islands, 67
Mathewson, John, 36
Maxwell, Robert, 29, 29b, 124
Maxwell Group Newspaper PLC, 29b
Mayer, Martin, 137n
Mexico
    SAR filings, 117
    US sting operation in, 91
microeconomic estimates
    of money laundering, 10, 19–23
Milosevic, Slobodan, 151n
MLCA. *See* Money Laundering Control Act
Mobutu Sese Seko, 151n
Moi, Daniel arap, 151n, 155
Monaco, 67
money laundering. *See also* self-laundering
    bank involvement in, 34, 133–35, 133n, 135n
    blue-collar crime, 41, 41t
    and cash smuggling, 28
    and corruption, 149, 156, 163–65, 164t
    and credit card advance payments, 31b
    criminalization of, 176
    and currency exchange, 31b, 122–23

data compilation for, 189
definition of, 9, 65n
domestic, 26
and drug trafficking, 34
economic modeling of, 191
and electronic finance, 73b
elements of, 25
and failed states, 156–63
financial penalties for, 113–14, 114f
and gambling, 28–29
impact of globalization, deregulation, 78
impact on developing countries, 93
informal value transfer systems, 30b
inmate survey regarding, 112–13
and insurance policies, 29–30
and kleptocracy, 156
and legitimate business ownership, 30b
phases of, 3
policy guidance, consequences, 23–24
and predicate crimes, 22–23, 69, 90, 111t
prevention efforts, 46. *See also* prevention pillar
prosecution, conviction data, 108–09, 109–12,
    109t, 110t, 111t, 187
prosecution of, 69
and purchase of goods, 31b
and real estate transactions, 31b
and relationship to national accounts, 18
research, lack of, 8, 188–89
risk of, in the US, 127–28
and securities transactions, 30–32
"shell" corporations, 30b–31b
"smurfing," 26b, 30b, 199
social consequences of, 42–43
US law enforcement of, 186–88
wire, electronic funds transfers, 30b
Money Laundering and Financial Crimes Strategy
    Act, 51t, 70, 197
Money Laundering Control Act (MLCA), 50t, 65,
    197
Money Laundering Prosecution Improvements
    Act, 197
Money Laundering Suppression Act, 51t, 197
money profiles, 174
money service bureaus, 56, 198
money-laundering estimates, 4, 5, 23
    approaches to, 10, 16. *See also* macroeconomic
        estimates; microeconomic estimates
    currency-demand approach to, 15–16
    macroeconomic approach to, 11–18
    microeconomic approach to, 19–23
    of OECD countries, 13, 14t
    UNECE report, 17–18
    for US, 9
money-laundering methods, 27–32
    and corresponding crimes, 32, 33t, 34
money-laundering offenses
    classification of, 40–43, 41t
    dimensions of, 40–41
money-laundering services
    agents of, 34–35

Other Publications from the Institute for International Economics

* = out of print

Job Loss from Imports: Measuring the Costs
Lori G. Kletzer
September 2001   ISBN 0-88132-296-2
No More Bashing: Building a New Japan–United
States Economic Relationship   C. Fred Bergsten,
Takatoshi Ito, and Marcus Noland
October 2001   ISBN 0-88132-286-5
Why Global Commitment Really Matters!
Howard Lewis III and J. David Richardson
October 2001   ISBN 0-88132-298-9
Leadership Selection in the Major Multilaterals
Miles Kahler
November 2001   ISBN 0-88132-335-7
The International Financial Architecture:
What's New? What's Missing?   Peter Kenen
November 2001   ISBN 0-88132-297-0
Delivering on Debt Relief: From IMF Gold to
a New Aid Architecture
John Williamson and Nancy Birdsall,
with Brian Deese
April 2002   ISBN 0-88132-331-4
Imagine There's No Country: Poverty, Inequality,
and Growth in the Era of Globalization
Surjit S. Bhalla
September 2002   ISBN 0-88132-348-9
Reforming Korea's Industrial Conglomerates
Edward M. Graham
January 2003   ISBN 0-88132-337-3
Industrial Policy in an Era of Globalization:
Lessons from Asia
Marcus Noland and Howard Pack
March 2003   ISBN 0-88132-350-0
Reintegrating India with the World Economy
T. N. Srinivasan and Suresh D. Tendulkar
March 2003   ISBN 0-88132-280-6
After the Washington Consensus:
Restarting Growth and Reform in
Latin America   Pedro-Pablo Kuczynski
and John Williamson, editors
March 2003   ISBN 0-88132-347-0
The Decline of US Labor Unions and
the Role of Trade   Robert E. Baldwin
June 2003   ISBN 0-88132-341-1
Can Labor Standards Improve under
Globalization?
Kimberly Ann Elliott and Richard B. Freeman
June 2003   ISBN 0-88132-332-2
Crimes and Punishments? Retaliation
under the WTO
Robert Z. Lawrence
October 2003   ISBN 0-88132-359-4
Inflation Targeting in the World Economy
Edwin M. Truman
October 2003   ISBN 0-88132-345-4
Foreign Direct Investment and Tax
Competition   John H. Mutti
November 2003   ISBN 0-88132-352-7

Has Globalization Gone Far Enough? The Costs
of Fragmented Markets
Scott Bradford and Robert Z. Lawrence
February 2004   ISBN 0-88132-349-7
Food Regulation and Trade: Toward a Safe
and Open Global System
Tim Josling, Donna Roberts, and David Orden
March 2004   ISBN 0-88132-346-2
Controlling Currency Mismatches in
Emerging Markets
Morris Goldstein and Philip Turner
April 2004   ISBN 0-88132-360-8
Free Trade Agreements: US Strategies
and Priorities
Jeffrey J. Schott, editor
April 2004   ISBN 0-88132-361-6
Trade Policy and Global Poverty
William R. Cline
June 2004   ISBN 0-88132-365-9
Transforming the European Economy
Martin Neil Baily and Jacob Kirkegaard
September 2004   ISBN 0-88132-343-8
Bailouts or Bail-ins? Responding to Financial
Crises in Emerging Economies
Nouriel Roubini and Brad Setser
September 2004   ISBN 0-88132-371-3
Chasing Dirty Money: The Fight Against
Money Laundering
Peter Reuter and Edwin M. Truman
November 2004   ISBN 0-88132-370-5

SPECIAL REPORTS

1   Promoting World Recovery: A Statement on
     Global Economic Strategy*
     by Twenty-six Economists from Fourteen Countries
     December 1982   ISBN 0-88132-013-7
2   Prospects for Adjustment in Argentina,
     Brazil, and Mexico: Responding to the Debt Crisis*
     John Williamson, editor
3   Inflation and Indexation: Argentina, Brazil,
     and Israel*   John Williamson, editor
     March 1985   ISBN 0-88132-037-4
4   Global Economic Imbalances*
     C. Fred Bergsten, editor
     March 1986   ISBN 0-88132-042-0
5   African Debt and Financing*
     Carol Lancaster and John Williamson, editors
     May 1986   ISBN 0-88132-044-7
6   Resolving the Global Economic Crisis: After
     Wall Street*
     by Thirty-three Economists from Thirteen
     Countries
     December 1987   ISBN 0-88132-070-6

7 World Economic Problems*
   Kimberly Ann Elliott and John Williamson,
   editors
   April 1988   ISBN 0-88132-055-2
   Reforming World Agricultural Trade*
   by Twenty-nine Professionals from Seventeen
   Countries
   1988   ISBN 0-88132-088-9
8 Economic Relations Between the United
   States and Korea: Conflict or Cooperation?*
   Thomas O. Bayard and Soogil Young, editors
   January 1989   ISBN 0-88132-068-4
9 Whither APEC? The Progress to Date and
   Agenda for the Future*
   C. Fred Bergsten, editor
   October 1997   ISBN 0-88132-248-2
10 Economic Integration of the Korean
   Peninsula
   Marcus Noland, editor
   January 1998   ISBN 0-88132-255-5
11 Restarting Fast Track*
   Jeffrey J. Schott, editor
   April 1998   ISBN 0-88132-259-8
12 Launching New Global Trade Talks:
   An Action Agenda   Jeffrey J. Schott, editor
   September 1998   ISBN 0-88132-266-0
13 Japan's Financial Crisis and Its Parallels to
   US Experience
   Ryoichi Mikitani and Adam S. Posen, eds.
   September 2000   ISBN 0-88132-289-X
14 The Ex-Im Bank in the 21st Century: A New
   Approach   Gary Clyde Hufbauer and
   Rita M. Rodriguez, editors
   January 2001   ISBN 0-88132-300-4
15 The Korean Diaspora in the World
   Economy
   C. Fred Bergsten and Inbom Choi, eds.
   January 2003   ISBN 0-88132-358-6
16 Dollar Overvaluation and the World
   Economy
   C. Fred Bergsten and John Williamson, eds.
   February 2003   ISBN 0-88132-351-9

WORKS IN PROGRESS

United States and the World Economy: Foreign
Policy for the Next Decade
C. Fred Bergsten, editor
New Regional Arrangements and
the World Economy
C. Fred Bergsten
The Globalization Backlash in Europe and
the United States
C. Fred Bergsten, Pierre Jacquet, and Karl Kaiser
Dollar Adjustment: How Far? Against What?
C. Fred Bergsten and John Williamson, editors

The Impact of Foreign Direct Investment
on Development: New Measures, New
Outcomes   Magnus Blomstrom, Edward
Graham, and Theodore Moran, editors
China's Entry into the World Economy
Richard N. Cooper
American Trade Politics, 4th ed.
I. M. Destler
The ILO in the World Economy
Kimberly Ann Elliott
Reforming Economic Sanctions
Kimberly Ann Elliott, Gary C. Hufbauer,
and Jeffrey J. Schott
Merry Sisterhood or Guarded Watchfulness?
Cooperation Between the IMF and
the World Bank   Michael Fabricius
Future of Chinese Exchange Rates
Morris Goldstein and Nicholas R. Lardy
NAFTA: A Ten-Year Appraisal
Gary Clyde Hufbauer and Jeffrey J. Schott
New Agricultural Negotiations in the WTO
Tim Josling and Dale Hathaway
Workers at Risk: Job Loss from Apparel,
Textiles, Footwear, and Furniture
Lori G. Kletzer
Responses to Globalization: US Textile
and Apparel Workers and Firms
Lori Kletzer, James Levinsohn, and
J. David Richardson
The Strategic Implications of China-Taiwan
Economic Relations
Nicholas R. Lardy
Making the Rules: Case Studies on
US Trade Negotiation
Robert Z. Lawrence, Charan Devereaux,
and Michael Watkins
US-Egypt Free Trade Agreement
Robert Z. Lawrence and Ahmed Galal
High Technology and the Globalization
of America   Catherine L. Mann
International Financial Architecture
Michael Mussa
Germany and the World Economy
Adam S. Posen
The Euro at Five: Ready for a Global Role?
Adam S. Posen, editor
Automatic Stabilizers for the Eurozone
Adam S. Posen
Global Forces, American Faces: US Economic
Globalization at the Grass Roots
J. David Richardson
Prospects for a US-Taiwan FTA
Daniel H. Rosen and Nicholas R. Lardy
Curbing the Boom-Bust Cycle: Stabilizing
Capital Flows to Emerging Markets
John Williamson